IMAGES
of America

MIDDLEBOROUGH

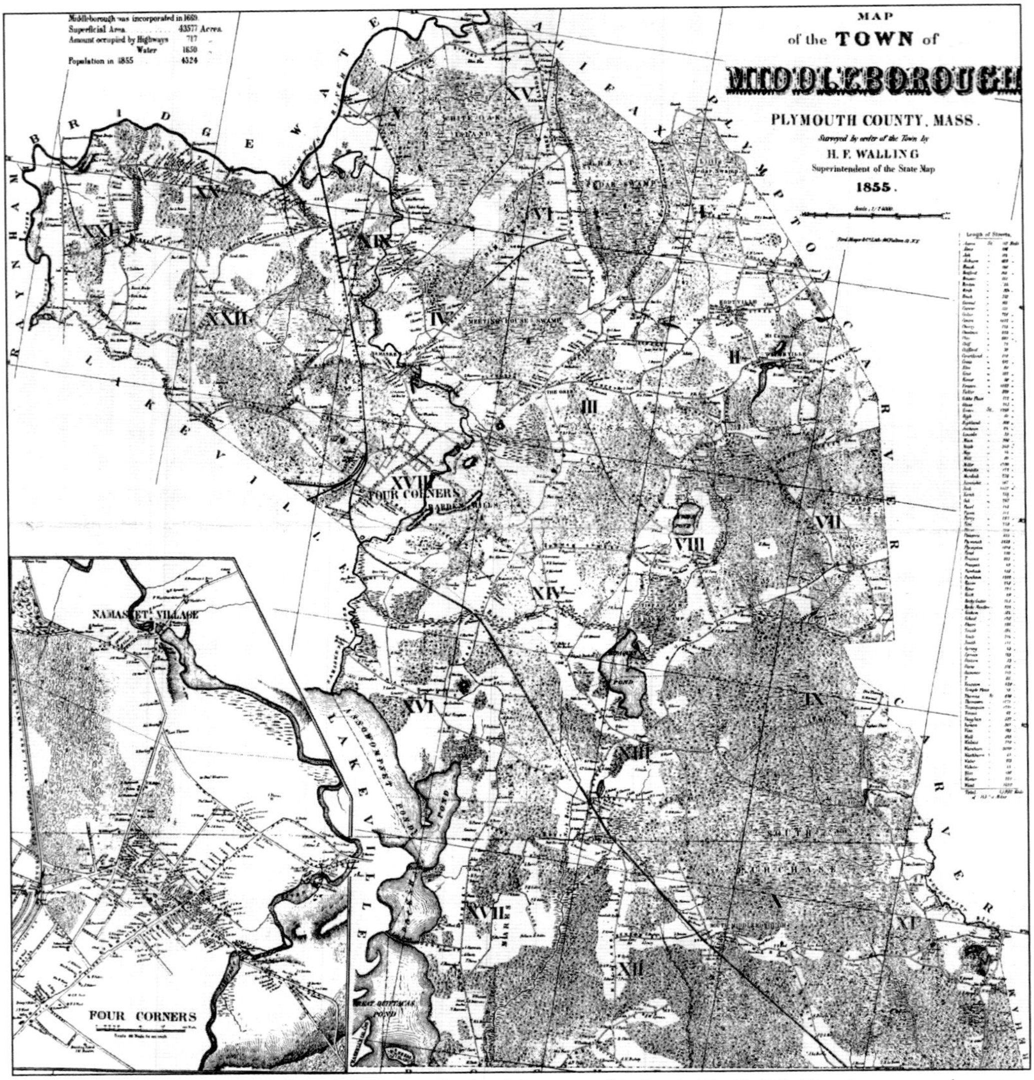

Although earlier maps of Middleborough had been published, H. F. Walling's comprehensive 1855 map had the greatest impact upon the community. As part of the drafting process, the town moved to name its numerous roadways that Walling included on his work. The large Roman numerals refer to the town's various school districts. The inset shows Middleborough Four Corners and Muttock, known at the time as Nemasket Village. (Courtesy of the Middleborough Historical Association.)

On the cover: Members of the Sullivan family enjoy a summer afternoon on the lawn of their house at the corner of Center and Lovell Streets in Middleborough's West Side neighborhood. Though photographed about 1900, the view anticipates the 20th-century residential growth of Middleborough's neighborhoods, the assimilation of its foreign-born residents, and the town's emergence as a middle-class suburban community. (Courtesy of the Middleborough Historical Association.)

IMAGES
of America

MIDDLEBOROUGH

Michael J. Maddigan and the
Middleborough Historical Association

ARCADIA
PUBLISHING

ISBN 978-0-7385-6559-0

Published by Arcadia Publishing
Charleston, South Carolina

Printed in the United States of America

Library of Congress Control Number: 2009924232

For all general information contact Arcadia Publishing at:
Telephone 843-853-2070
Fax 843-853-0044
E-mail sales@arcadiapublishing.com
For customer service and orders:
Toll-Free 1-888-313-2665

Visit us on the Internet at www.arcadiapublishing.com

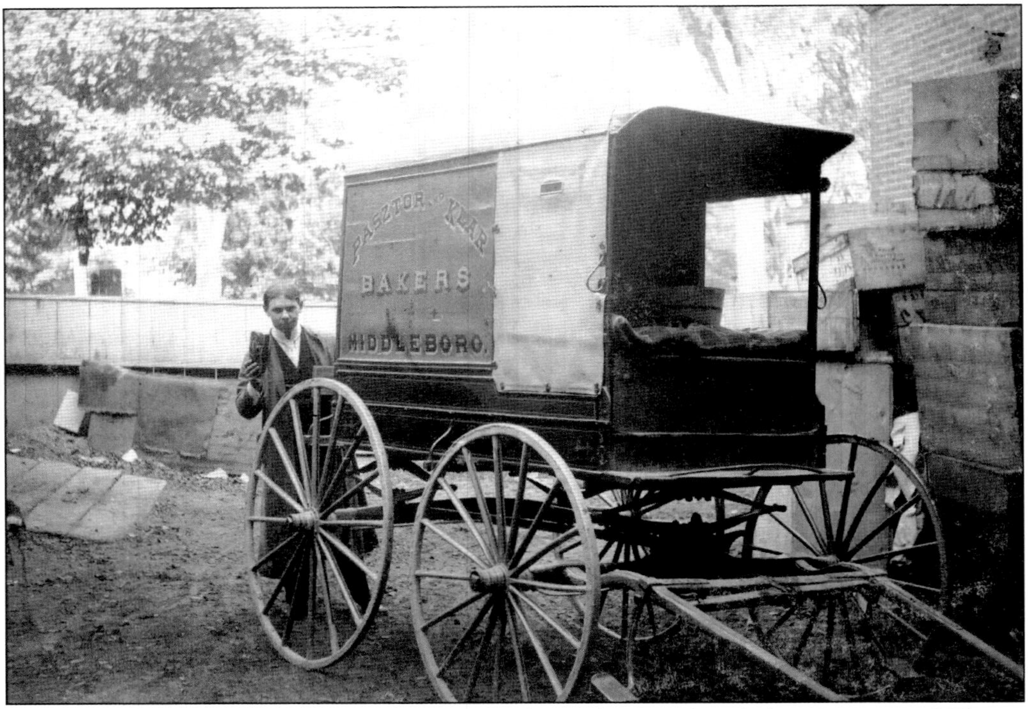

Amateur photographer John A. Belden takes a break from work at bakers Pasztor and Klar to pose for this portrait in the late 1890s. Leaving high school in order to help support his mother, Belden was also employed by Middleborough Four Corners druggist Clarence Hathaway. Still Belden found time to pursue his hobby and in the process left behind a delightfully informal record of Middleborough at the dawn of the 20th century. (Courtesy of the Middleborough Historical Association.)

Contents

Acknowledgments

This volume would not have been possible were it not for the work of a number of dedicated professional and amateur photographers practicing their craft over the past 150 years in Middleborough. Since Levi Thatcher opened the town's first daguerreotype rooms on Center Street, Middleborough and its residents have been well documented on glass, tin, paper, and film. Besides later professional portrait photographers, such as George T. Putnam, William C. Butman, George H. Wilbur, and William J. Thibault, amateur photographers with their cumbersome box cameras, glass plates, and then with Kodak's revolutionary Brownie, captured faces and places long since past. Particularly notable among these were Walter L. Beals, whose large collection of glass-plate negatives elegantly depicts Middleborough at the dawn of the 20th century; John A. Belden, a young high school student, whose work, though limited in output, displays a remarkable informality; and Fred F. Churbuck, many of whose photographs of local scenes were later published by picture-postcard publishers so good were they deemed.

Fortunately, the works of these photographers and countless other unknown enthusiasts are now part of the collections of the Middleborough Public Library and the Middleborough Historical Association. The present work focuses upon the collections of the Middleborough Historical Association, which was established in 1922 and part of whose ongoing mission is to make more readily available the history of this special New England town. Many of the association's images contained herein are published for the first time. Unless otherwise noted, images are taken from its collection.

Thanks go to Nancy Gedraitis, president of the association, for her unflagging enthusiasm in driving this project, as well as her invaluable input; to Dotty Thayer, past president of the association, for her wealth of ideas and for proofreading the manuscript; to the many individuals who have donated images over the years; and finally to the Middleborough Historical Association itself for making available its collections and, more importantly, for the role it assumes every day in preserving Middleborough's rich and varied history.

INTRODUCTION

The history of Middleborough, given its large geographical size, is a history of its numerous villages. At 69 square miles, it is the second largest town in area in Massachusetts. Like other large towns, Middleborough developed a number of small communities that provided the earliest residents with much-needed services, such as mills, schools, churches, and, inevitably, cemeteries. These villages ranged in size from Middleborough Four Corners, which, by the 1850s, had emerged as the municipal, commercial, industrial, and social center of the town, to smaller village centers like Titicut-North Middleborough, Eddyville, Rock, and South Middleborough. Even smaller were neighborhoods, including Fall Brook, Wapanucket, Highlands, Warrentown, Thompsonville, the Soule Neighborhood, Purchade, France, and Tribou, where the presence of a schoolhouse, cemetery, or both tended to give identity to the surrounding area.

The area that became Middleborough was initially settled by Native Americans, whose presence in the vicinity dates back some 10,000 years, as indicated by excavations in the mid-20th century at Wapanucket on the northern shore of Lake Assawompsett and later excavations elsewhere. Attracted by the area's large bodies of water and the winding river that they found full of fish, the Wampanoag eventually named the area Nemasket, meaning "place of fish." Conflicting worldviews between the local Native Americans and the English colonists who arrived in 1620, however, culminated in King Philip's War (1675–1676), which devastated the Native Americans of Middleborough and virtually destroyed their culture. Those who survived were either sold into slavery or placed on reservations such as the one established at Titicut.

As a consequence of the war, Middleborough, in common with other neighboring towns, saw an influx of English settlers. One development that differentiated Middleborough, however, from other communities within the Old Colony was the large presence of Baptists, led by Elder Isaac Backus, a renowned leader in the American Baptist movement. Baptist churches were established at North and South Middleborough, as well as at Beechwoods in what is now Lakeville. By 1793, while Middleborough had three Congregational churches, it had an equal number of Baptist parishes that distinguished it from most of its neighbors. And despite the influence wielded locally by loyalist Judge Peter Oliver, the community became radicalized in the third quarter of the 18th century under the dynamic leadership of ministers like Backus and Sylvanus Conant of the First Congregational Church, including one young soldier named Robert Shurtleff, who was better known as Deborah Sampson.

A generation later, on the eve of the Industrial Revolution, Middleborough was a thriving agricultural town—one of the most productive in southeastern Massachusetts. And despite rapid industrialization following 1850, Middleborough continued to foster its agricultural tradition well into the 1900s. With much of its area not proving conducive to cultivation, Middleborough turned towards those agricultural pursuits that its sandy soils would permit, including lumbering, cranberry cultivation, dairying, and haying. By the 1880s, Middleborough had developed as the principal lumber producer in the commonwealth (due largely to its vast tracts of white pine). Following rapid expansion of the cranberry industry in the late 19th and early 20th centuries, Middleborough similarly emerged as the self-proclaimed "cranberry capital of the world." It was in Middleborough that the New England Cranberry Sales Company, the first cranberry growers' cooperative in Massachusetts, was headquartered following its 1907 organization. Numerous herds of Holstein cattle that were commonly seen throughout Middleborough in the century following 1875 also attested to the community's success in dairying, as did the expansive hay and corn fields that grew the fodder that fed these animals.

However, Middleborough, with its industrial roots in iron making and the Nemasket River as a source of power, keenly sought new industrial opportunities, an aspiration facilitated by the arrival of the railroad in 1848. Middleborough Four Corners, now the center of Middleborough, owed its earliest commercial and industrial development to an energetic Baptist community led by Levi Peirce. As the most industrialized area of town, the four corners literally boomed in the early 1850s when numerous industries located there. This growth continued unabated throughout the remainder of the century despite periodic recessions, spawning new working-class neighborhoods like the West Side, Peaseville, and the Star Mills. By the 1870s, Middleborough boosters were even vying with their counterparts in Brockton, intent upon becoming the principal town in Plymouth County. Circumstances dictated that that position would be achieved by the "shoe city" to the north, but to Middleborough's advantage, it was better able to diversify industrially and therefore suffered less when the shoe industry collapsed. Not only boots and shoes but also straw hats, trunks, milled lumber, spools, cotton and woolen cloth, needles, parlor grates and cast iron work, varnish, stove blacking, organs, paper boxes, print work, fire apparatus, ice bags and heating pads, and calendars and novelties all were produced in Middleborough's manufactories.

Industrialization brought with it technological advances that remade the face of the community. Transportation was revolutionized with the introduction of railways, trolleys, and automobiles, all of which connected Middleborough's outlying villages more closely with the center and the center more closely with the proverbial outside world. Modern municipal services quickly followed in the last half of the 1800s when fire and police protection, street numbering and naming, water and sewerage service, gas and electric lighting, telegraphs, and telephones were introduced, creating a modern, advanced community centered about the four corners. Located here too were the town's public library and hospital.

Meanwhile, the growing demand for consumer goods in the 19th century solidified the role of Middleborough Four Corners as a commercial center for both Middleborough and its surrounding communities. Grocery stores, apparel and dress shops, drugstores, fruit stands, bakeries, sporting goods establishments, jewelers, hardware stores, and numerous other retail operations sold their wares to shoppers from far and wide, while physicians, opticians, lawyers, insurance brokers, bankers, and other professionals offered their services to a growing population. Through the 1950s, downtown Middleborough remained an economically vibrant center where residents could shop, dine, or even catch a film. Besides movies, the options for leisure-time activities were varied, including sports, outdoor activities afforded by the river and nearby lakes, frequent parades, lectures, and concerts, and the numerous shows sponsored by the many local civic, fraternal, and social organizations.

Given its economic diversity, the regional decline in manufacturing that followed World War II affected Middleborough less than other nearby communities, and during the postwar period, the community began transitioning toward a service-based economy. More radical were the changes wrought by the automobile, which led to the decline of Middleborough Four Corners as the principal commercial center for the area. As the automobile facilitated the mobility of Middleborough's residents, formerly wooded and agricultural areas between Middleborough's traditional villages were covered with houses, and the distinctions between these formerly well-defined neighborhoods began to blur.

It is hoped that these images will encourage Middleborough's residents to learn more about the history of the community and to remain not only cognizant but also protective of its past.

One

The Green, East Middleborough, and Muttock

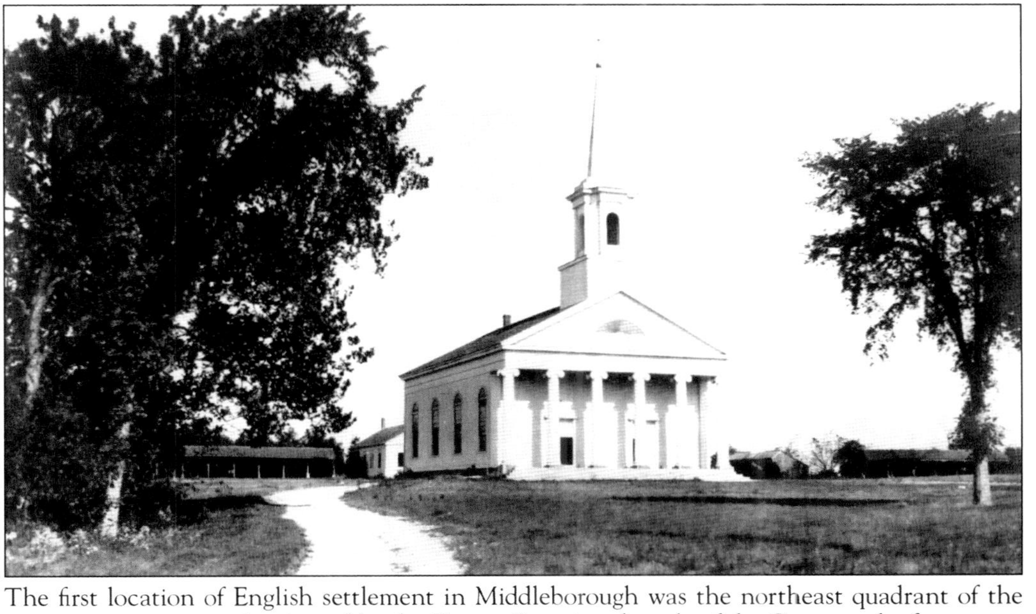

The first location of English settlement in Middleborough was the northeast quadrant of the present town, an area dominated by the Green. Securing the role of the Green as the first center of Middleborough was the location of the First Congregational Church, known familiarly as the "Church of the Green." The present church pictured here was built in 1828 from a design by James Sproat. (Courtesy of James G. MacDonald III.)

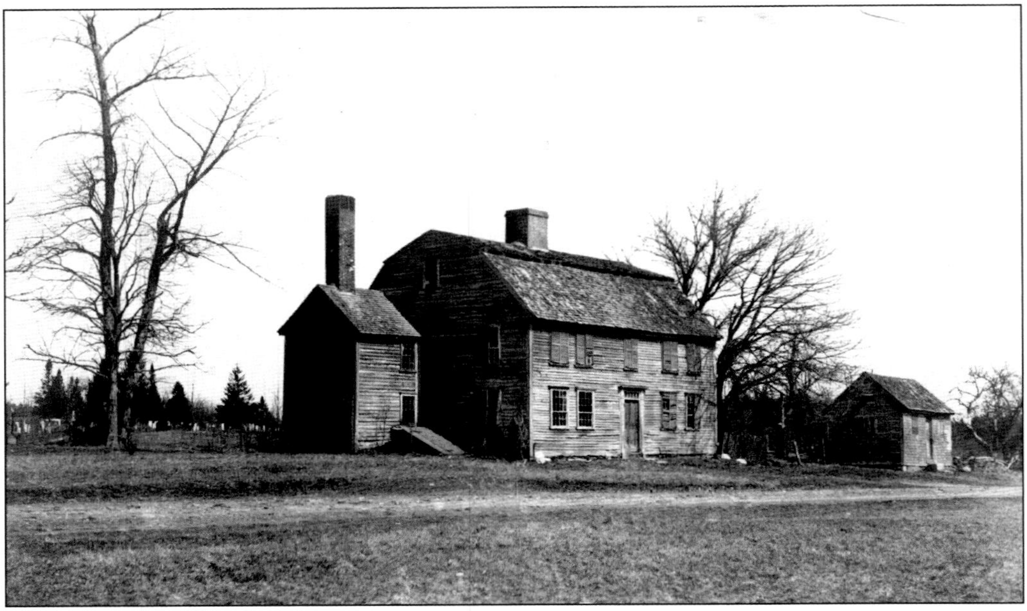

Lending further credence to the Green's claim as the center of Colonial Middleborough was the presence of the Sproat Tavern, which stood upon the east side of the training green. The tavern was a noted social center, figuring prominently as a scene of debates at the time of the Revolutionary War. It was demolished in the late 19th century. Behind it lies the Cemetery at the Green.

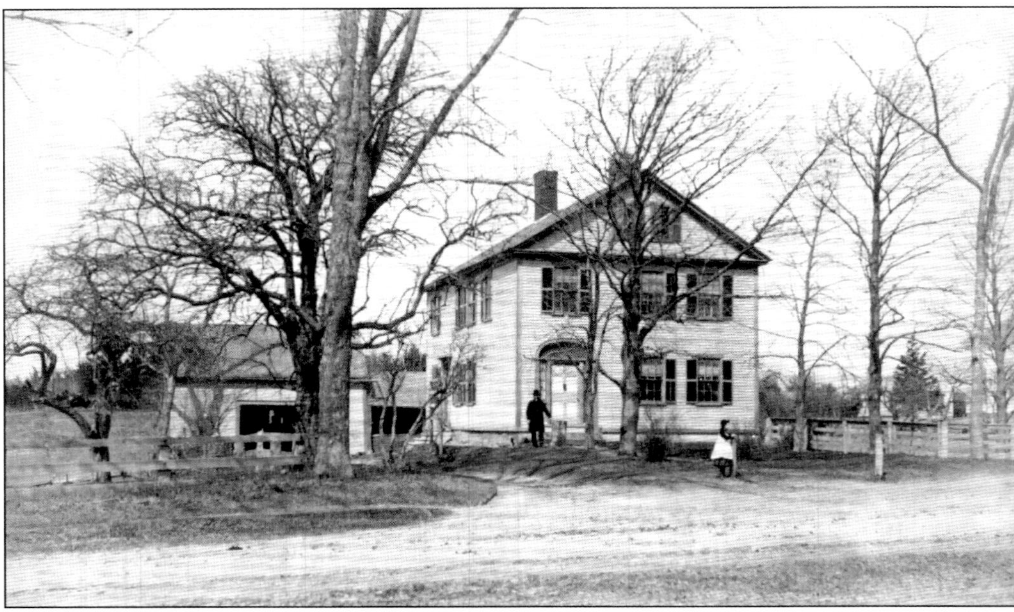

The First Congregational Church parsonage was a substantial home constructed facing the green in the early 1800s and was intended for the use of the minister and his family. Of its various occupants, the Reverend Israel W. Putnam in the 19th century and the Reverend Arthur G. Cummings in the 20th century held the longest, most-influential pastorates. It remains standing on Plympton Street as an interesting architectural counterpoint to the neighboring church.

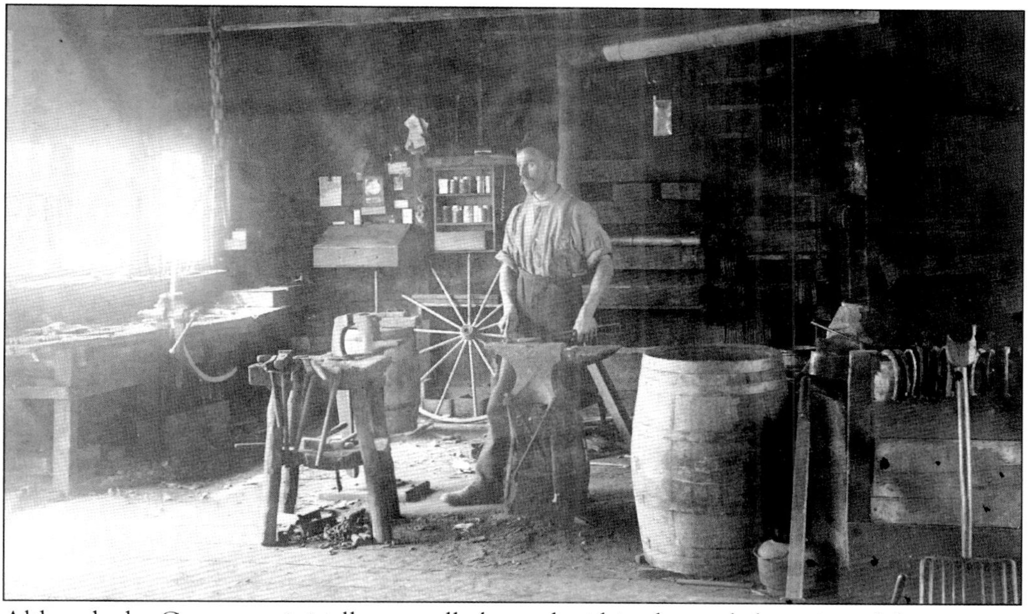

Although the Green was initially centrally located within the settled portion of the town, as other outlying districts became more populated, the Green became increasingly marginalized. After 1800, Middleborough Four Corners began to replace it in importance. The Green was nonetheless able to support small-scale commercial activity, including a store and a blacksmith shop, which was operated by Edward W. Fessenden, who is seen pictured at his anvil.

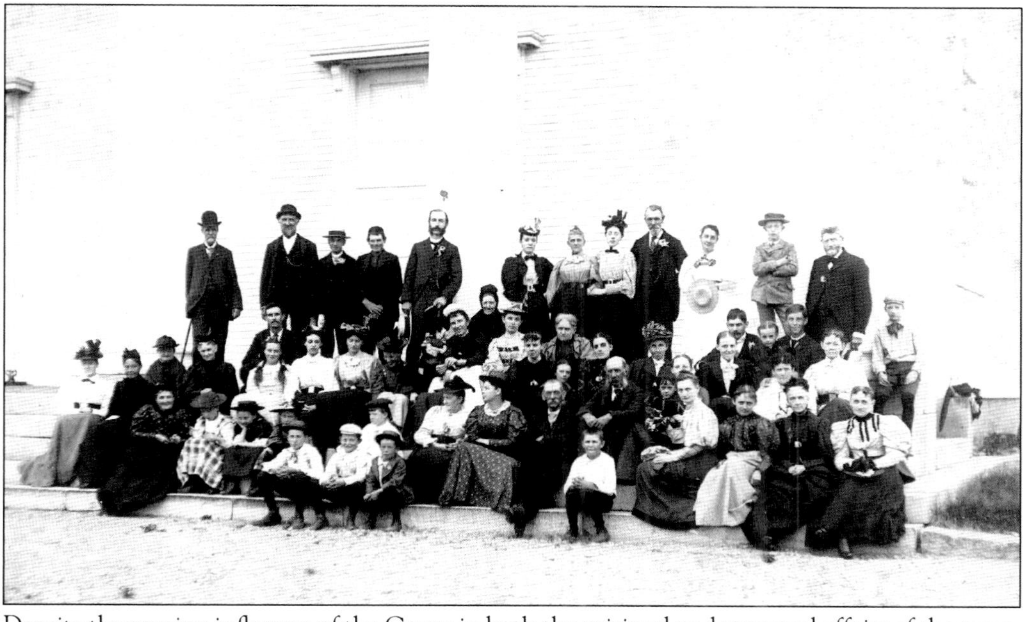

Despite the waning influence of the Green in both the spiritual and temporal affairs of the town, the First Congregational Church remained a powerful influence in the life of local residents both as a religious force and as a social outlet. Here members of the church have gathered for an Independence Day picnic in 1895. Pastor George Stearns stands in the back row, fifth from the left.

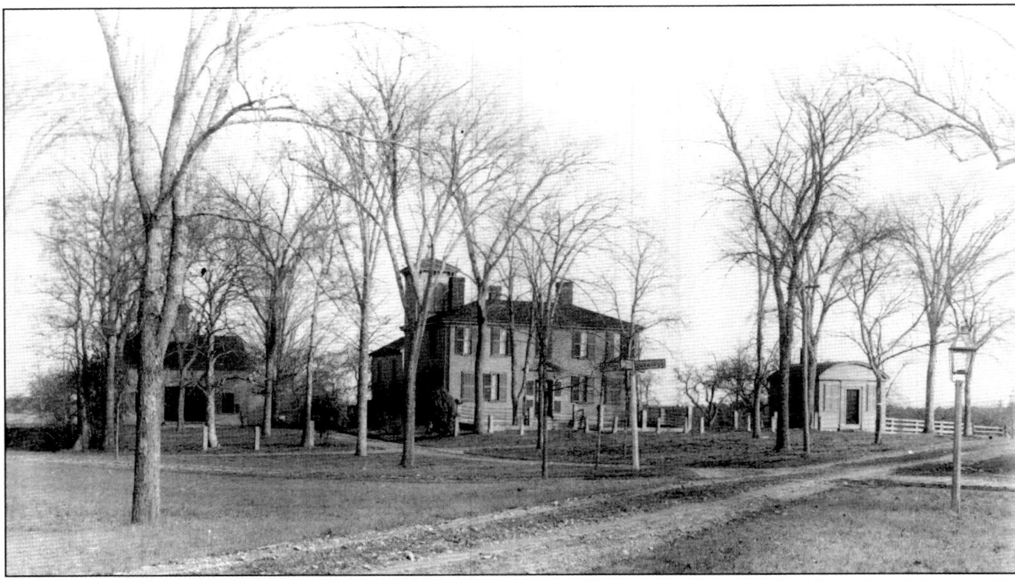

Northeast of the Green was a series of early villages, including Eddyville, Waterville, Thompsonville, and the Soule Neighborhood, which became collectively known as East Middleborough. Of these villages, it was Eddyville and particularly its green, as seen here with the Eddy homestead in 1904, which came to be considered the heart of the area. While an early attempt at industrialization was made at Waterville, East Middleborough remained an agricultural community.

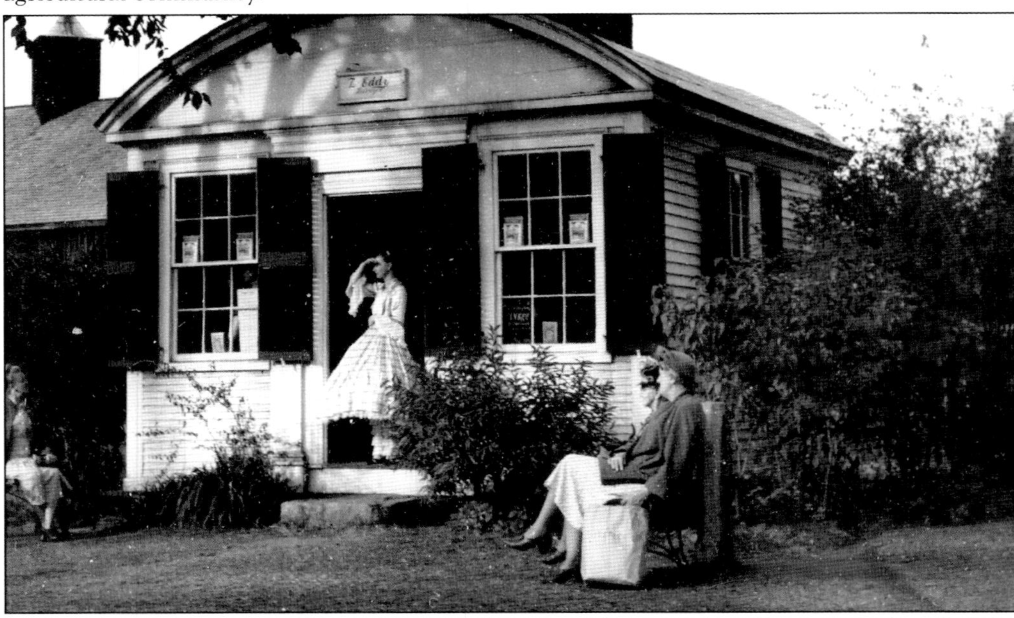

Most prominent of the Eddys who settled and resided at Eddyville was Zachariah Eddy (1780–1860). His 1806 law office with its unusual barrel-vaulted roof is pictured following its relocation from Eddyville to Storrowtown on the grounds of the Eastern States Exposition at Springfield where it was photographed in 1955. Besides being a prominent local attorney, Eddy was an early local historian of note who penned Middleborough's first published history.

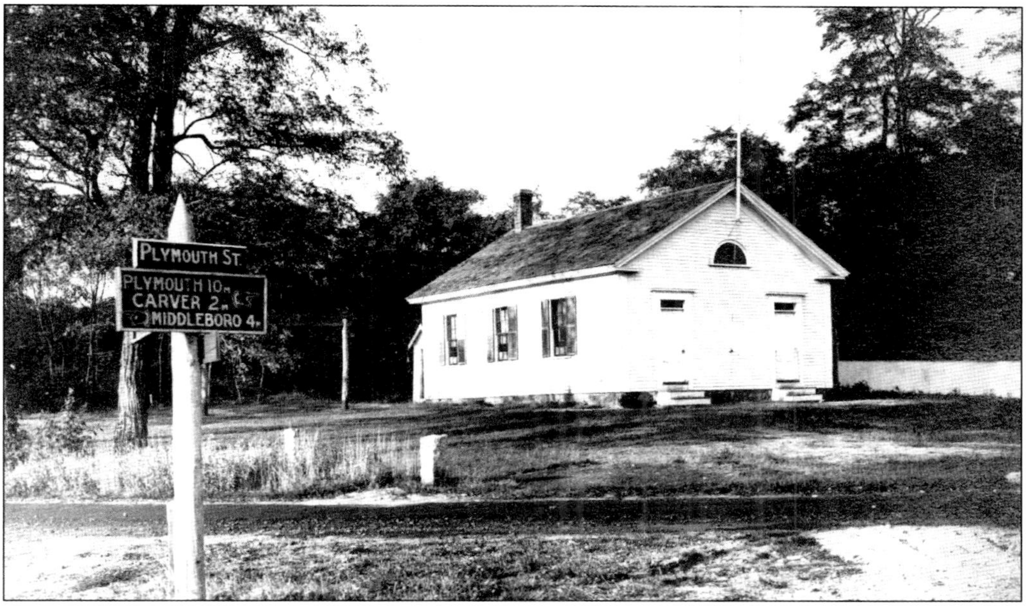

Waterville developed along Plymouth Street at Savery's Pond as the site of the Eddy family's industrial enterprises. The Waterville Schoolhouse (1877) on the corner of Plymouth and Carmel Streets served both its namesake village as well as Eddyville. The schoolhouse was typical of those built at the time in Middleborough, and residents "spared no pains to make it pleasant inside as well as out." Today it survives as a private residence.

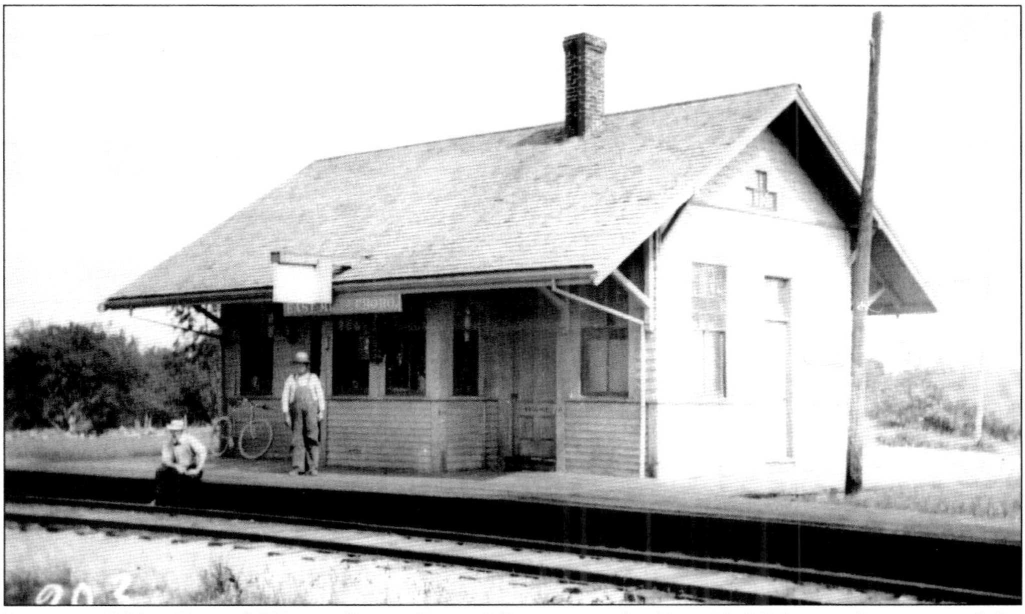

Between Eddyville and Waterville on Carmel Street was the East Middleborough station of the Plymouth and Middleboro Railroad. The line linking the two namesake communities opened with much fanfare in 1892 but was never well patronized. Nonetheless, the small East Middleboro station helped give an identity to the community until the railroad line was abandoned in the late 1930s. (Courtesy of James G. MacDonald III.)

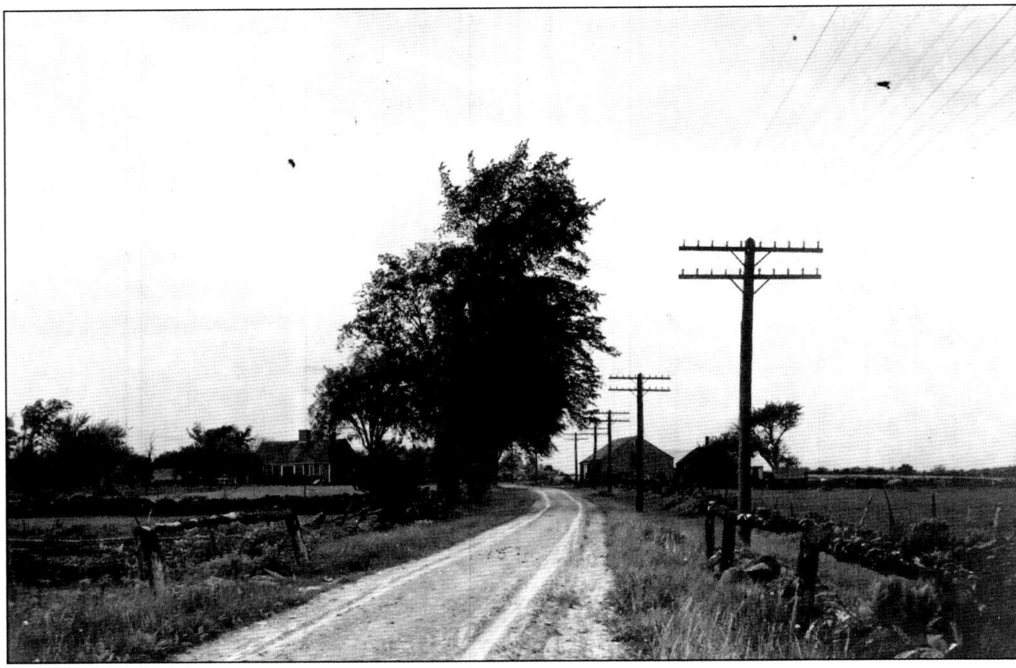

Historic Thompson Street, linking the Green with Halifax, was one of the earliest areas of Middleborough settled and was named for the large number of its residents who bore that name, all descendants of John Thompson. This view looks northwards from Danson's Brook towards Elmwood Farm, owned in the mid-1800s by Philander W. Thompson and in the early 1900s by the Kinsman Brothers, who established an extensive dairy operation there.

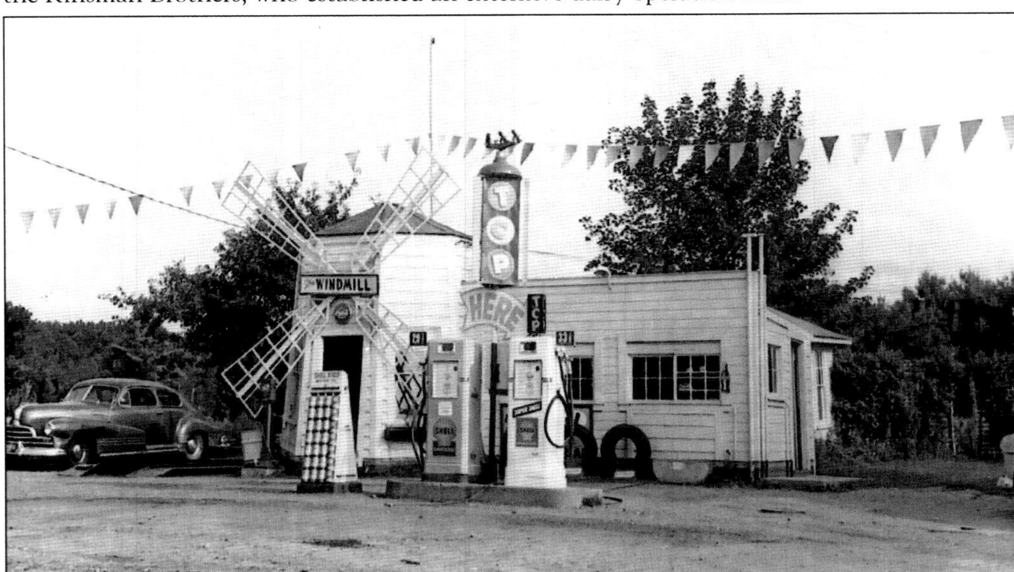

In the 20th century, Routes 44 and 105 were routed through East Middleborough, prompting the development of a number of small businesses to cater to motorists, including the Windmill filling station that was situated on Plympton Street between the Green and Thompson Street. At the time the photograph was taken, the Shell gasoline sold here retailed for just over 29¢ a gallon.

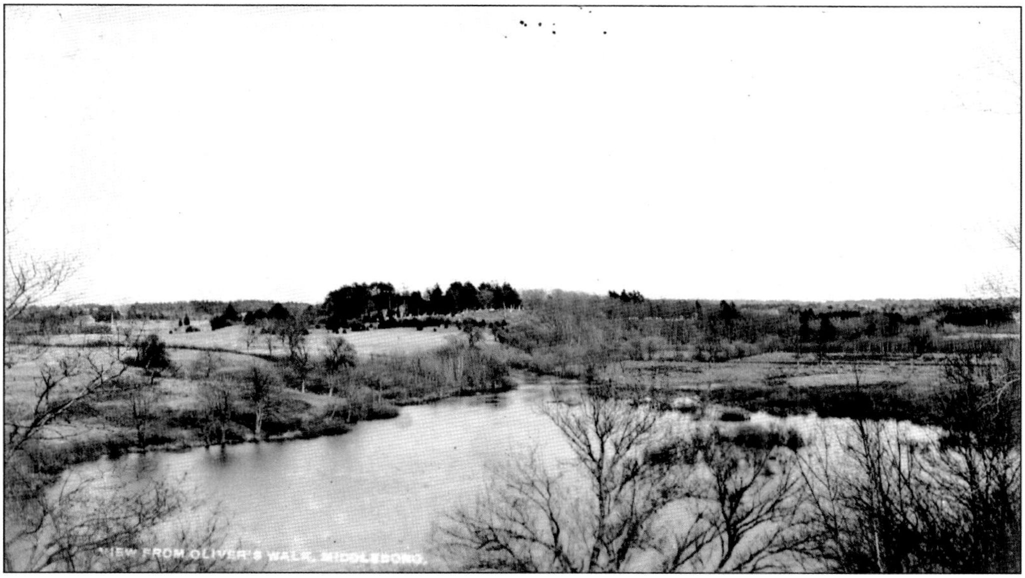

Located just west of the Green was Muttock through which the Nemasket River flowed. The earliest Native American inhabitants of Middleborough were attracted by the large bodies of fresh water locally as well as the abundance of fish in the Nemasket River, a name itself meaning "place of fish." The river also served as a transportation corridor, linking Lake Assawompsett with the Taunton River and ultimately Mount Hope Bay.

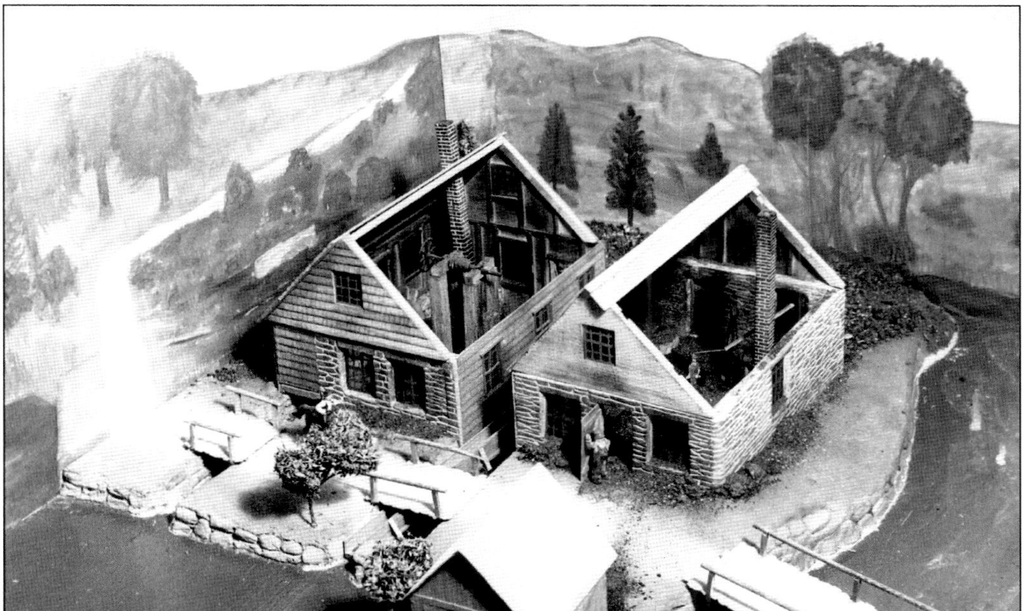

In the mid-1700s, early settlers transformed the earlier Native American village of Muttock into the industrial heart of Middleborough with a gristmill, sawmill, and a small-scale iron works. Under the influence of Judge Peter Oliver, Muttock emerged as the principal seat of local industry. A dioramic display constructed in the 1960s by Frederick Eayrs Jr. gives a good conception of how the Oliver ironworks must have appeared originally.

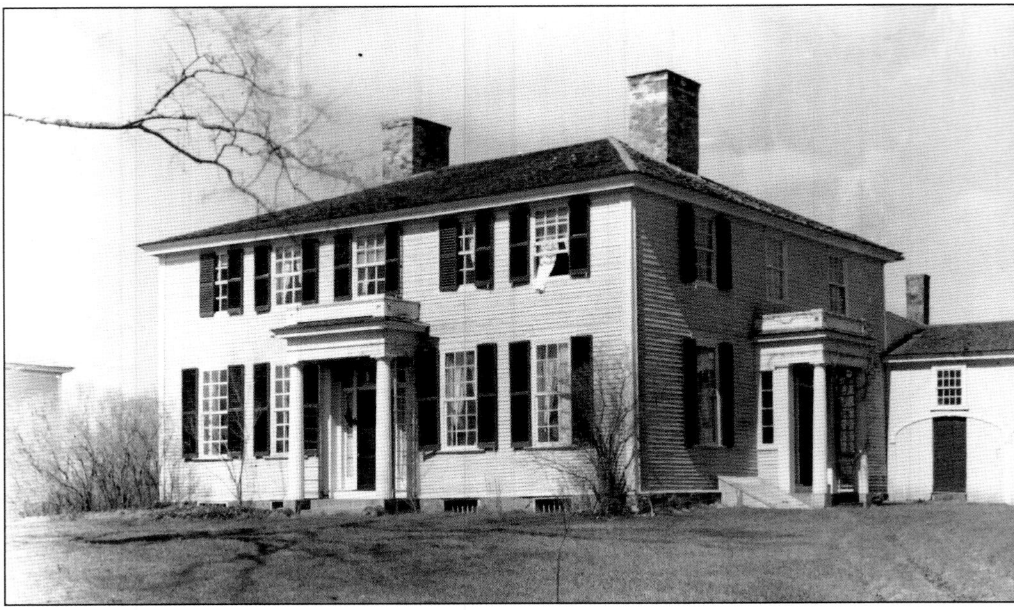

Built in 1769 for Judge Peter Oliver's son, Dr. Peter Oliver Jr., was the small Oliver house on Plymouth Street, a modest home in contrast to the judge's much grander home, Oliver Hall, which was deliberately burned during the American Revolution in retaliation for the Oliver family's Royalist sympathies. The small Oliver house survived and was documented as part of the Historic American Buildings Survey in 1936.

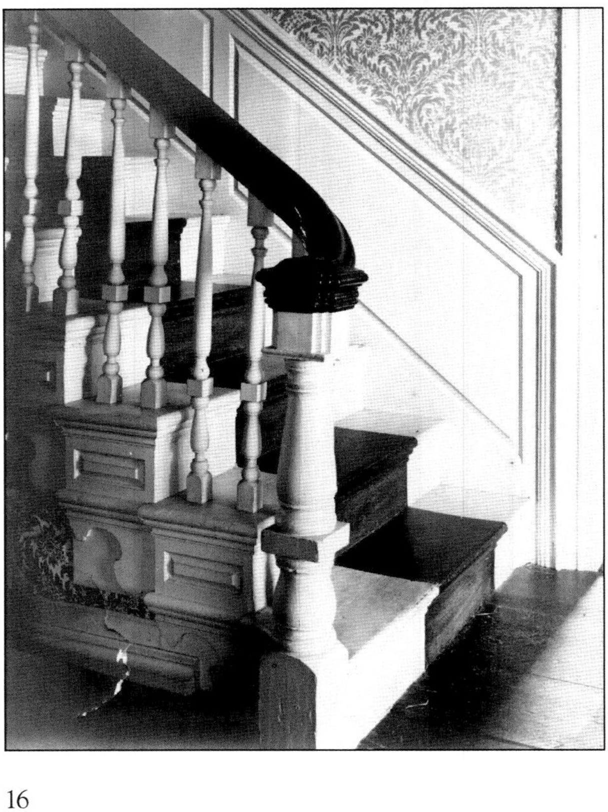

The fine craftsmanship of the artisans hired by Oliver is clearly reflected in the intricate woodwork of the house, which is perhaps best exemplified by the ornate staircase pictured here in the 1930s. The house was later owned by the Sproat family who maintained an interest in the mills at Muttock. In the 1940s, the house was reacquired by a branch of the Oliver family and remains in their ownership today.

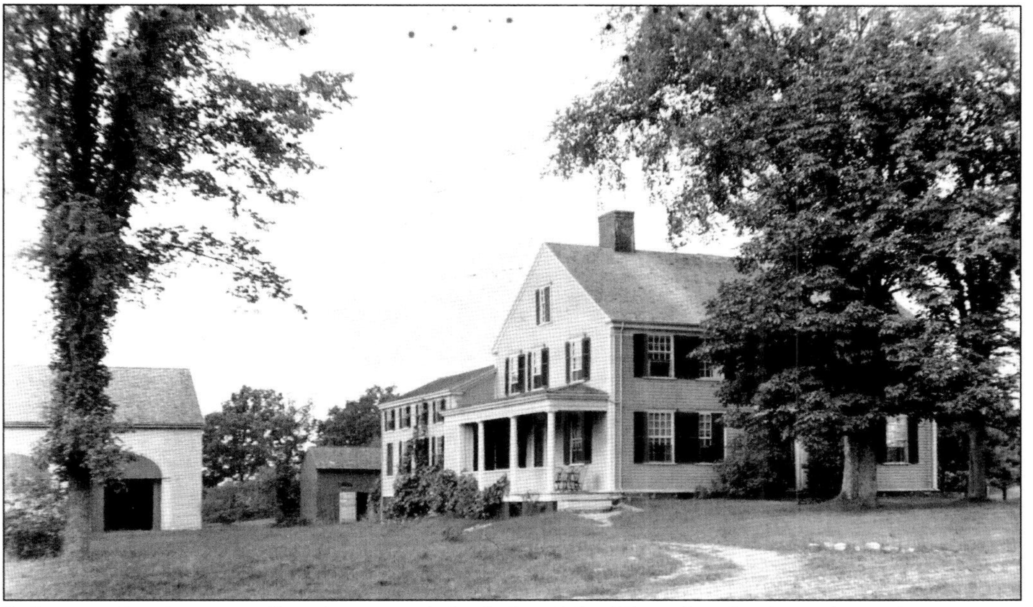

Following the American Revolution and the flight of the Oliver family, the industrial operations at Muttock were overseen by the Washburn and Sproat families. Gen. Abiel Washburn was the dominating personality of Muttock during the Federal era, producing shovels at the former Oliver mills site and operating a store nearby. Washburn had this Georgian-style home erected on Plymouth Street facing the Nemasket River. It still stands facing the KOA Campground.

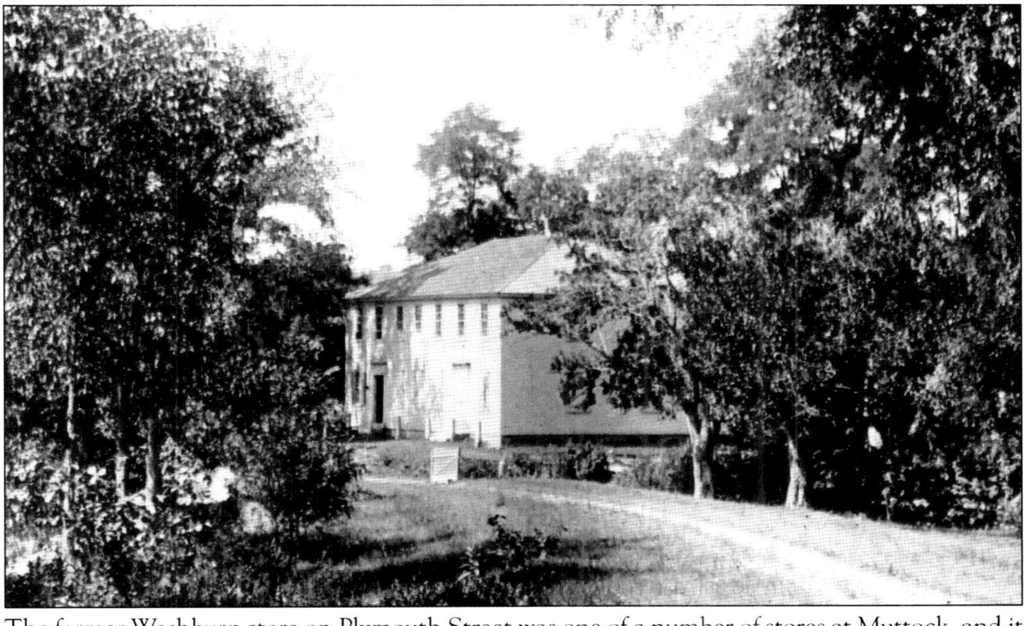

The former Washburn store on Plymouth Street was one of a number of stores at Muttock, and it remained a thriving commercial enterprise until the late 1840s when owner Philander Washburn simply closed shop one day. His somewhat deprecating wife is said to have subsequently referred to it as her husband's "place of no business." It was later converted to a two-tenement home before being burned down in 1963.

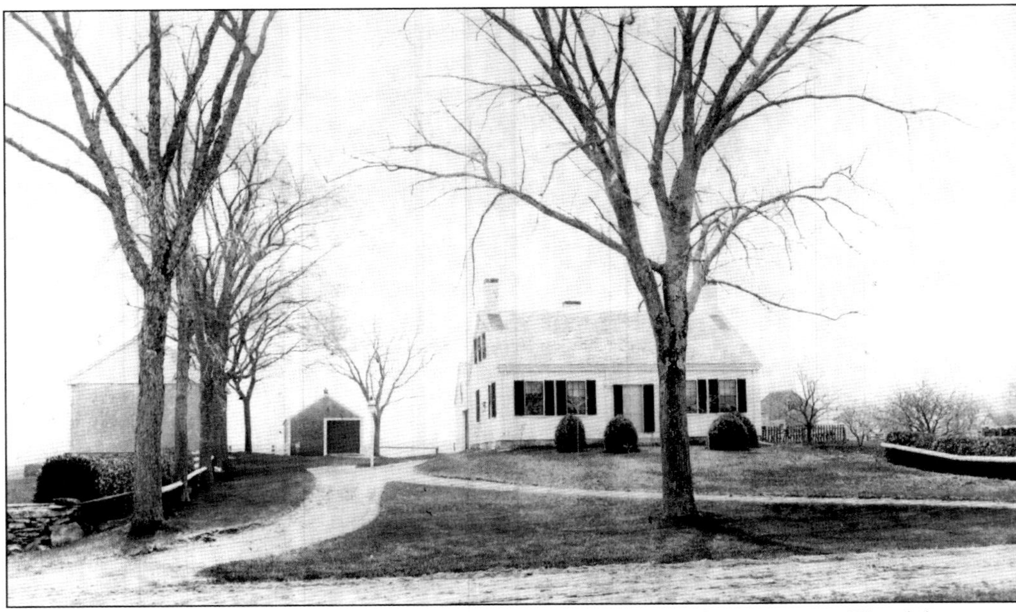

In contrast to the Oliver and Washburn houses was the modest Lorenzo Wood house on Plymouth Street near Nemasket Hill Cemetery. The house was occupied by a succession of men named Lorenzo Wood, two of whom were later owners and editors of the *Middleboro Gazette*. For many years, Lorenzo Wood Jr. (1906–1968) penned the popular "Echoes from Shad Row, or By the Clear Nemasket" local history column. (Author's collection.)

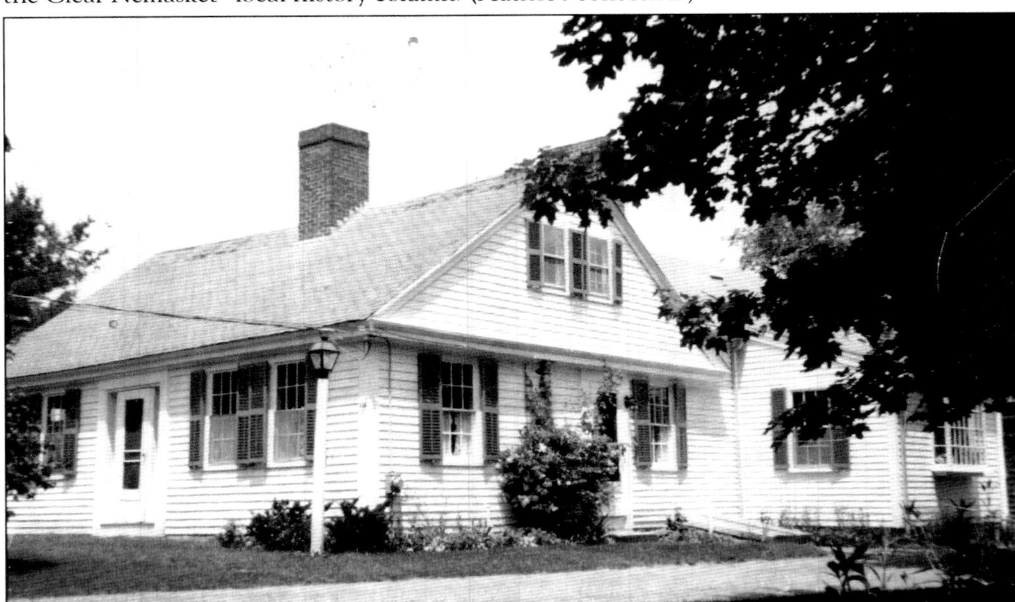

Located on North Street above the Oliver works was the Davis Wilder house, seen in this mid-20th-century snapshot. The Wilder house was typical of those built and occupied by workers in the iron and shovel works below. The Wilder family was long associated with the local iron industry both as workers and later as blacksmiths. The house is now part of the Muttock National Register Historic and Archaeological District.

One of the distinctive features at Muttock was the dry laid stone slab bridge over the Nemasket River. The largest such bridge in Plymouth County when it was constructed in 1857, here it is shown some 20 or so years later looking north towards Washburn's former store. A Works Progress Administration project during the 1930s replaced the rails along its sides with more substantial stone walls.

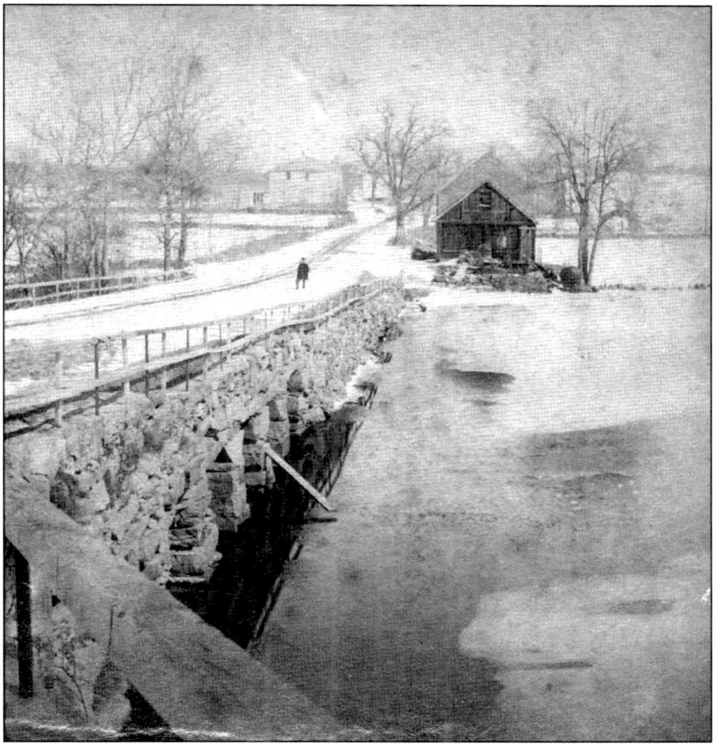

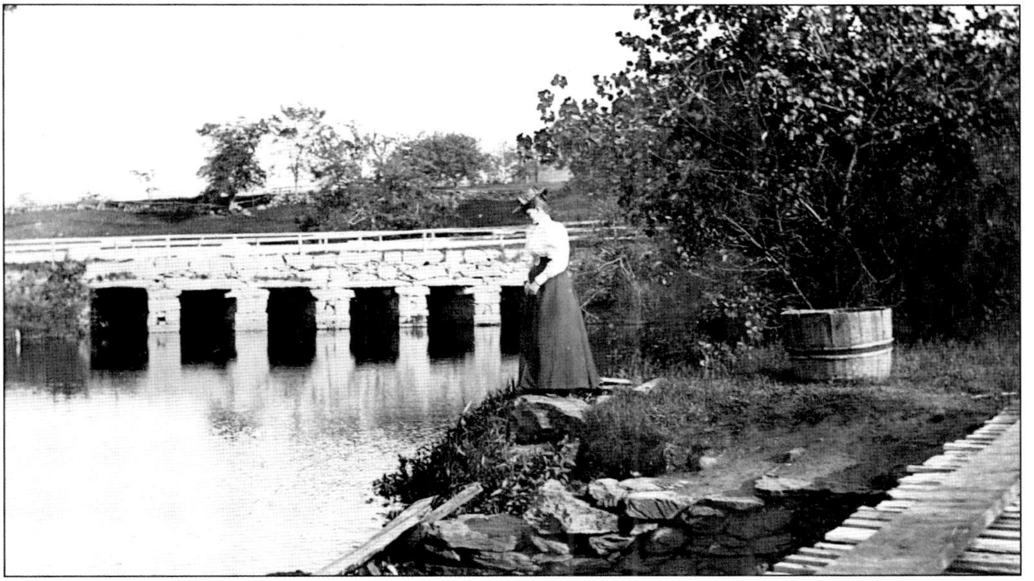

Late-19th-century Muttock, devoid of both industrial and commercial activity, became a quiet, residential neighborhood. Abandoned by industry, the former Oliver mills proved a scenic setting for the work of amateur photographers attracted by its rustic qualities. Numerous cabinet and stereographic views were produced, capturing the vicinity's rural Gothic character. Here a solitary woman contemplates the Nemasket River, with the Nemasket Street bridge visible in the background.

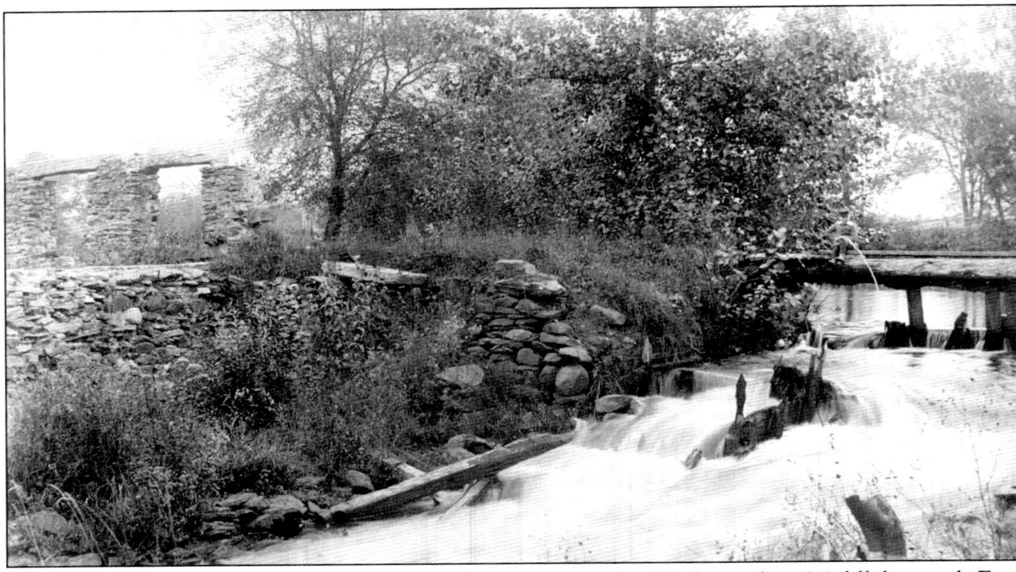

In the mid-1800s, the neighborhood entered a long period of decline when Middleborough Four Corners finally eclipsed Muttock as the center of local industry and commerce. Although the area attempted to forestall the inevitable and restyled itself under the short-lived name Nemasket Village in the 1850s, the former industrial works were left to fall into ruin following 1865, and efforts to revive the site failed. (Author's collection.)

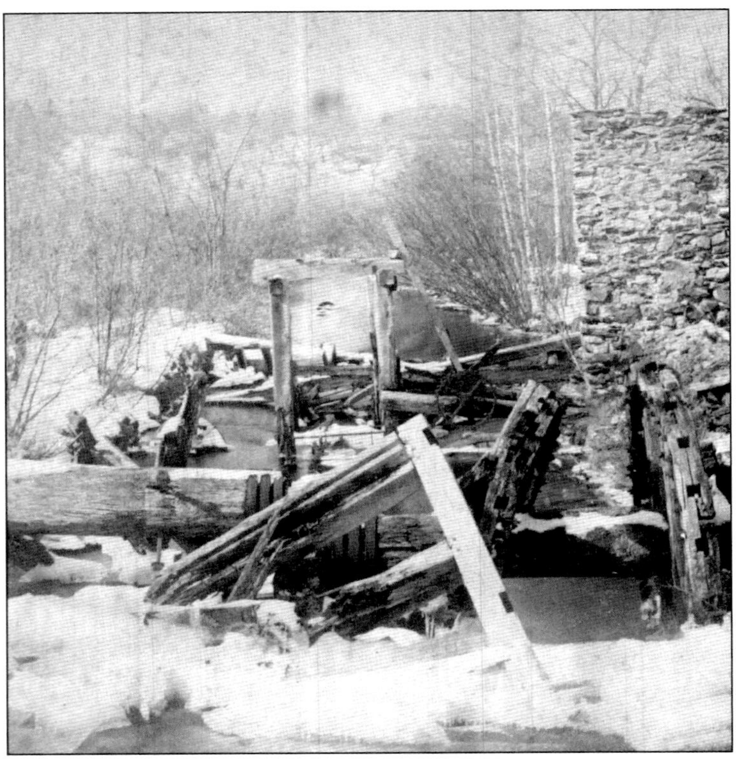

The ruins of the Oliver family mills continued to decay, eventually collapsing into the river and becoming overgrown with vegetation. The site was largely forgotten when, during the 1960s, archaeological work was undertaken to reveal the remaining features of the Colonial-era site. Today the site is Oliver Mill Park, one of Middleborough's most noted features, and it is the centerpiece of the Muttock National Register Historic and Archaeological District. (Courtesy of James G. MacDonald III.)

Two

North Middleborough and Warrentown

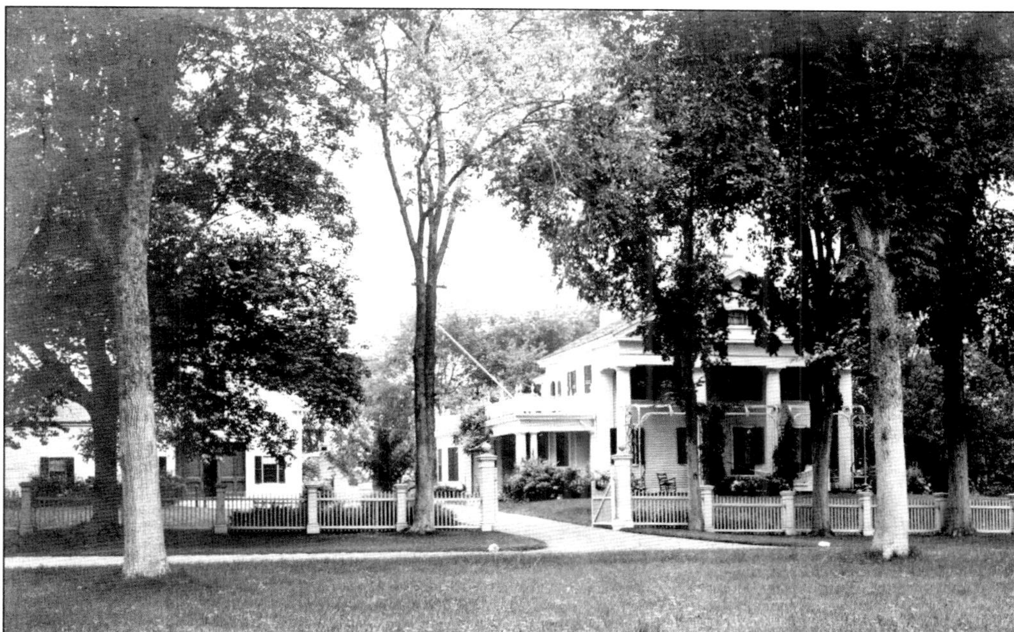

Like East Middleborough, North Middleborough encompassed a number of villages, including Titicut and Purchade, all located in the northwest corner of town. Long considered the green heart and center of North Middleborough, however, was Titicut Green, a former training field at the junction of Plymouth and Pleasant Streets. The David Gurney Pratt house, now owned by the Chamberlain School, fronts an elm tree–shaded Titicut Green in this view from about 1900.

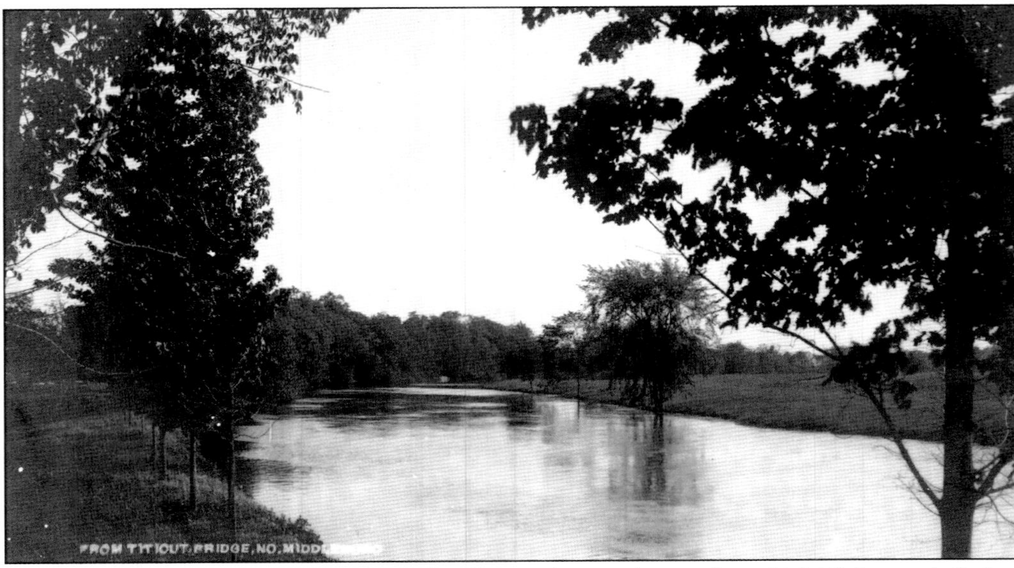

The Ketiticut or Taunton Great River bordering the northern edge of Middleborough linked the Nemasket River with the sea at present-day Fall River. A short distance downstream from Plymouth Street was the Native American village of Titicut, which straddled the river and where a fishing weir and a ford were located. This view dates from about 1900 and was taken from Plymouth Street. (Courtesy of James G. MacDonald III.)

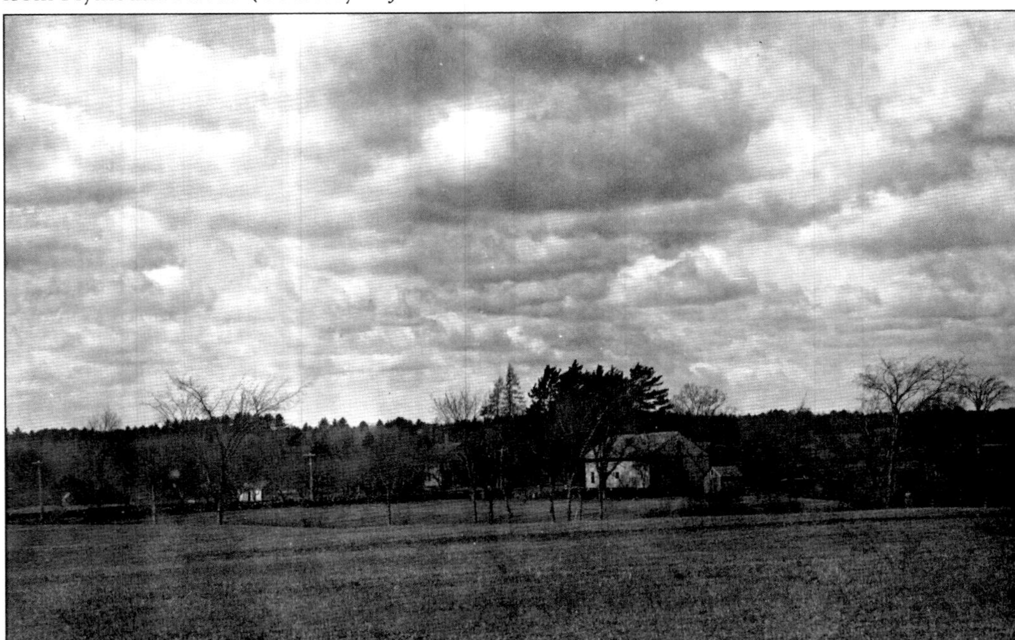

The Albert Pratt farm on Vernon Street, seen about 1900 from Fort Hill, was long known as the site of the Native American village of Titicut. Archaeological finds substantiating the location were commonplace on the farm throughout the 19th century, prompting more serious consideration of the site a century later. In the mid-20th century, extensive archaeological excavations on the farm, then owned by the Taylor family, confirmed a Native American presence.

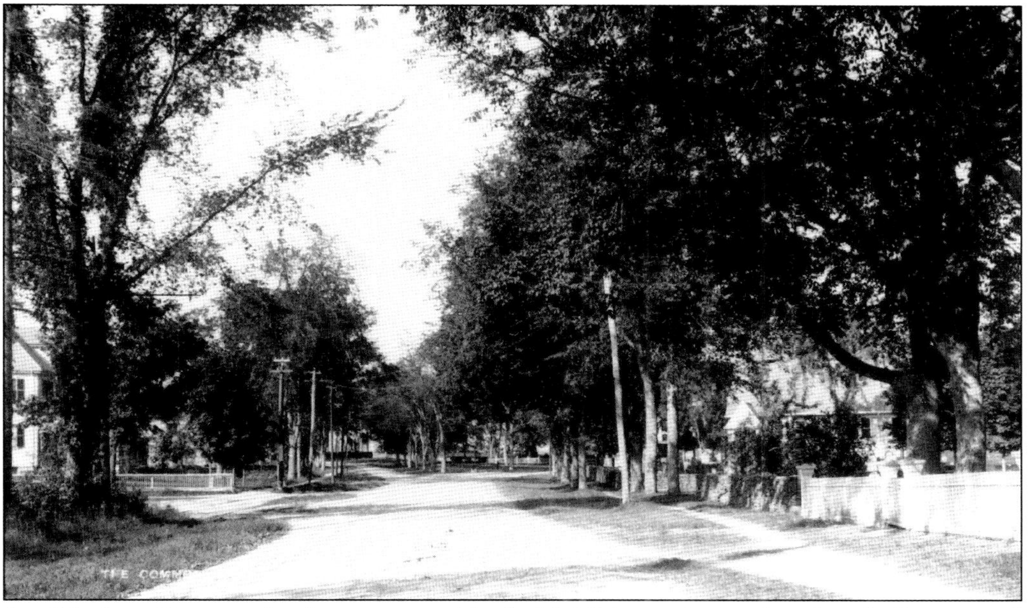

As did the village at the four corners, North Middleborough developed with Baptist and Congregational churches, an academy, schools, a cemetery, and a prominent family—the Pratts—to drive improvement of the community. Unlike Middleboro Four Corners, however, North Middleborough was centered about an attractive green, which is seen in the distance looking westwards along Plymouth Street about 1900.

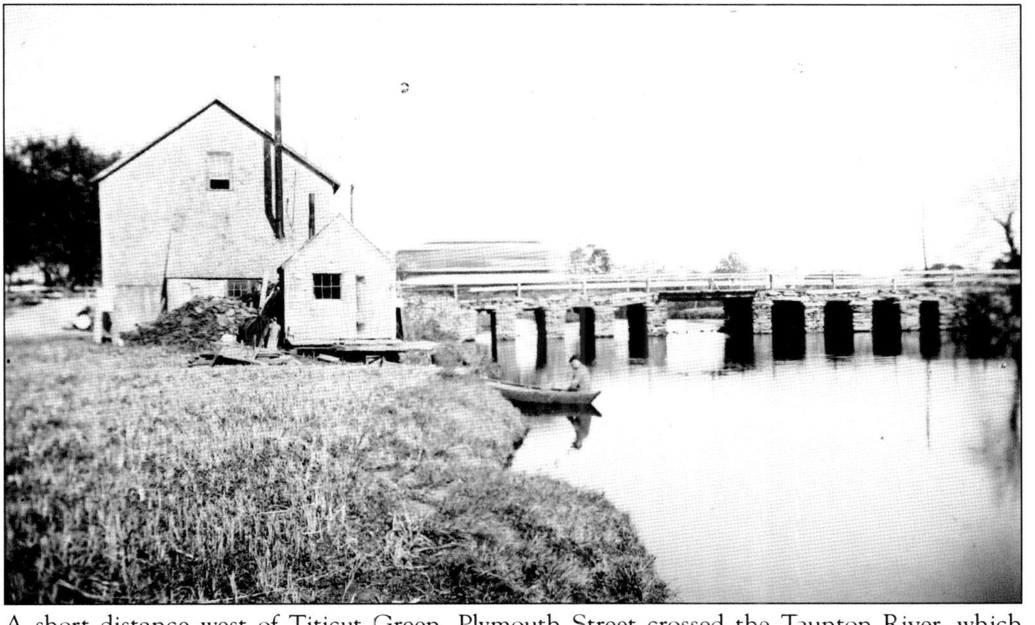

A short distance west of Titicut Green, Plymouth Street crossed the Taunton River, which remained important in the economic and cultural life of North Middleborough. For a brief period around 1800, ships were constructed in the vicinity by Capt. Benjamin Pratt and Deacon Holmes. This view shows Sturtevant's or Titicut Bridge about 1900. The blur atop the bridge is a fast-moving trolley bound for Brockton.

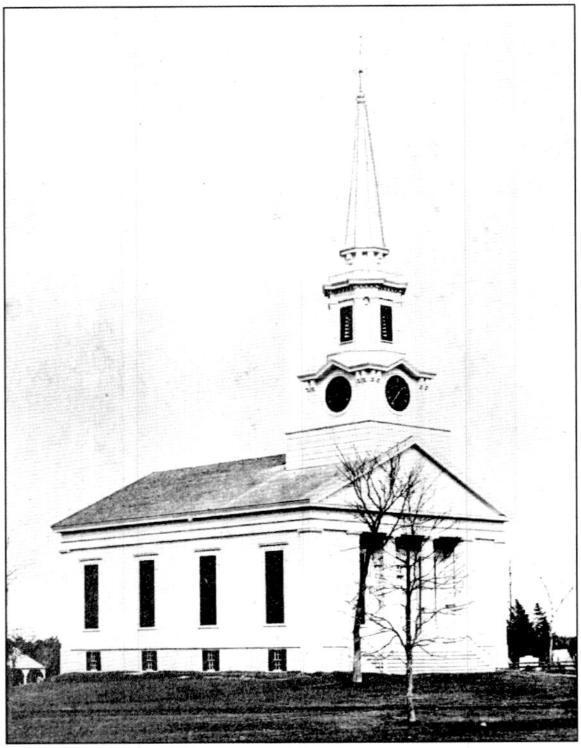

Facing the training green at Titicut was the North Congregational Church, which served both North Middleborough and the neighboring portion of Bridgewater. In 1744, Titicut residents successfully petitioned for the creation of a separate parish at North Middleborough "so that we may enjoy the gospel privileges by ourselves," and four years later, a church was established. Although the architect of the second structure to house the church (seen at left) is unknown, it bears hallmarks of Solomon K. Eaton, a North Middleborough native and architect of several local churches and buildings, including Middleborough Town Hall. The Greek Revival church was struck by lightning the night of March 15, 1898, and burned to the ground. Soon afterwards, it was replaced with a striking Craftsman-inspired church, which today continues to occupy a position of prominence on the north side of Titicut Green.

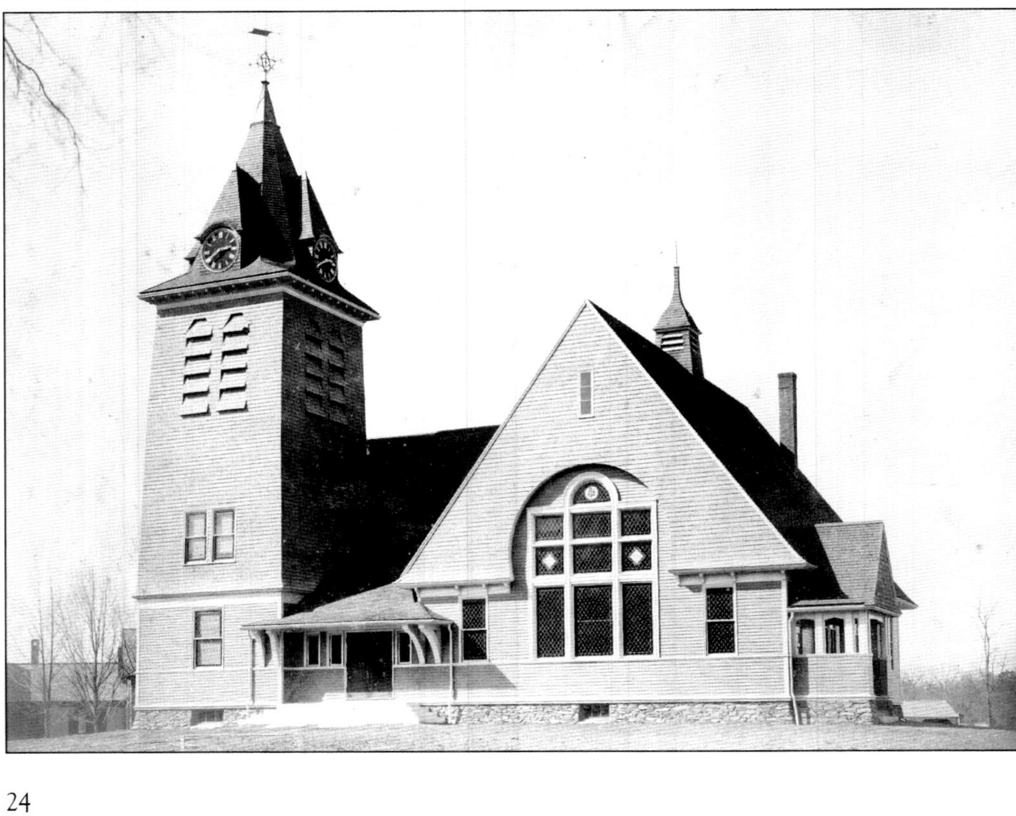

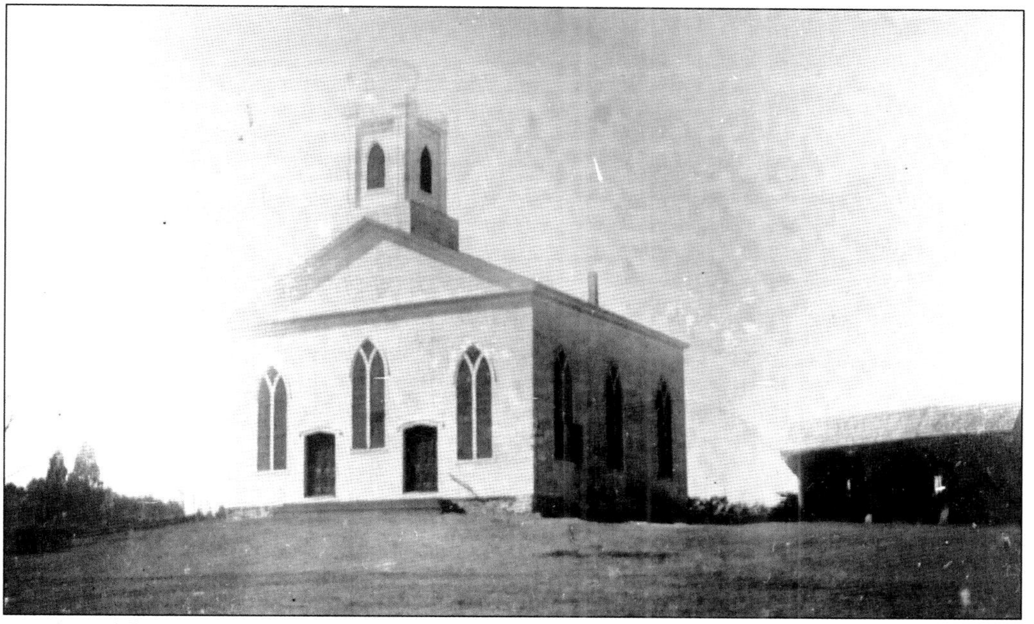

North Middleborough had the first Baptist church in southeastern Massachusetts, and from this, later churches were established at Beechwoods (1757), South Middleborough (1761), Lakeville (1800), and Middleborough Four Corners (1828). The second structure to house the First Baptist Church of Middleborough was this simple wood-frame structure with its Gothic-inspired lancet windows, which stood near the junction of Plymouth and Bedford Streets.

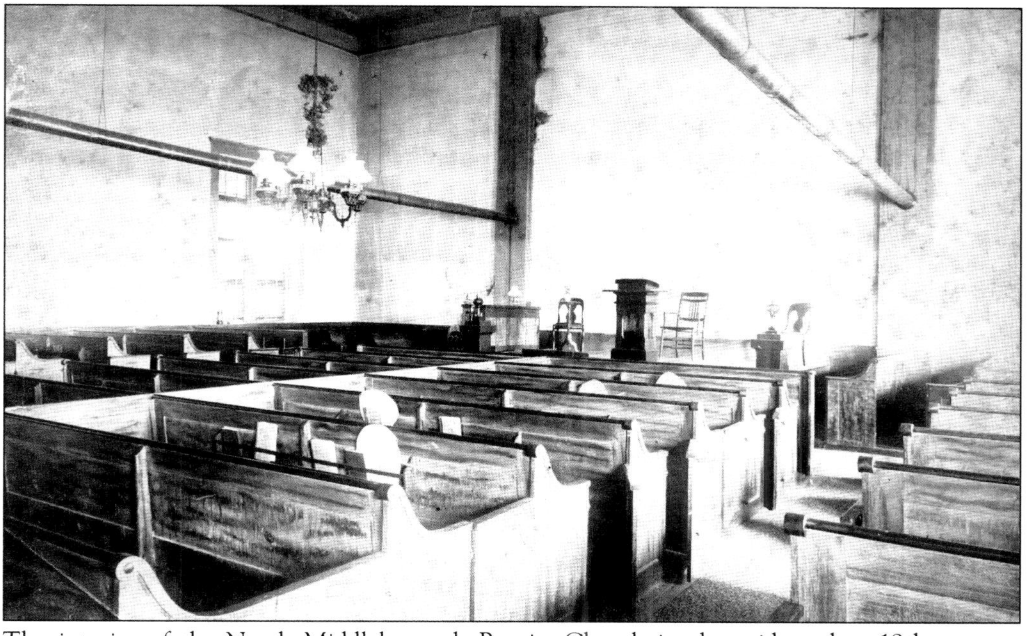

The interior of the North Middleborough Baptist Church in the mid- to late 19th century reveals its Spartan furnishings and rustic character. Most Middleborough meetinghouses of the era were typically furnished and equally poorly heated, much to the dismay of congregations on cold, raw days. The church was demolished in 1894 and replaced with the present structure.

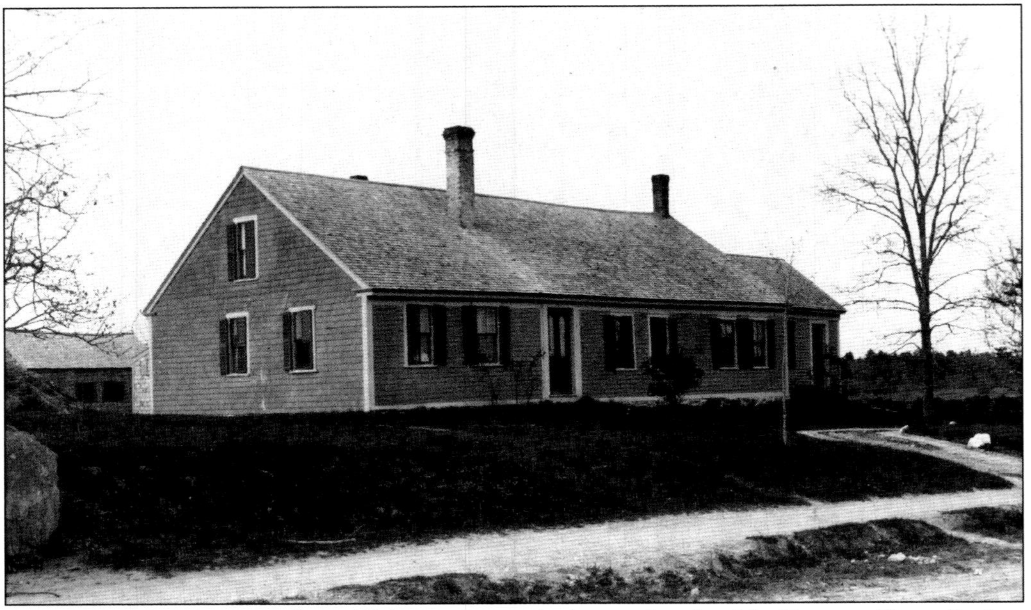

The Baptist church at North Middleborough was the home church of the Reverend Isaac Backus (1724–1806), a recognized leader in the early American Baptist movement and an advocate of religious tolerance. Although Backus traveled frequently for his work, he found an occasional respite at his North Middleborough home, which still stands on Plymouth Street midway between Titicut Green and Bedford Street.

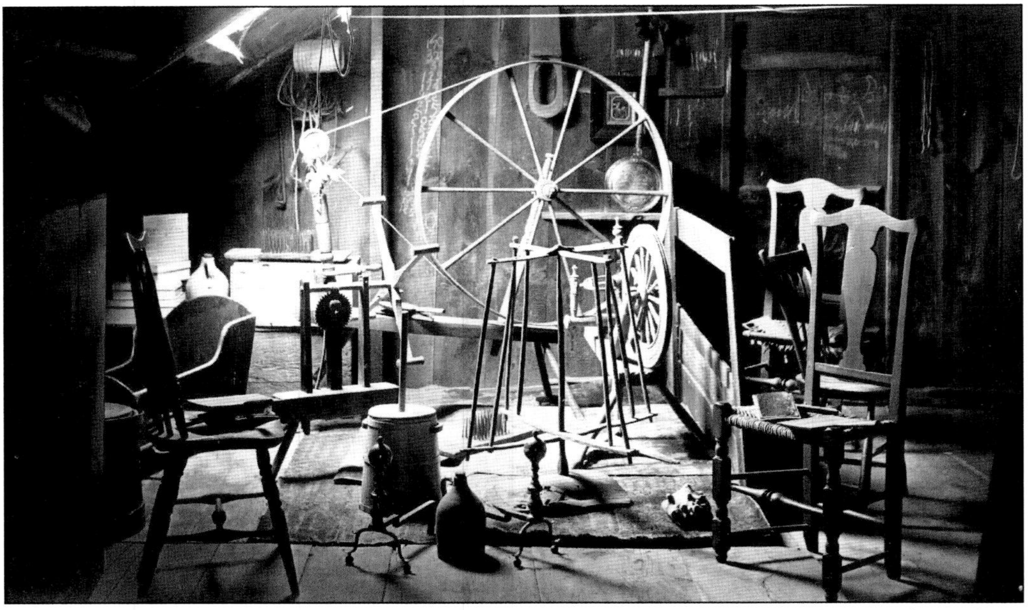

The earliest Middleborough homes later became troves for heirloom artifacts such as those depicted in the garret of the Backus house in 1902, which were eagerly sought by antique hunters when Colonial Revivalism came into vogue following 1876. Woolen and flax spinning wheels, chairs, andirons, a bed warmer, a yarn winder, a butter churn, and a cradle all add greatly to the Colonial atmosphere despite its somewhat staged appearance.

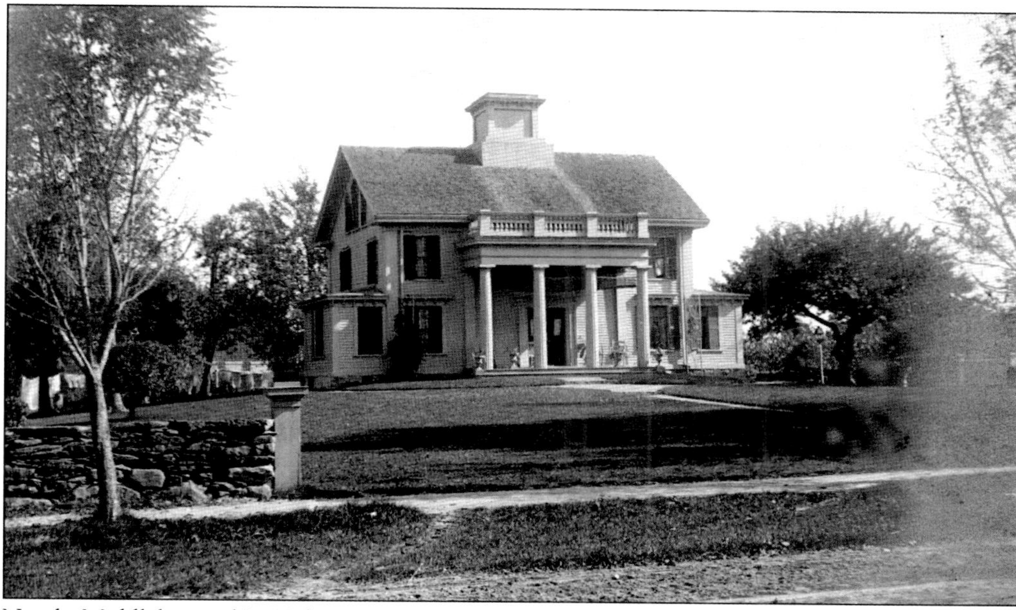

North Middleborough's 19th-century growth was fostered by the Pratt family. Among the influential members of the family was Augustus Pratt, who resided in the stately home on Pleasant Street, pictured here about 1900. Pratt was well known throughout the state for his model farm, his advanced views on agriculture, and his prizewinning specimens. A member of the state board of agriculture, Pratt was also a sponsor of the cooperative movement.

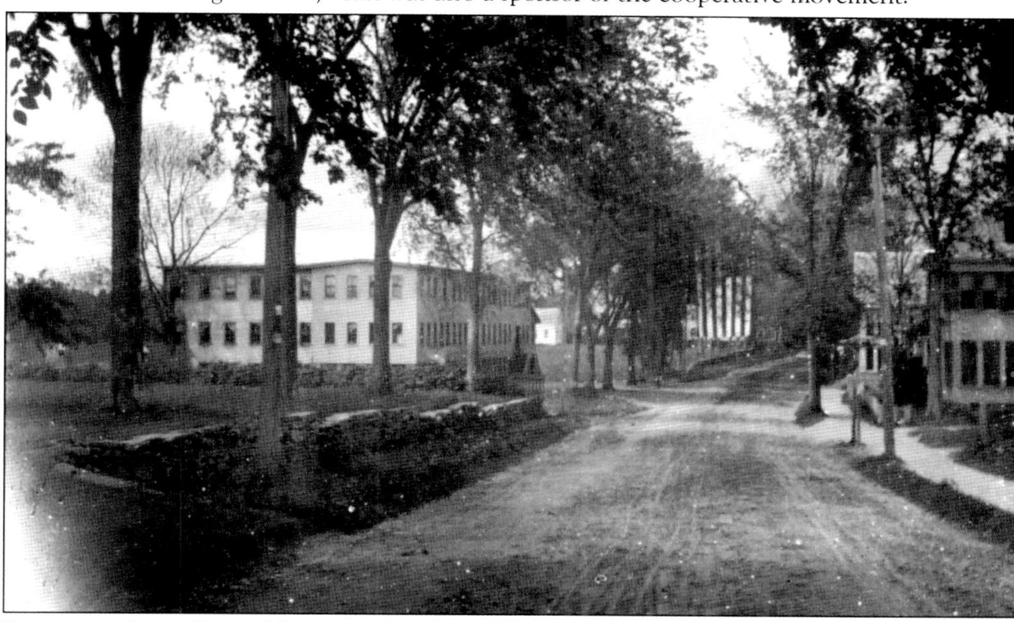

Despite the best efforts of the Pratts, North Middleborough was somewhat inconveniently located to both transportation links and sources of power and failed to develop a broad industrial base. Nonetheless, industry was represented by the Alden and Pratt shoe manufactory, seen here in a rare view of Plymouth Street looking northwest in 1898. The building was destroyed by fire two years later on October 17, 1900.

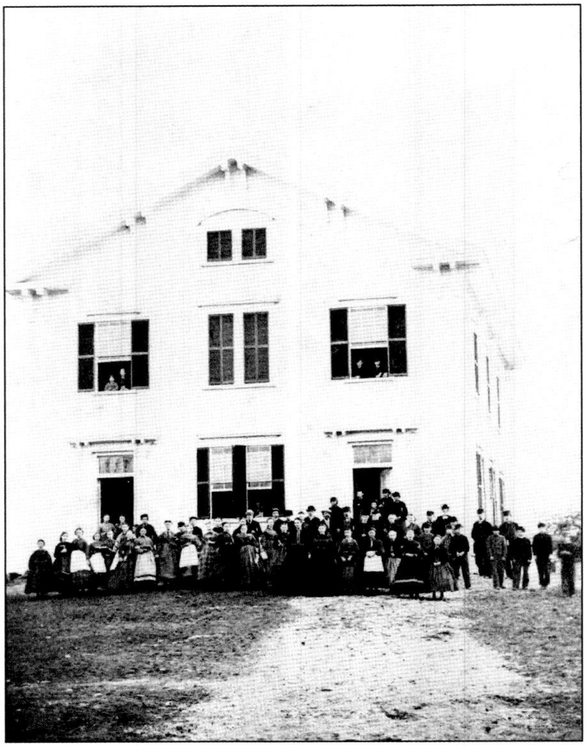

Among the best known of Middleborough's educational institutions was the Pratt Free School. Originally established as Titicut Academy in 1856, the school provided education to both sexes. Here, a group of schoolchildren from about 1856 have gathered to be photographed in front of the academy building that faced Titicut Green. Titiuct Academy offered a comprehensive curriculum, as indicated by this promotional circular for the 1859–1860 academic year. Academy trustees touted the advantages of being located in rural North Middleborough. "Here are none of those '*grog shops*' and '*eating saloons*' to be met with in more thickly settled villages, and which tend to corrupt the morals and vitiate the characters of the young and inexperienced . . . The Institution will be found surrounded by the *peaceful quiet* so admirably adapted to the mind searching for the hidden treasures of knowledge."

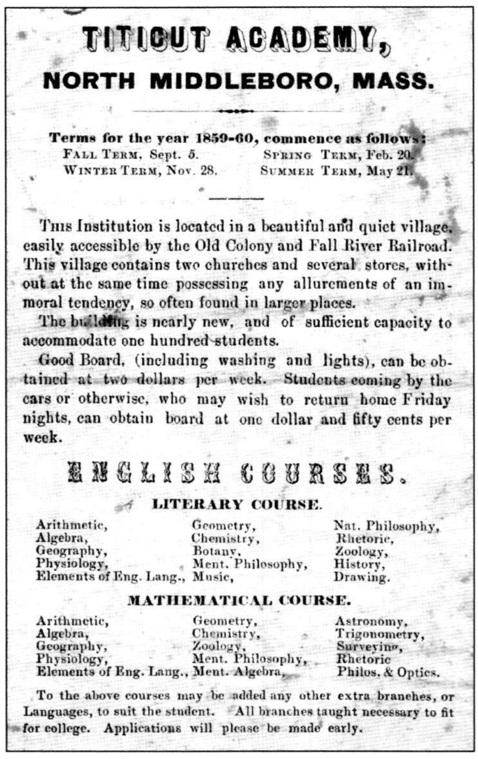

TITICUT ACADEMY,

NORTH MIDDLEBORO, MASS.

Terms for the year 1859-60, commence as follows:

Fall Term, Sept. 5.	Spring Term, Feb. 20.
Winter Term, Nov. 28.	Summer Term, May 21.

This Institution is located in a beautiful and quiet village, easily accessible by the Old Colony and Fall River Railroad. This village contains two churches and several stores, without at the same time possessing any allurements of an immoral tendency, so often found in larger places.

The building is nearly new, and of sufficient capacity to accommodate one hundred students.

Good Board, (including washing and lights), can be obtained at two dollars per week. Students coming by the cars or otherwise, who may wish to return home Friday nights, can obtain board at one dollar and fifty cents per week.

ENGLISH COURSES.

LITERARY COURSE.

Arithmetic,	Geometry,	Nat. Philosophy,
Algebra,	Chemistry,	Rhetoric,
Geography,	Botany,	Zoology,
Physiology,	Ment. Philosophy,	History,
Elements of Eng. Lang.,	Music,	Drawing.

MATHEMATICAL COURSE.

Arithmetic,	Geometry,	Astronomy,
Algebra,	Chemistry,	Trigonometry,
Geography,	Zoology,	Surveying,
Physiology,	Ment. Philosophy,	Rhetoric
Elements of Eng. Lang.,	Ment. Algebra,	Philos. & Optics.

To the above courses may be added any other extra branches, or Languages, to suit the student. All branches taught necessary to fit for college. Applications will please be made early.

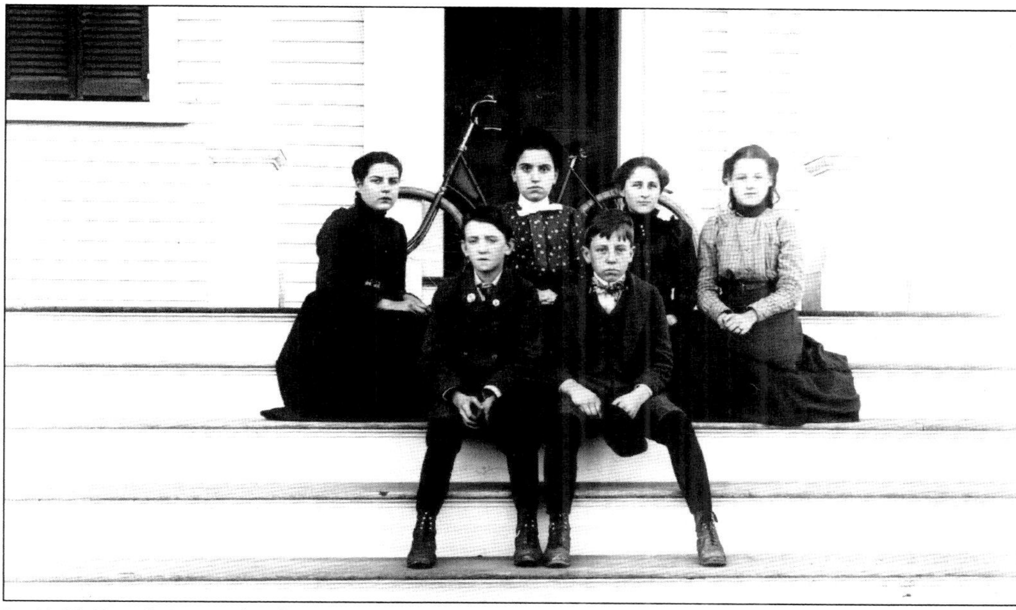

In 1865, Enoch Pratt of Baltimore, Maryland, a North Middleborough native, proposed financing the academy with tuition free for local students. "I make this endowment solely for the benefit of the constant rising generation of my native place," Pratt stated at the time of his initial gift. Students like those pictured above on the school's steps about 1900 benefited greatly. Following 1951, the school was operated by the Town of Middleborough.

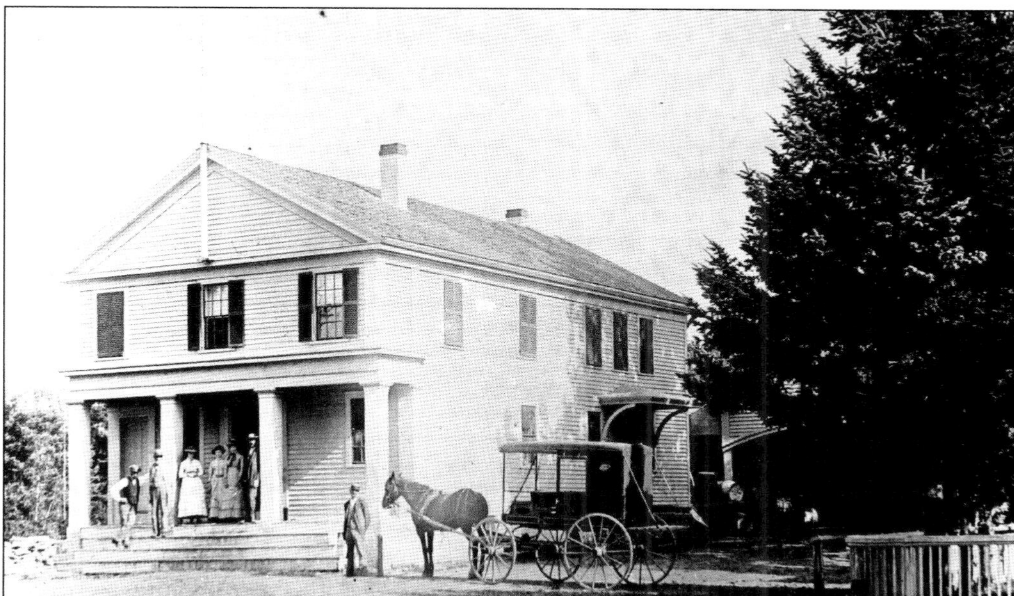

As elsewhere, informal village social life at North Middleborough was centered about the local mercantile, here represented by Nathan Pratt's store, which also housed the local post office and stood on the south side of Titicut Green. Pratt's store, "a rendezvous for the kindred spirits of the village years ago," was destroyed by fire on August 21, 1899, when a kerosene lamp tipped over. The Pratt operation was succeeded by Caswell Brothers.

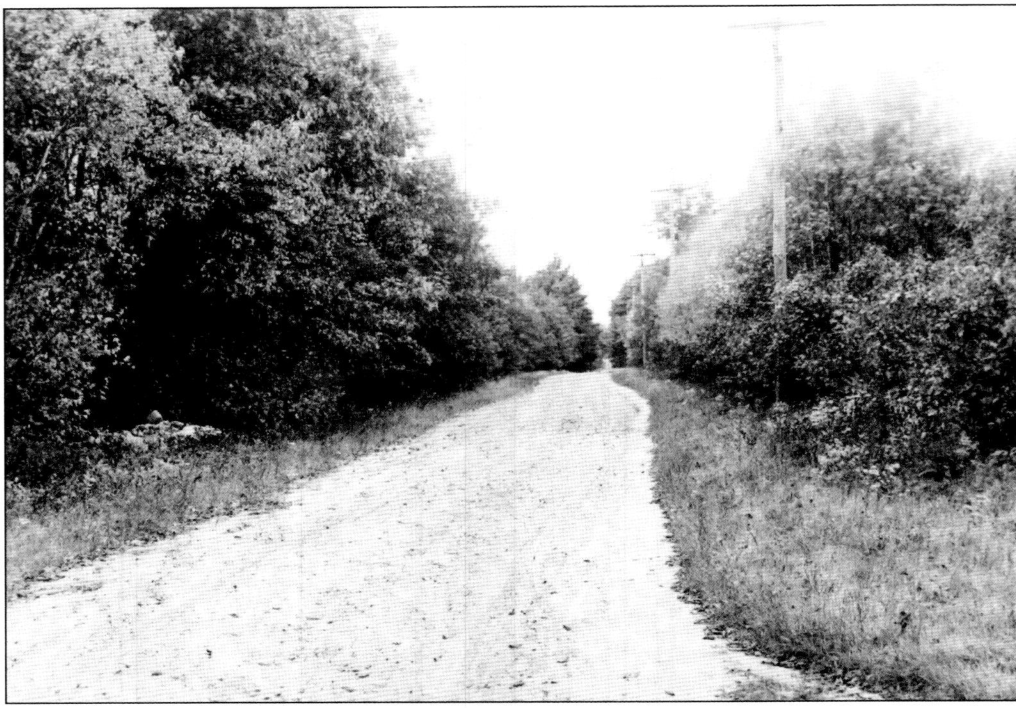

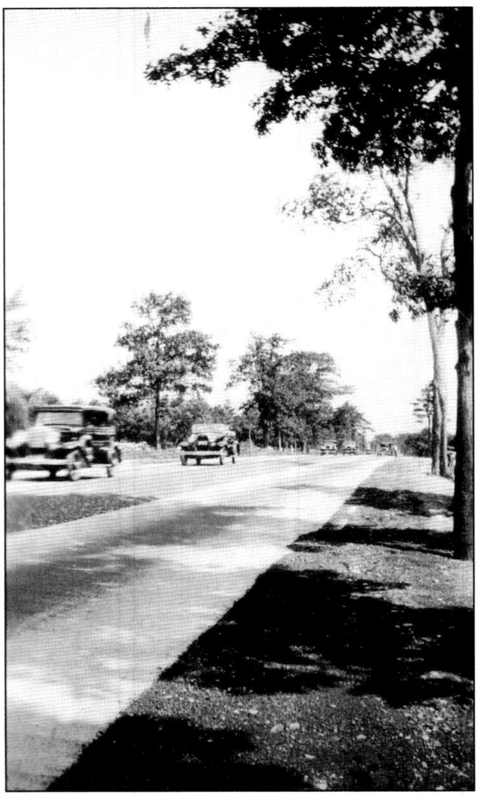

Linking North Middleborough to a wider world was Bedford Street, which was built following 1804 as a toll road originally known as the New Bedford and Bridgewater Turnpike. Bedford Street, as it came to be known, remained a narrow gravel road as late as October 1901, when the above photograph was taken. Although the condition of the road was better than most, it well illustrates the difficulties of road transportation a century ago. In 1930 and 1931, Bedford Street was rebuilt with the construction of two concrete strips separated by a macadamized median. An intrepid photographer captured this line of automobiles passing down the newly opened road in North Middleborough on July 19, 1931. This was not the only transportation advance for North Middleborough. In the mid-20th century, an airport operated on Pleasant Street, the runway of which is now Otis Pratt Lane.

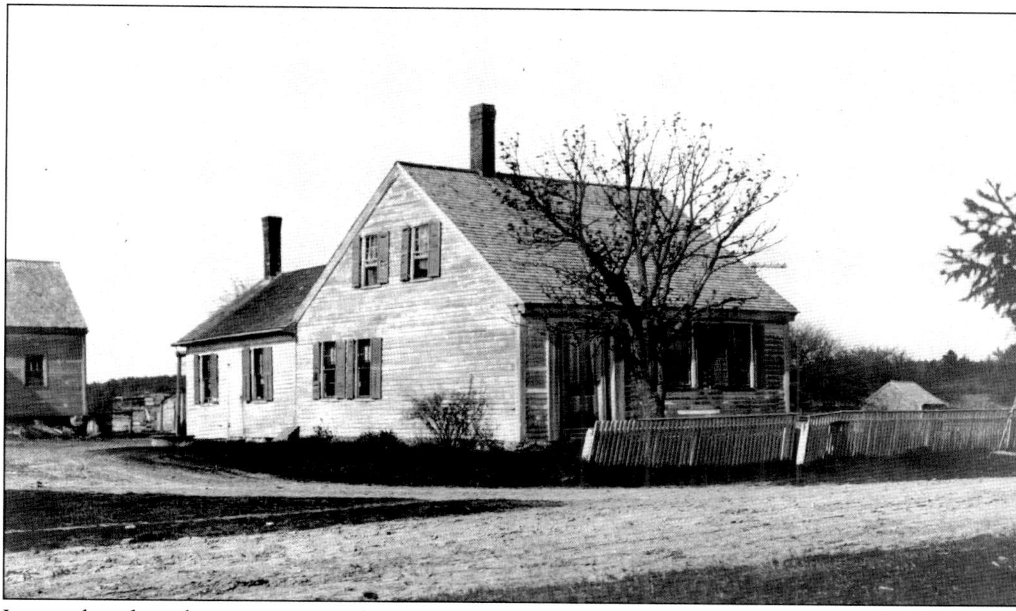

Located midway between Muttock and North Middleborough was Warrentown, a small village once populated by descendants of Richard Warren. Among them was Lavinia Bump (1841–1919), who, as an adult, stood less than a yard tall. She was able to parlay her talent and unique size into a show-business career noted for its longevity. The house in which she was born still stands on Plymouth Street near the intersection of Summer Street.

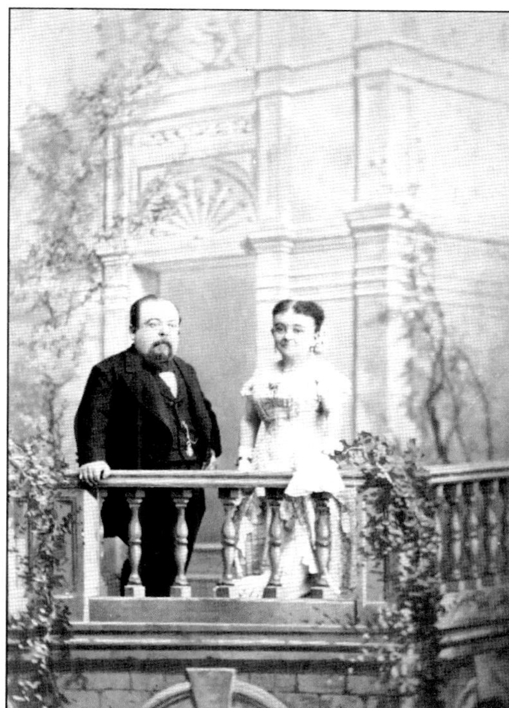

Bump, better known as Lavinia Warren, was a diminutive performer noted for her charm who became one of the most famous American women of the 19th century. Her first husband, Tom Thumb (Charles Sherwood Stratton), a protégé of P. T. Barnum, was a worldwide celebrity at the time of their 1863 marriage. The couple constructed a comfortable home for themselves at Warrentown, the interior of which was scaled to their small size.

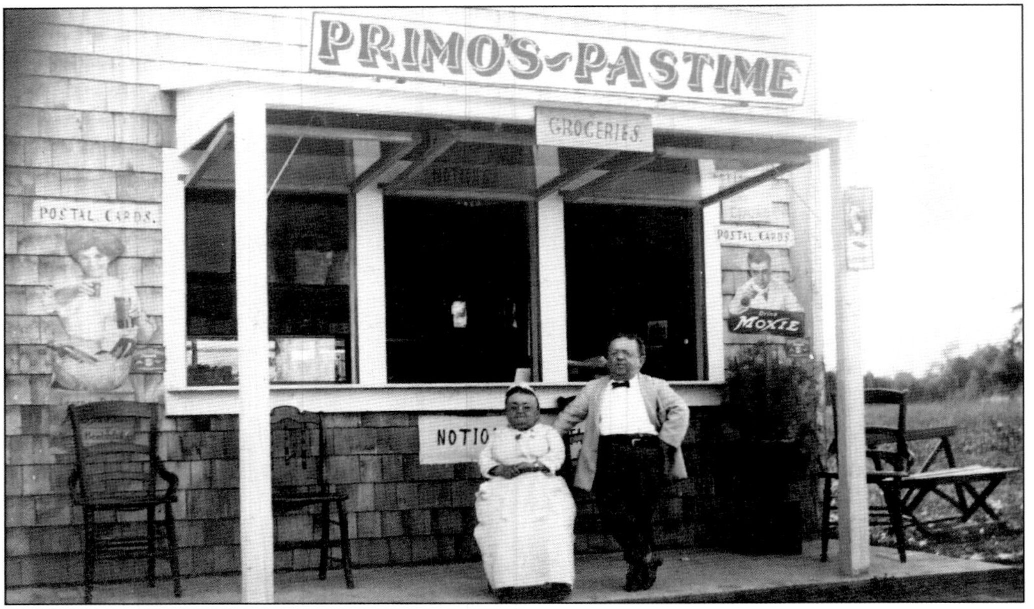

Following Tom Thumb's death at Warrentown in 1883, Lavinia Warren married Count Primo Magri, another tiny performer, in 1885. For a number of years, the couple continued to perform and tour. Following their retirement, they operated a refreshment stand known as Primo's Pastime on Plymouth Street near their home. While ice cream and souvenirs were sold, most came to catch a glimpse of the remarkable pair.

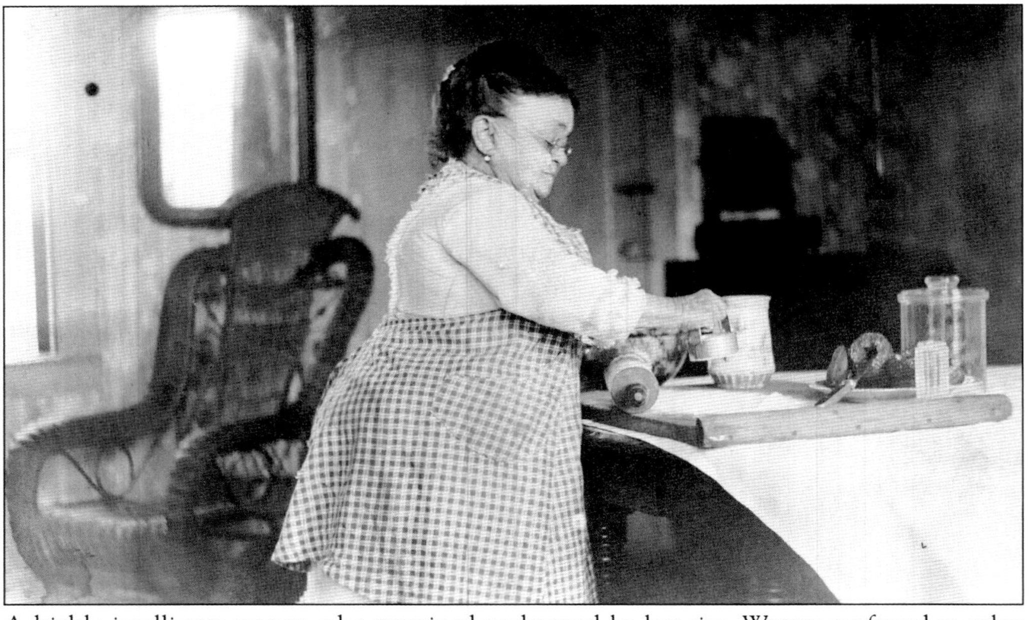

A highly intelligent woman who remained undaunted by her size, Warren preferred to relax through domestic tasks such as baking and particularly sewing. Her Warrentown home featured both a cooking range and a sewing machine scaled to her small size. Later in life, she became interested in Christian Science and was a supporter of patriotic organizations such as the Daughters of the American Revolution.

Three

South Middleborough and Rock

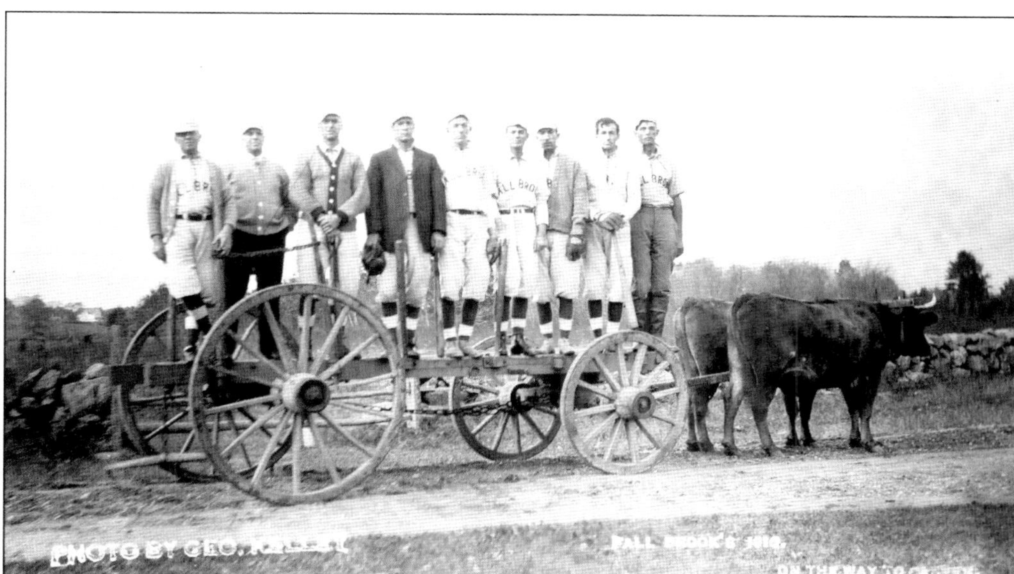

An independent social life was enjoyed by the southern districts of town, as exemplified by the Fall Brook baseball team, which was one of the best in the area. Here they pause for a photograph by George Kelley in 1910. South Middleborough and Rock's self-reliant spirit was a result of their development as Baptist communities established in the latter half of the 18th century.

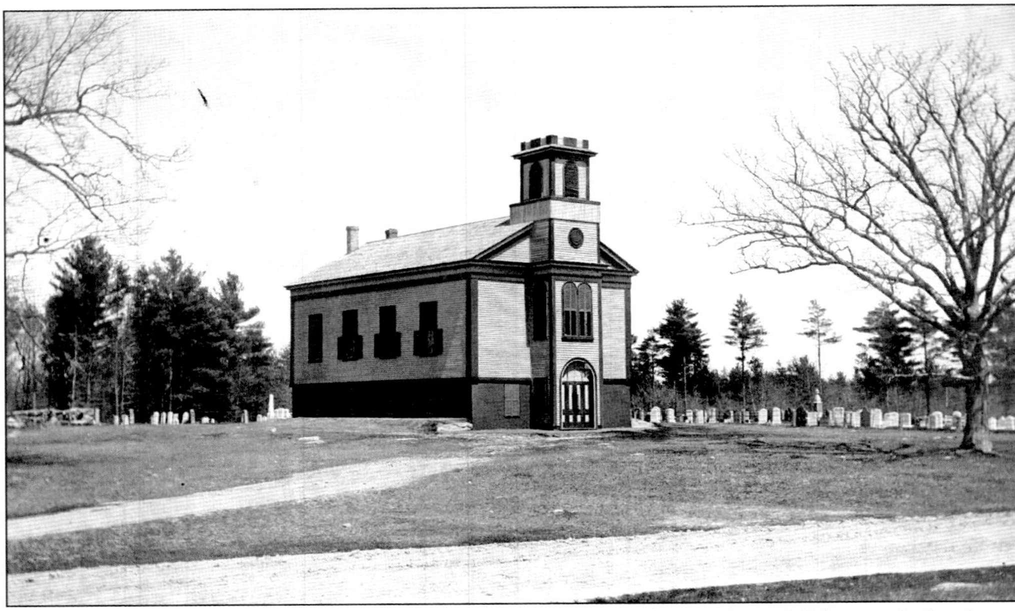

Of the communities in the southern portion of Middleborough, South Middleborough developed earliest, and by 1761, a Baptist church was established. Following the removal of the Baptists to Rock Village in the late 1700s, the Reformed Methodists established a following at South Middleborough and in 1841 constructed the church shown here on Wareham Street. The congregation remains an active organization within the community.

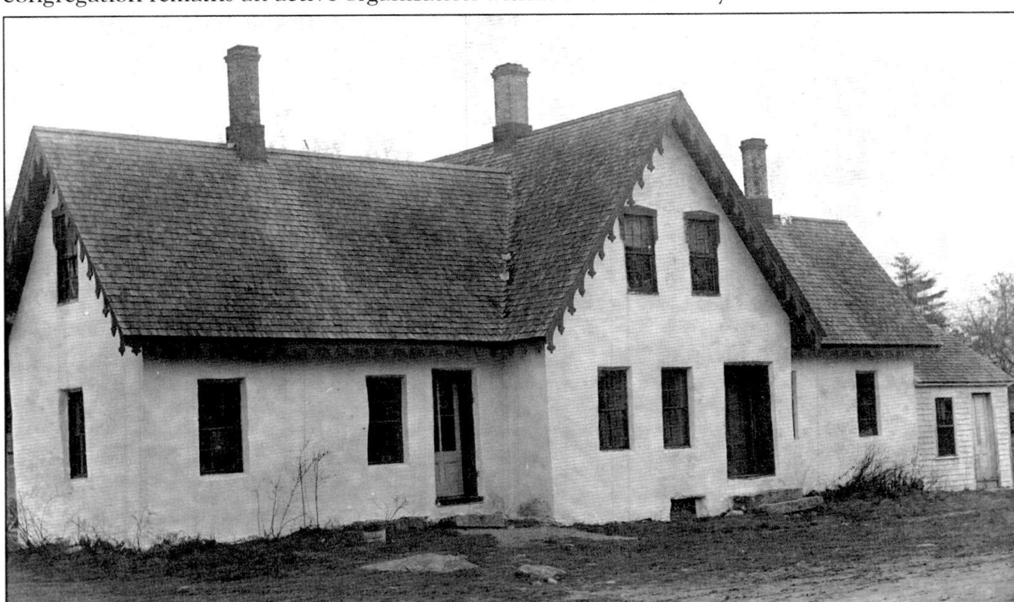

A short distance to the east of the South Middleborough church and cemetery is the Stone House, named for the material used in the construction of its walls. Begun about 1828, the house took a number of years to complete and was first occupied by the family of Calvin Gammons. Since then, it has served as an overnight camp, an antiques shop, and a private residence once again.

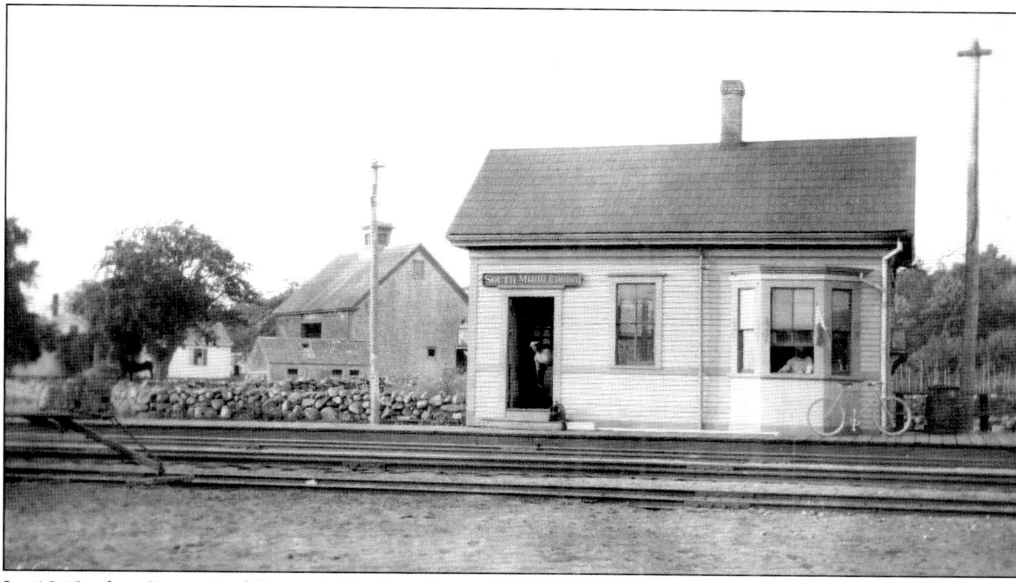

In 1848, the Cape Cod Branch Railroad constructed a rail line through South Middleborough. A small station was located at the Spruce Street crossing, and for years, staple products such as lumber, boxboards, trunks, and cranberries were shipped from South Middleborough. Throughout the period, however, passenger traffic remained light, and in 1939, the New York, New Haven and Hartford Railroad, which then operated the line, permanently discontinued passenger service.

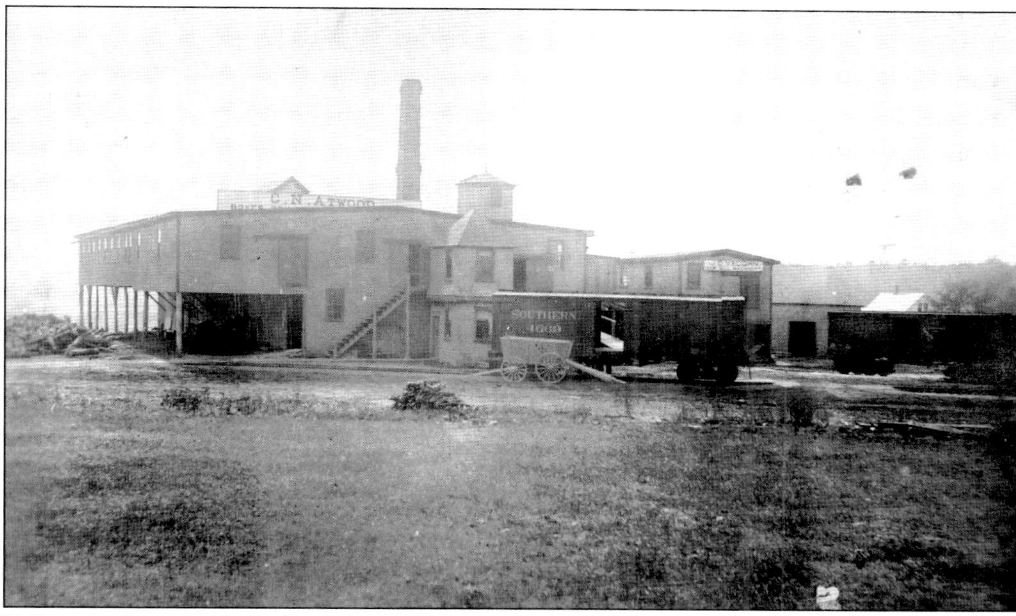

Following the arrival of the railroad in 1848, South Middleborough transformed itself into a lumbering center with mills like Benson's, Witham's, and Hunt's exploiting the vast tracts of standing white pine in the vicinity. In nearby Rock, Charles N. Atwood's mill (seen here) also flourished with the coming of the railroad, operating successfully at Miller and Walnut Streets until destroyed by fire in the mid-19th century. (Courtesy of Dorothy Thayer.)

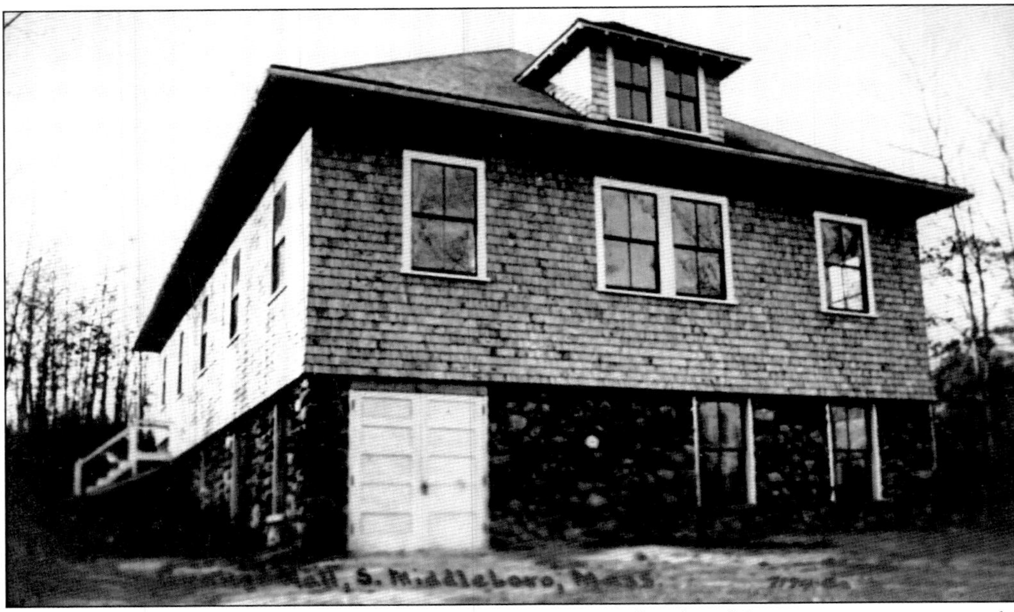

As a farming community, Middleborough not surprisingly played host to two granges, the Nemasket Grange at Middleborough center organized in 1888 and the South Middleborough Grange formed in 1913, both of which sought to support agriculture. In 1916, the large Grange Hall at South Middleborough was built, and it continues to serve its original purpose. The local Granges also played an important social role in both communities.

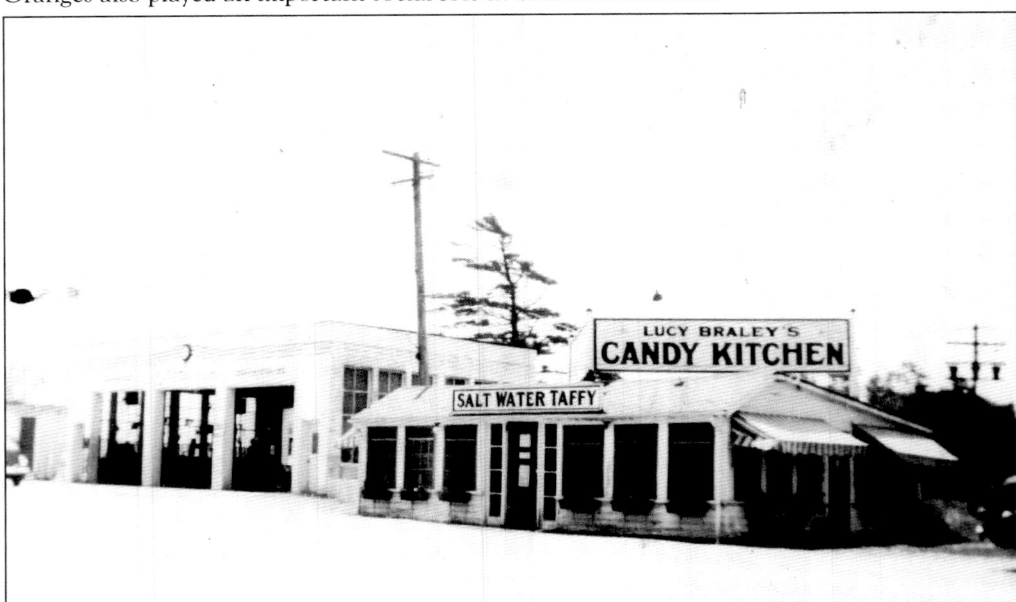

The 20th-century economic fortunes of South Middleborough were saved by the rebuilding of Wareham Street and its designation as Route 28, one of two modern roads linking Boston with Cape Cod. To take advantage of the enormous volume of traffic, small businesses like Sisson's Filling Station and Lucy Braley's Candy Kitchen were established along Wareham Street following 1925. Nearby, Sisson's Diner still operates today. (Author's collection.)

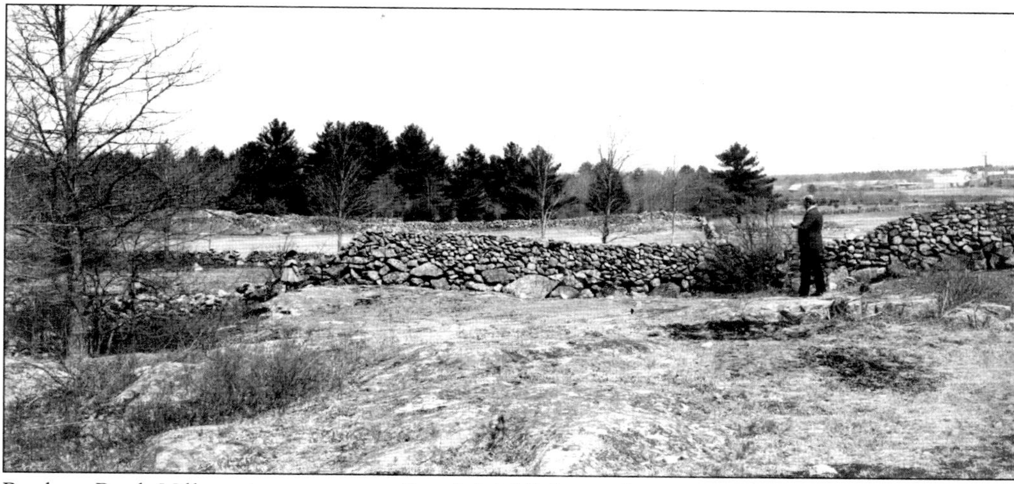

Rock or Rock Village, in contrast to South Middleborough, remained a quiet, rural residential village. Originally known as Beaver Dam for the natural obstruction settlers found along one of the branches of Black Brook, the village later came to be known as Rock, named for the large granite outcropping situated west of Miller Street. Here two visitors, a man and a young girl, stand upon a portion of the rock.

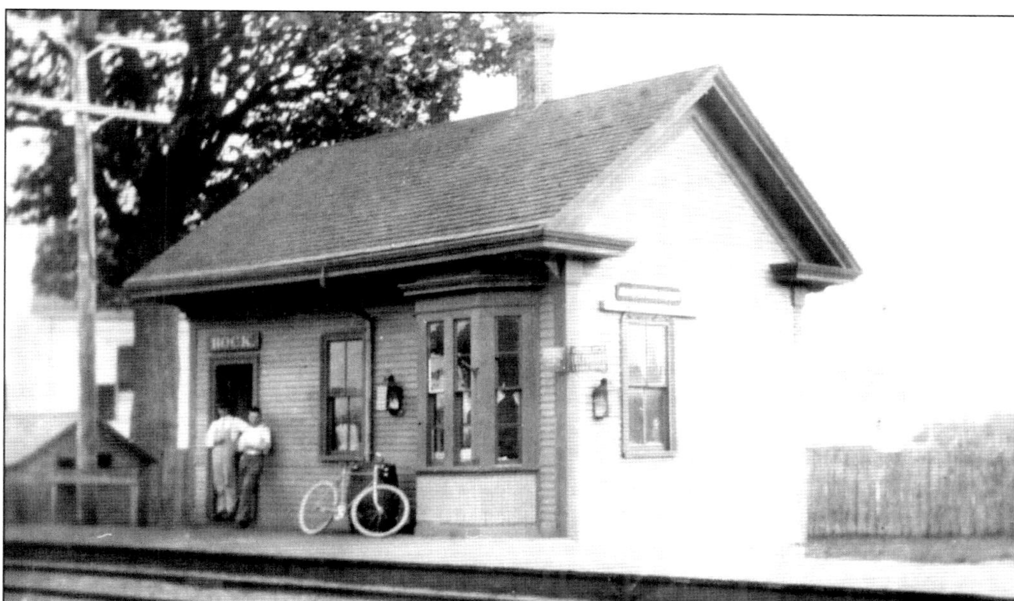

Like South Middleborough, Rock benefited from the arrival of the Cape Cod Branch Railroad in 1848. Because of the proximity of the two stations, however, railroad officials for many years sought to consolidate the two, a move resisted by Rock residents who strove to maintain their community's identity. The station remained at the Miller Street crossing near the Rock Village Church until the discontinuation of passenger service in 1939.

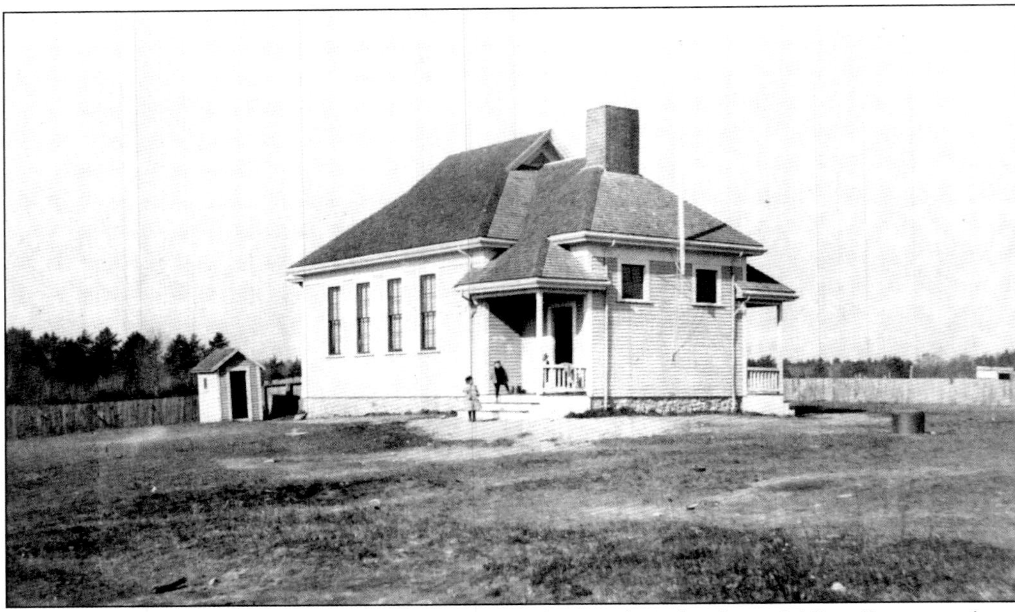

Designed by Warren H. Southworth in 1897, the Rock School on Miller Street with its 36 adjustable desks and "good blackboard surfaces" was described at the time of its construction as "a model country schoolhouse, and every resident of town may well feel proud of it." The school was added to in 1951 and finally closed in 1990, at which time it housed the first grade and kindergarten for the area.

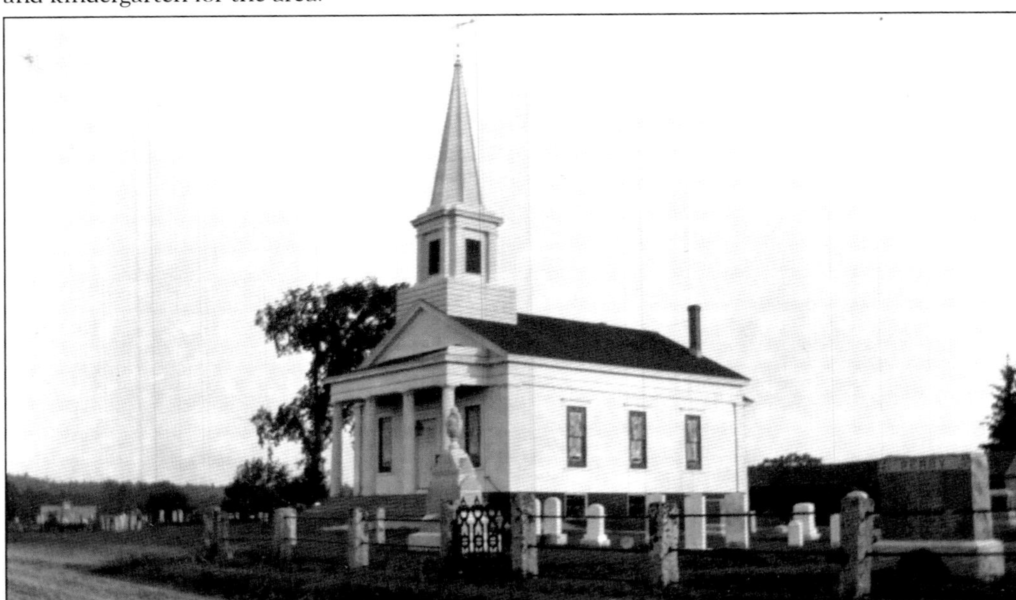

In 1792 and 1793, a number of Rock residents defected from the South Middleborough church and began holding services closer to home, ultimately prompting the relocation of the entire church to Rock. In 1795, a church was erected on Highland Street next to the Rock Burying Ground, which had been established in 1791. The second structure to house the church, seen above, was built in 1852 and stood until 1918.

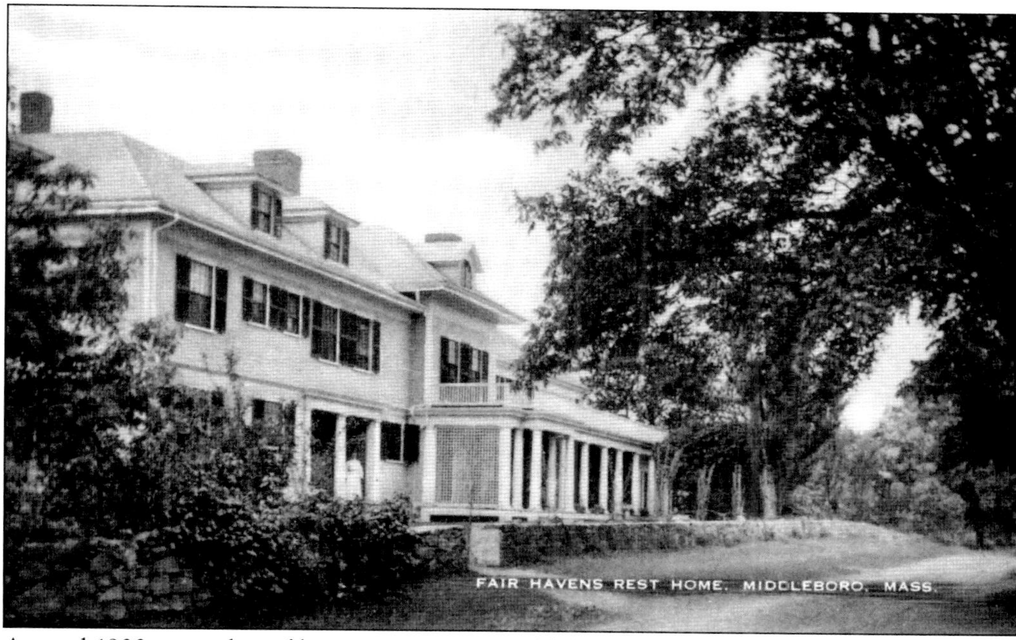

Around 1900, a number of large estates were established along Marion Road just west of Rock Village, as Boston businessmen established summer residences near the Middleborough ponds. Among them was Clifford R. Weld, whose estate was created about 1904. The Weld home later became the Fair Havens Rest Home, which for a time catered largely to the local Finnish community. (Courtesy of James G. MacDonald III.)

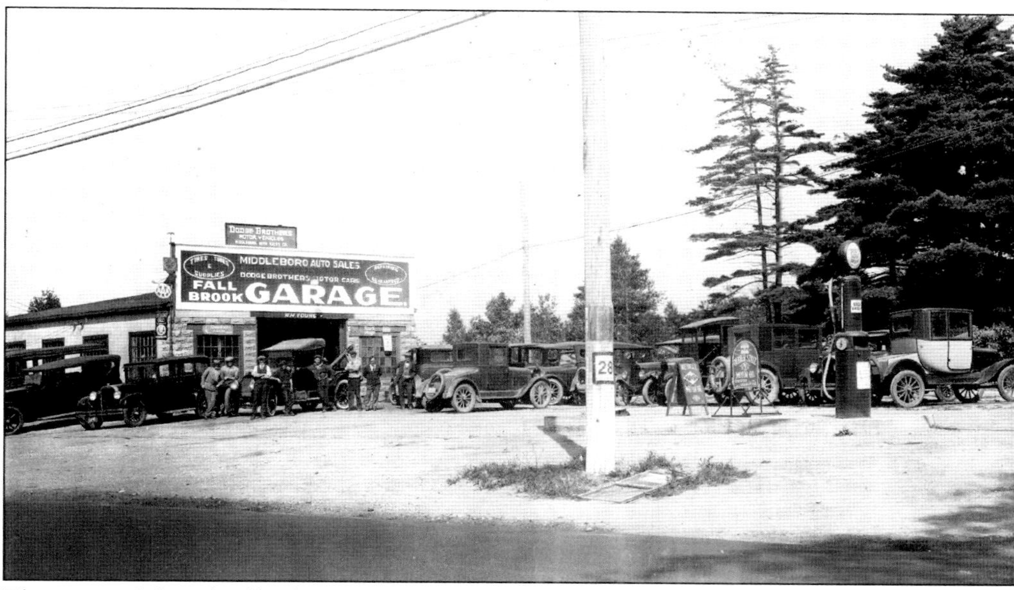

The automobile radically changed rural southern Middleborough, including Fall Brook, where the Fall Brook Garage was built at the intersection of Wareham and Sachem Streets. At the time, Wareham Street remained a part of Route 28, as indicated by the number painted on the telephone pole, and the garage was undoubtedly more successful selling gasoline and performing repairs than in selling the Dodge automobiles for which it held the franchise.

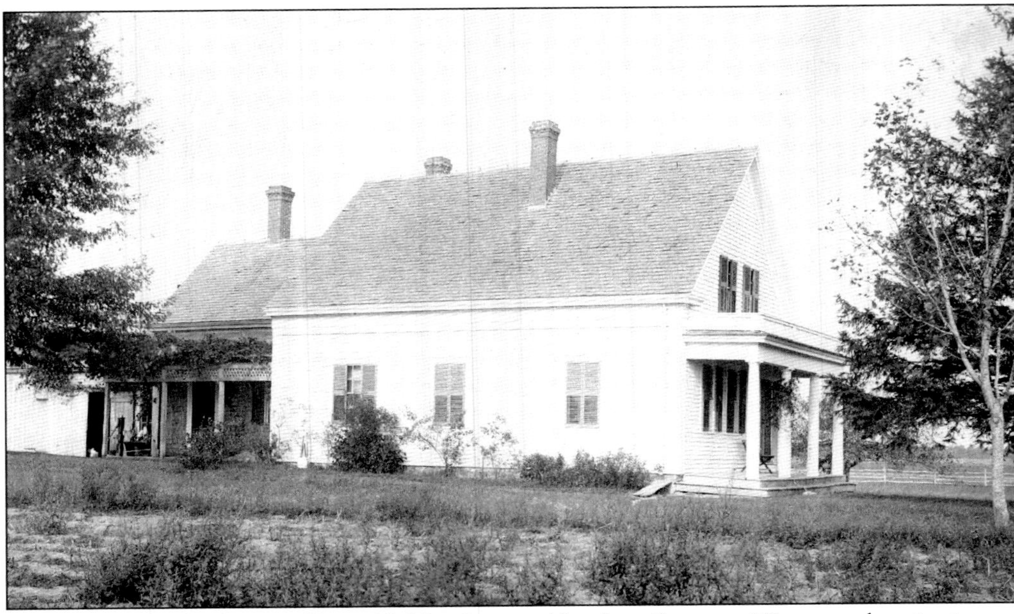

Lakeside Farm, the home of Isaac N. Vaughan on Vaughan Street at Wappanucket, is pictured in August 1893. For generations, the Vaughan family had been prolific in this section of Middleborough, situated immediately north of Lake Assawompsett along the eastern side of the Nemasket River. The home was later occupied by the Freitas family, which continues to farm much of the Vaughan property.

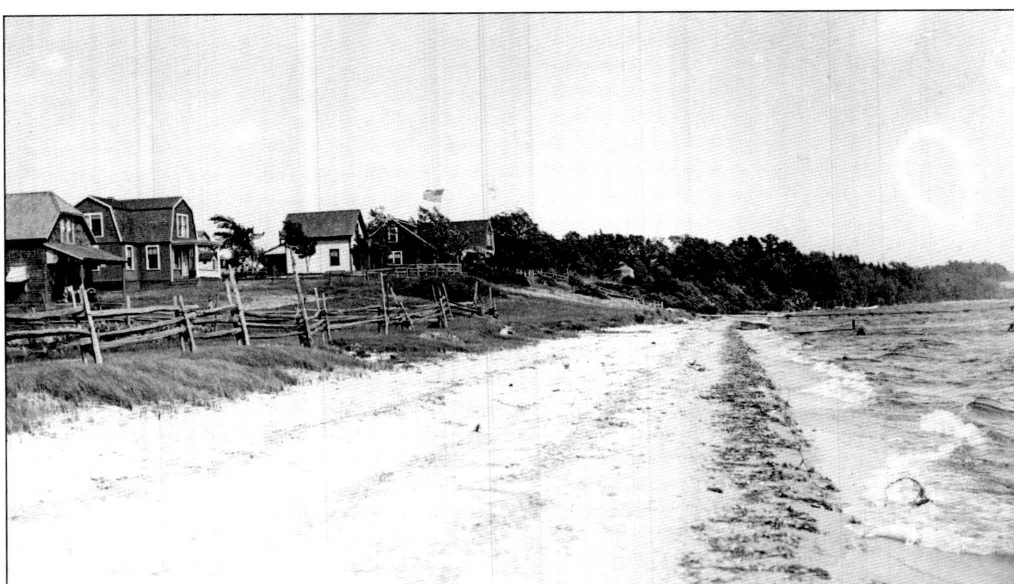

Vaughan began selling small lakefront parcels on his Vaughan Street farm in 1879, intending them to be used for cottage development. Several adjoining parcels were sold, and the area became known as Lakeside shortly thereafter. Each of Vaughan's later deeds prohibited the establishment at Lakeside of dance halls, billiard rooms, and bowling alleys and specifically prohibited the use of any building there to either manufacture or sell alcohol.

Four

Middleborough Four Corners

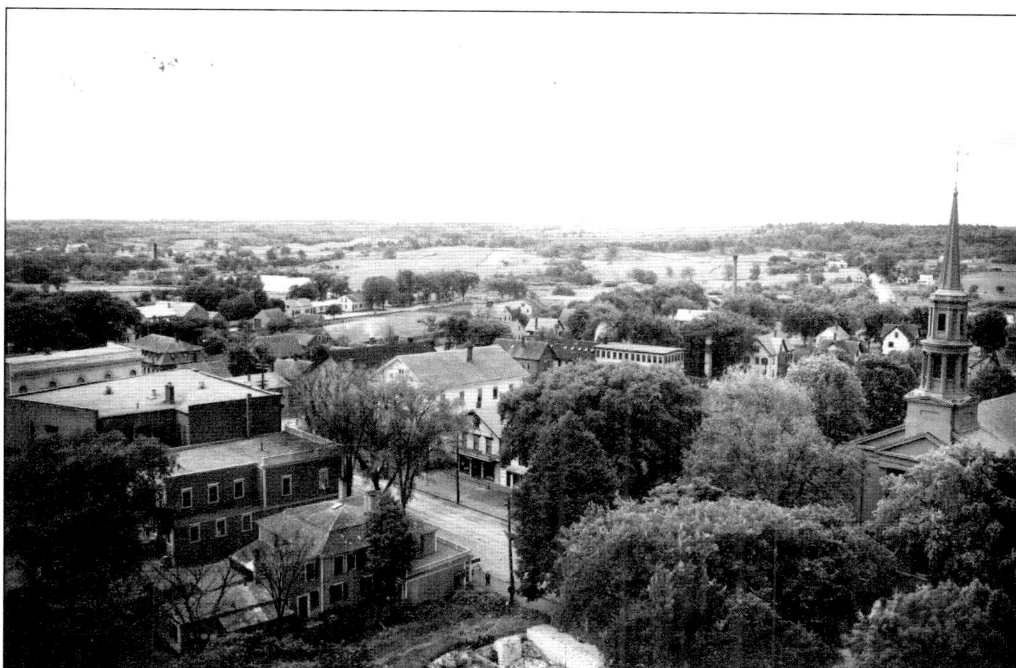

Located about the intersection of what are now Center, South Main, Wareham, and North Main Streets, the village of Middleborough Four Corners emerged as the center of Middleborough following 1850. Despite its rise to become the predominant and most populous district within town, the village still maintained an idyllic atmosphere, ringed by open fields and forests, as seen in this view from the town hall about 1900.

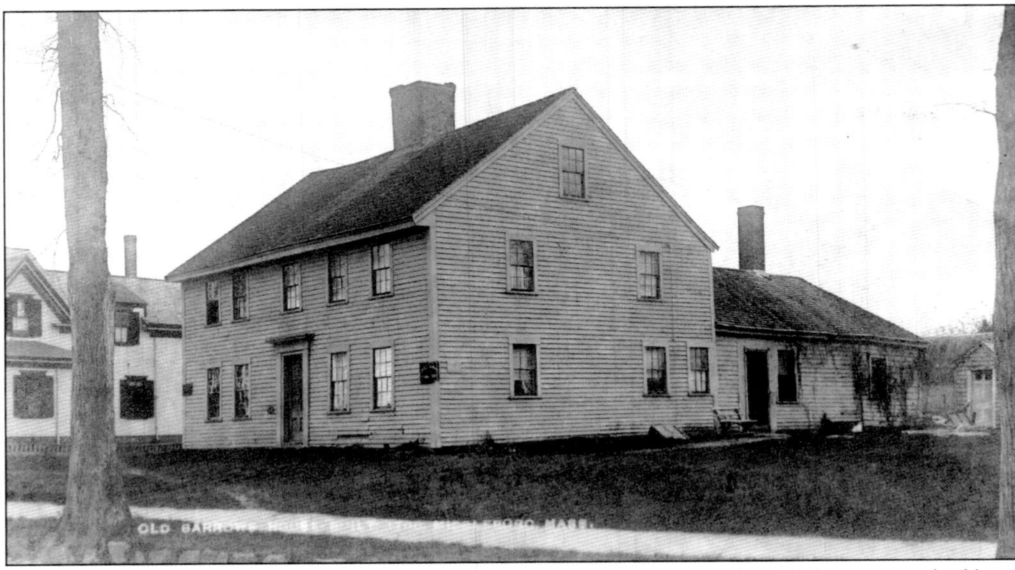

Settlement that existed near Middleborough Four Corners prior to the 1800s consisted of large farms extending to the river. Few houses stood along the main roadway (North and South Main Streets), which linked Plymouth and Dartmouth. The Barrows garrison house stood on North Main Street on the site of the later Nemasket Grange hall. Built about 1700 by Samuel Barrows, it was demolished in 1919.

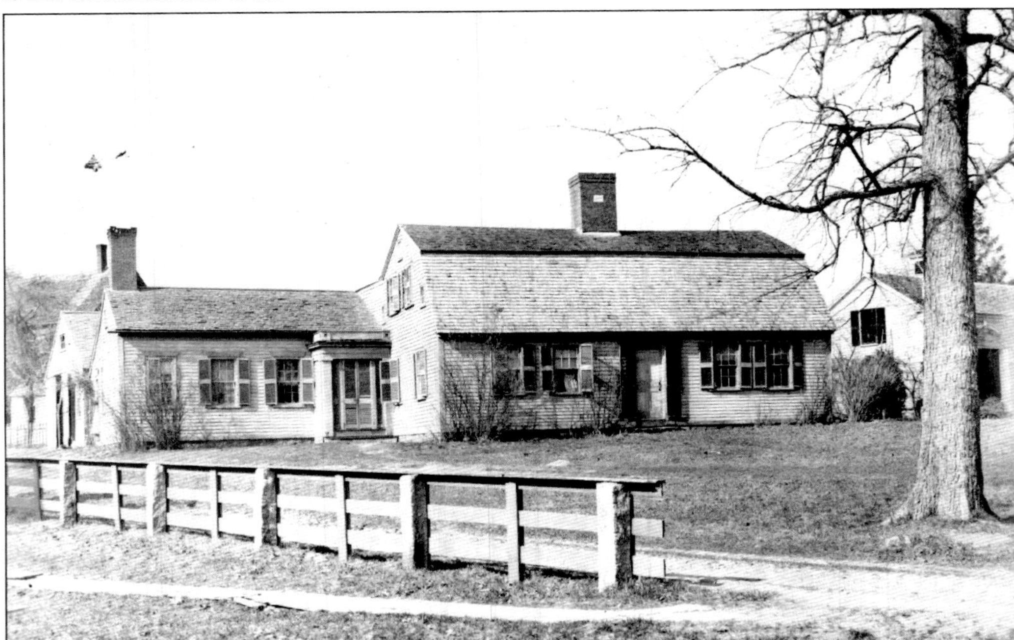

The Silas Wood house was the earliest home standing between the four corners and Mortontown and is extant. Although the date inscribed in its chimney is 1771, some have maintained that the house dates to as early as 1710. Wood's grandson Deacon Abiel Wood later occupied the house, during which time he compiled a record of Middleborough deaths that has become an important resource for genealogists today.

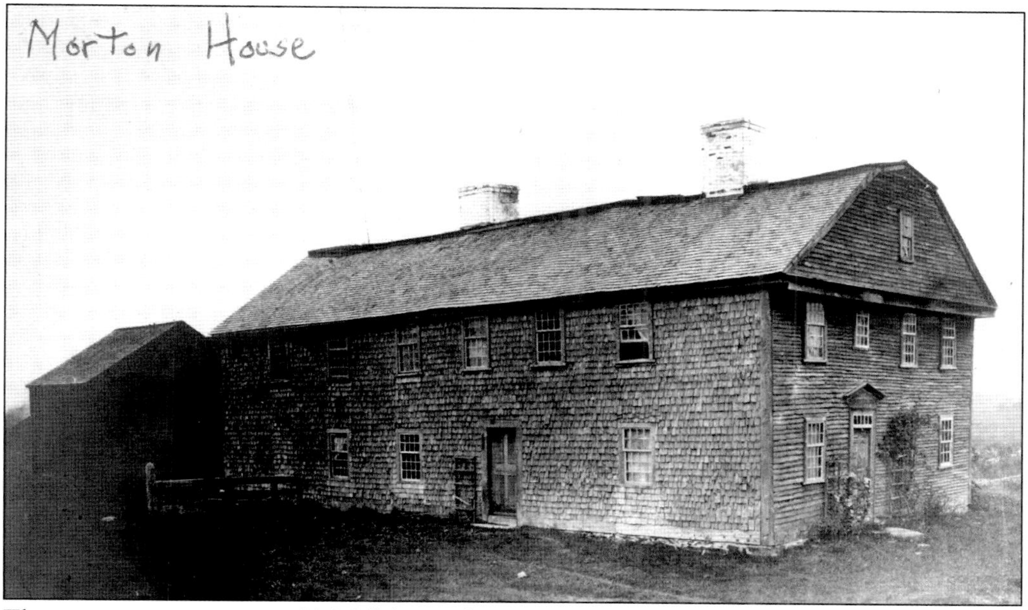

The most active section of Middleborough center prior to the rise of the four corners was Mortontown, situated along South Main Street just south of Grove Street. The area was dominated by the ancient gambrel-roofed Morton house, which stood in the middle of the present roadway and was a landmark for generations until being demolished in 1870. "Fans made from the wood are being hawked about," reported a newspaper at that time.

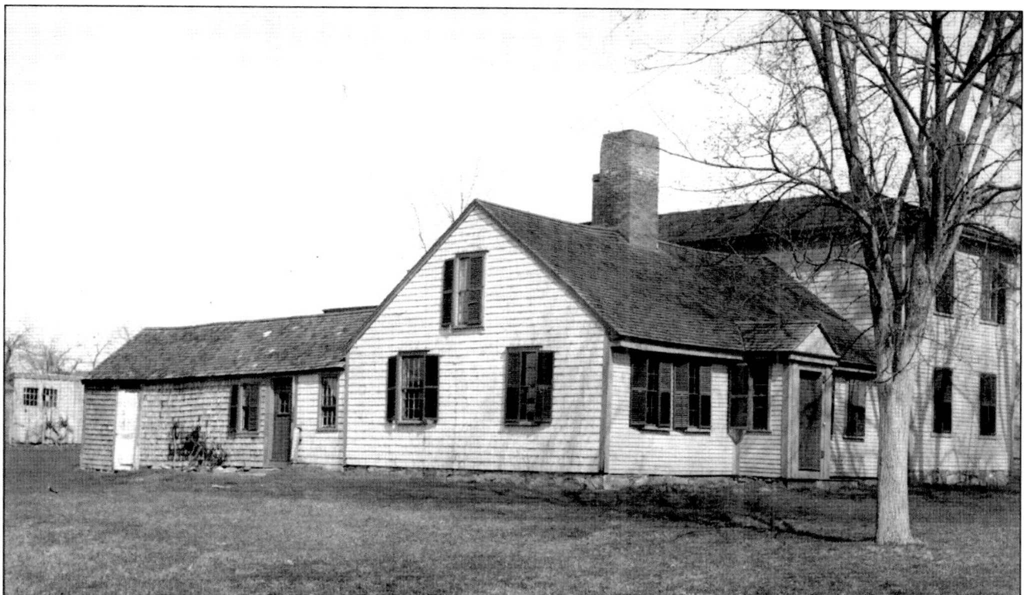

Although the exact age of the Clark house is unknown, it was described as being of "ancient vintage." Built by Seth Morton and later occupied by Dr. Samuel Clark and his son Dr. Joseph Clark, the small cape-style house stood on South Main Street near Clark Street and was typical of the modest nature of Middleborough homes of the 18th century. It was demolished for Route 25 in the 1960s.

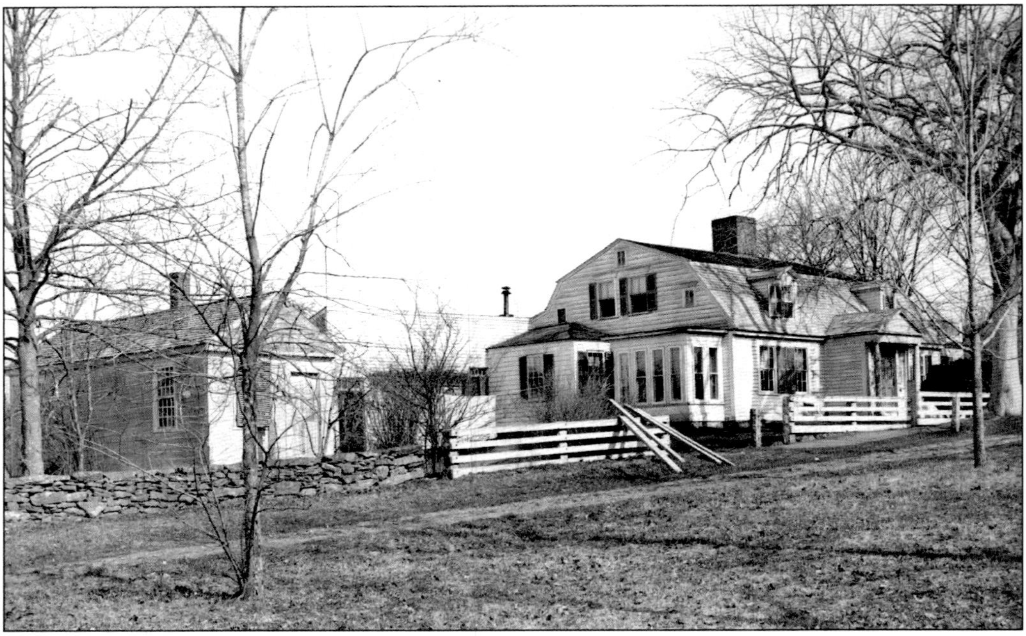

The Judge Wilkes Wood house was also a prominent feature at Mortontown where it stood on the site now occupied by the Rite-Aid pharmacy. Like other houses in the neighborhood, it was built in the early 1700s by a member of the Morton family. Occupied by Wood and his descendants throughout the 19th century, it was demolished in 1966 for Fernandes Supermarket.

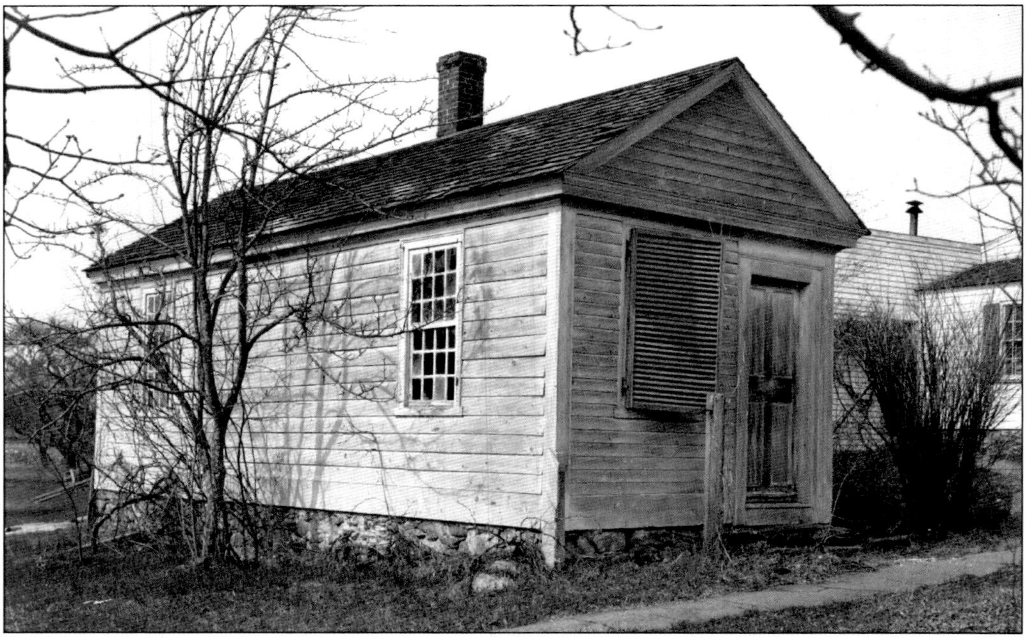

Standing just south of the Wood house (and seen also in the previous photograph) was Judge Wilkes Wood's law office. Wood's son William H. Wood also practiced law and utilized the office for a period. Saved at the time the Wood house was demolished, the office was moved to the grounds of the Middleborough Historical Museum where it has been restored to its original appearance.

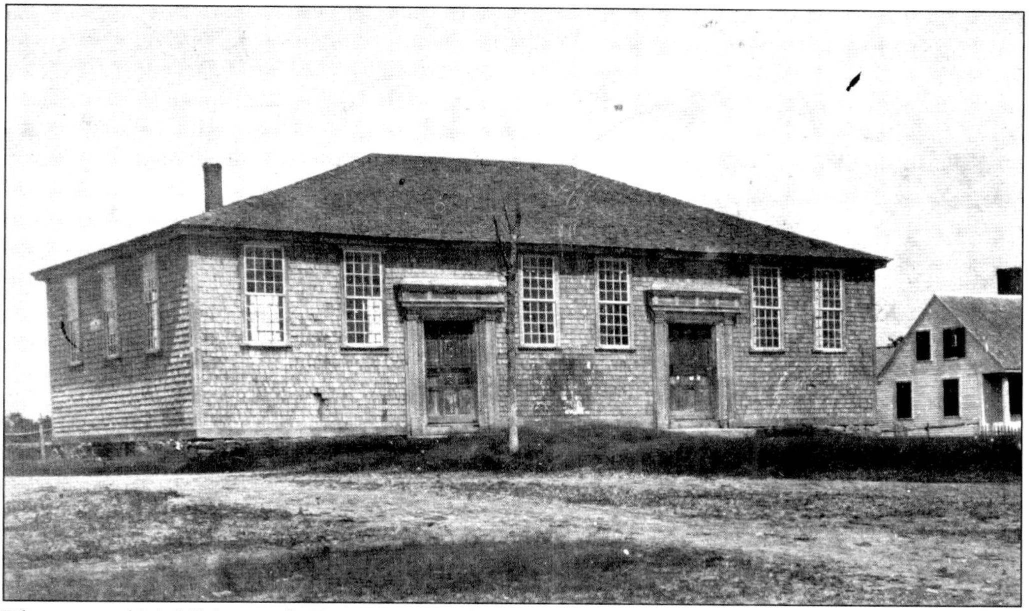

The area of Middleborough Four Corners (and Mortontown in particular) was geographically more central within the town that then included Lakeville, and it was consequently selected as the site of a new town house, which was erected at South Main and West Grove Streets in 1796. Later, the town house came to be much criticized. It was replaced by the present town hall in 1874 and sold for scrap lumber.

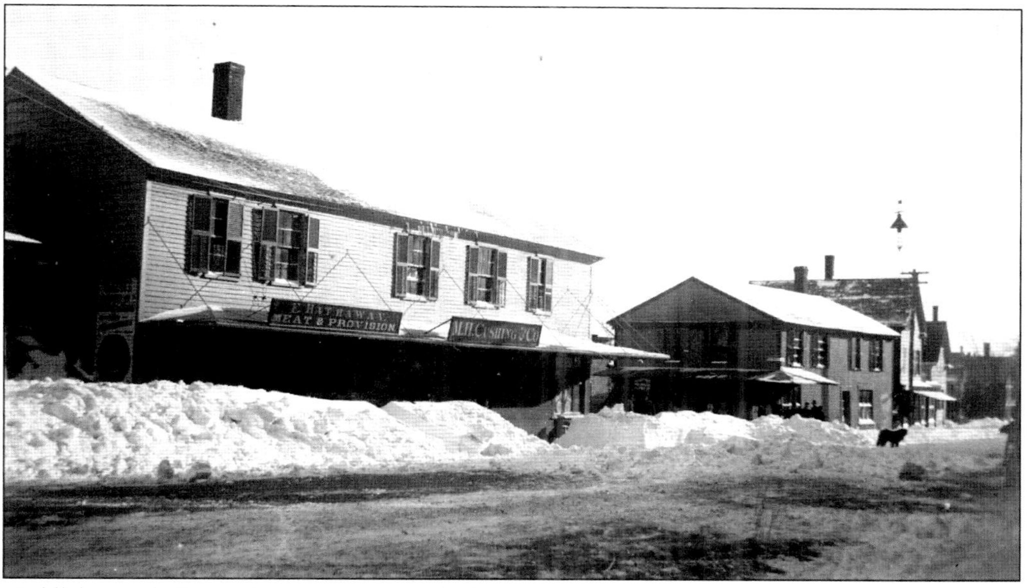

Middleborough Four Corners was propelled towards becoming the civic, industrial, religious, social, and educational center of Middleborough by an ambitious group of Baptist activists headed by Levi Peirce (1773–1847). Peirce took advantage of the crossroads, where roads from Wareham, Plymouth, Taunton, and New Bedford met, to establish a mercantile operation (front left). Frequently referred to as the "old store," Peirce's original building was replaced in 1900 by the Peirce Block.

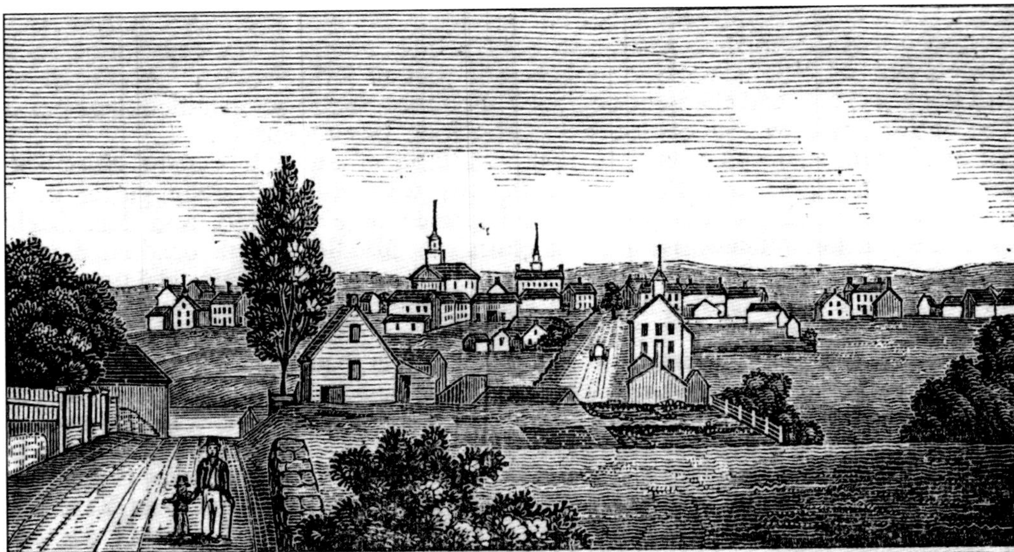

Village of Four Corners, Middleborough.

By 1831, when the above woodcut was produced, Levi Peirce and the coterie of entrepreneurs that surrounded him had successfully promoted expansion of Middleboro Four Corners, seen here from midway up Barden Hill. Through the efforts of Peirce and his associates, the Central Baptist Church, Peirce Academy, and the Nemasket Manufacturing Company were founded, and the spires of those three institutions, from left to right, may be seen interrupting the horizon.

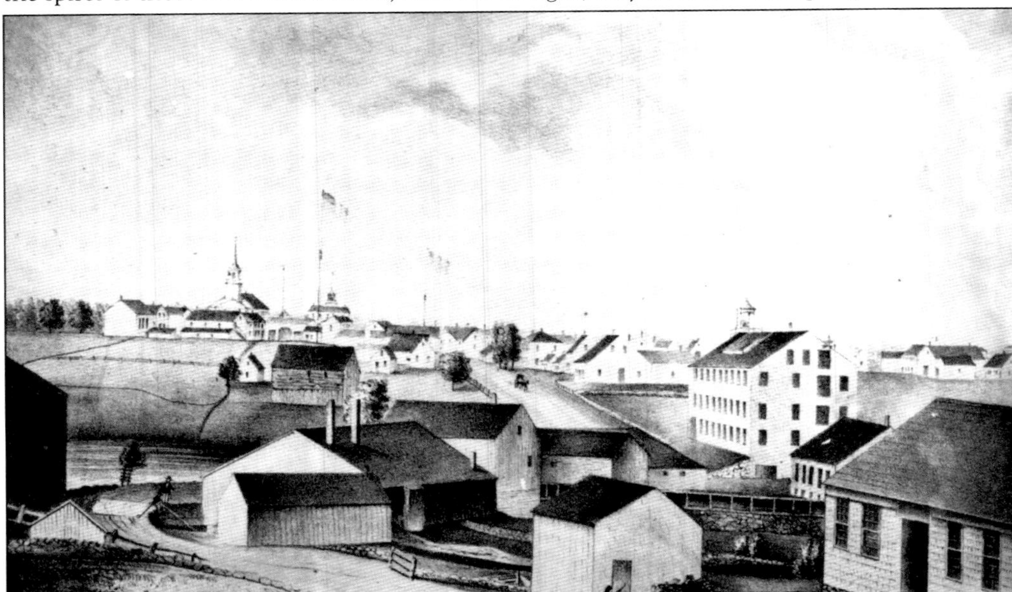

This 1850 view of the same area shows the growth experienced by the village during the second quarter of the 19th century, although the Baptist church, Peirce Academy, and Nemasket cotton mill remain. The operation of the cotton mill, particularly, and the development of the shovel works (the buildings at front center) promoted residential and commercial development near the four corners that continued unabated for another century and a half.

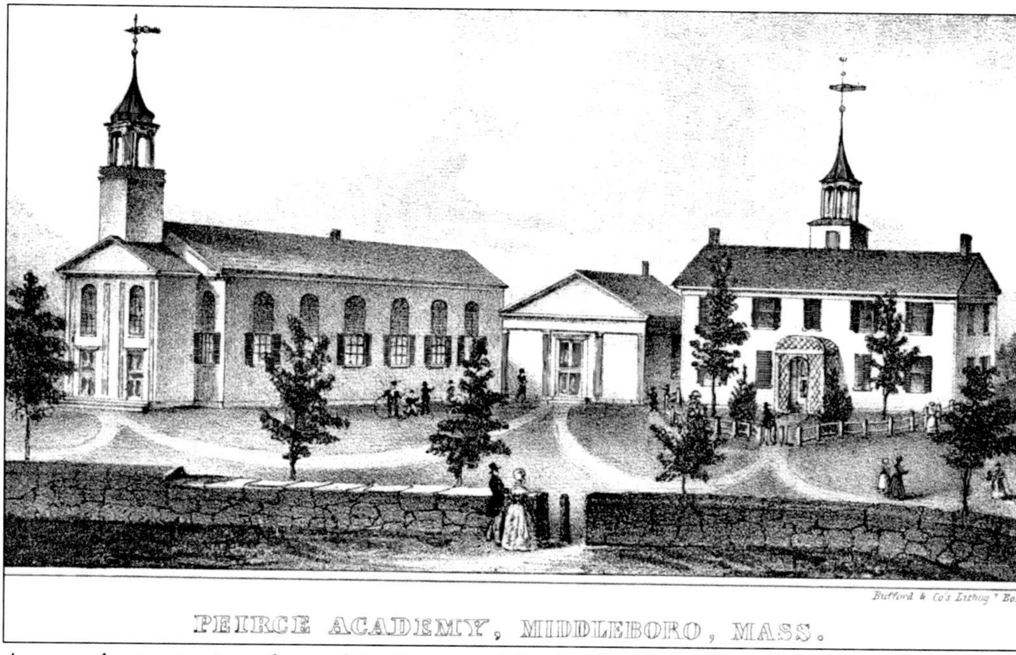

Among the institutions fostered by Peirce and his Baptist contemporaries were a new church that became known as the Central Baptist Church and an educational institution named Peirce Academy in his honor. Originally, Baptist services were held in the small chapel building in the center of the engraving above. The chapel was moved to School Street where it was used as a dormitory and gymnasium for Peirce Academy. Still later, it served the local Methodists as a chapel before their own church was built in 1868 and 1869. It was last moved to the West Side where it was known as the chapel house before being demolished in 1932. The structure on the right is the original Peirce Academy building, which stood on the site of the present post office. The same site from nearly the same vantage point is depicted about 1830 (above) and 1850 (below).

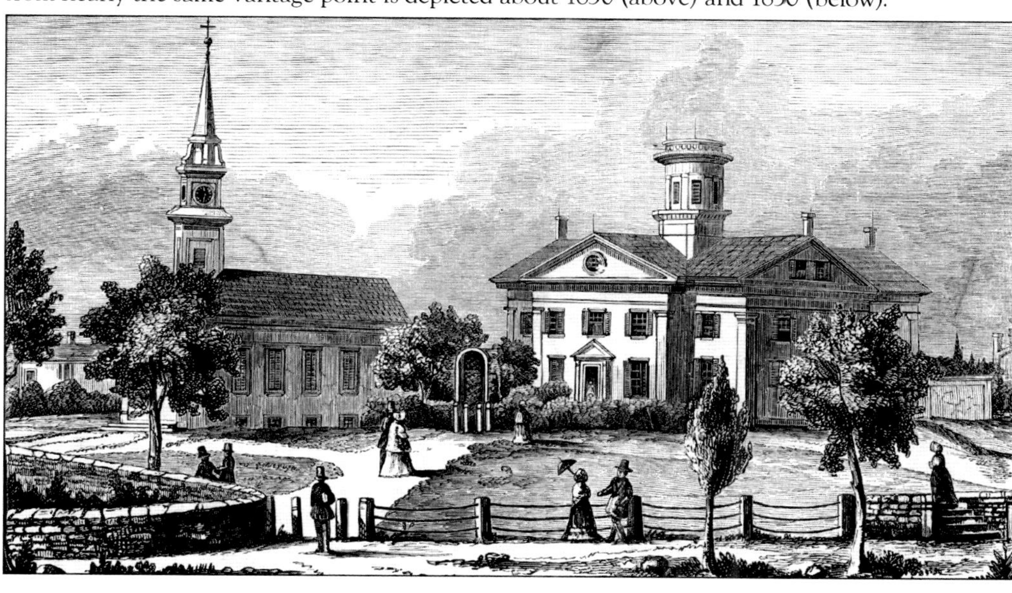

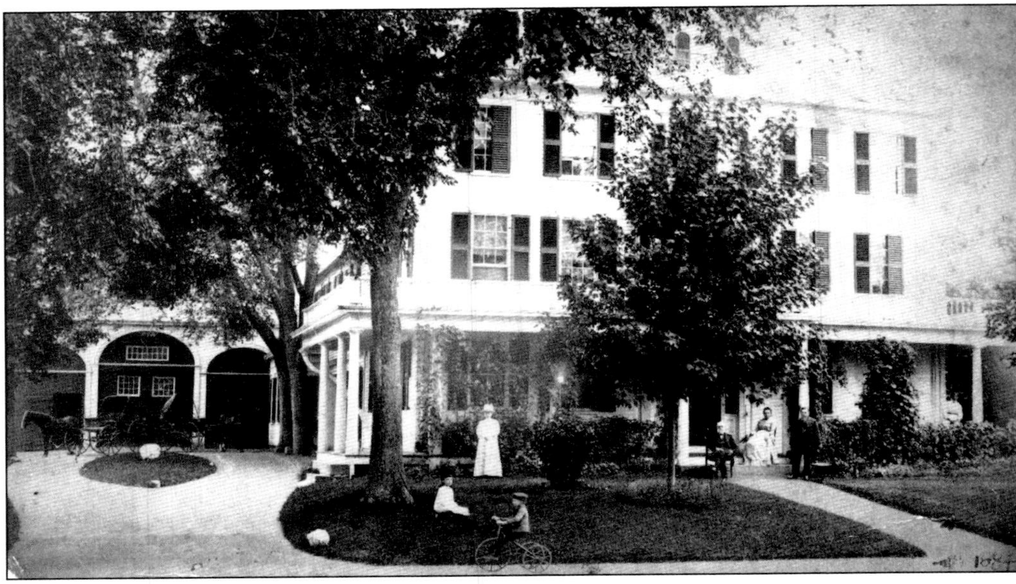

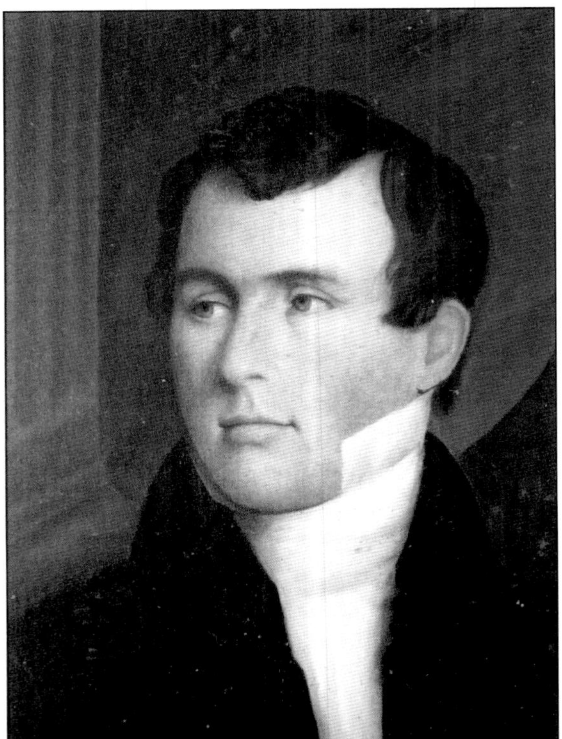

Typical of the homes built at Middleborough Four Corners by its Federal-era entrepreneurs was the Tucker-Jenks house on the corner of North Main and Peirce Streets. Constructed by Levi Peirce's son-in-law Elisha Tucker, the house was later occupied by Tucker's descendants, including the Jenks family seen posed for a summertime portrait sometime after 1881. The house was last operated as a hotel known as the Martinique before being demolished in 1957 to make way for a filling station. Along with his in-laws, the Peirces, the Bournes, and the Thatchers, Tucker became associated with a number of industrial and commercial enterprises at Middleborough Four Corners founded by his wife's father. Tucker served as treasurer of both the Central Baptist Church and Peirce Academy, maintaining the family's connection with those institutions.

Most successful of Middleborough Four Corners's entrepreneurs, however, was Peter H. Peirce (1788–1861), Levi's younger brother. Peter was a partner with other family members in the shovel and cotton industries along the Nemasket River and, in the days prior to local banks, he was a large lender of money. His parsimonious ways permitted him to accumulate a modest fortune, much of which was left to the town following 1901.

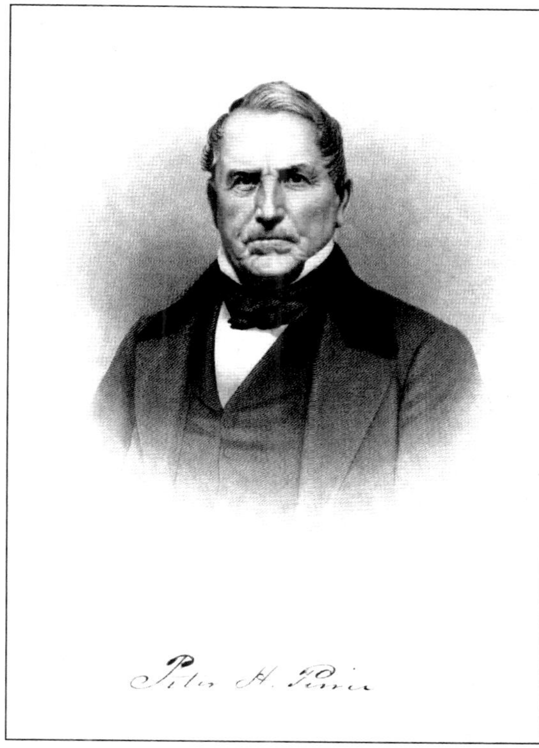

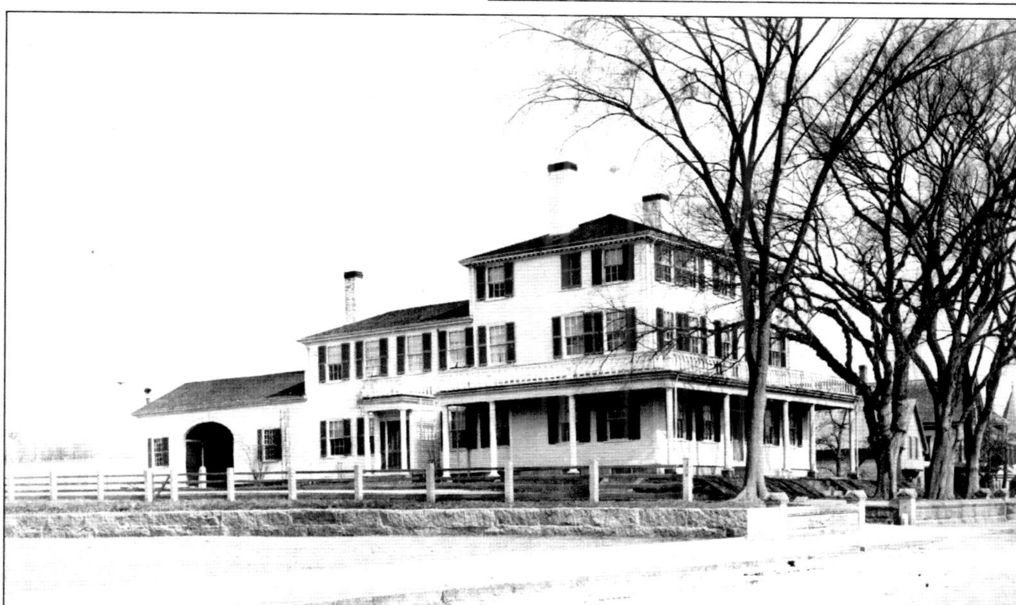

Although Peter seemed to have had little use for his fortune, which today constitutes the Peirce Trust, he did spend money on his North Main Street home. Peirce enjoyed the luxury of running water, which was forced into the house from the Nemasket River below by means of a hydraulic ram. The house has been painstakingly restored by attorney George C. Decas, author of a biography of Peter.

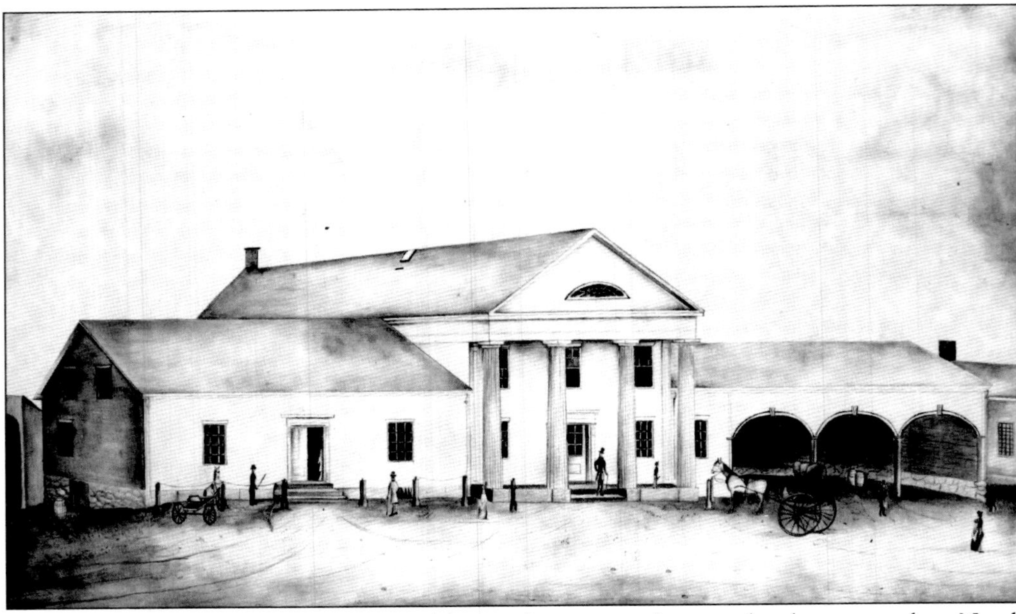

Another source of Peter H. Peirce's wealth was the mercantile store that he operated on North Main Street under the firm name Peter H. Peirce and Company. To house the store, Peirce constructed a large Greek Revival store building with attached carriage sheds, the original appearance of which was documented in this wash drawing, which is believed to have been done by his daughter Judith.

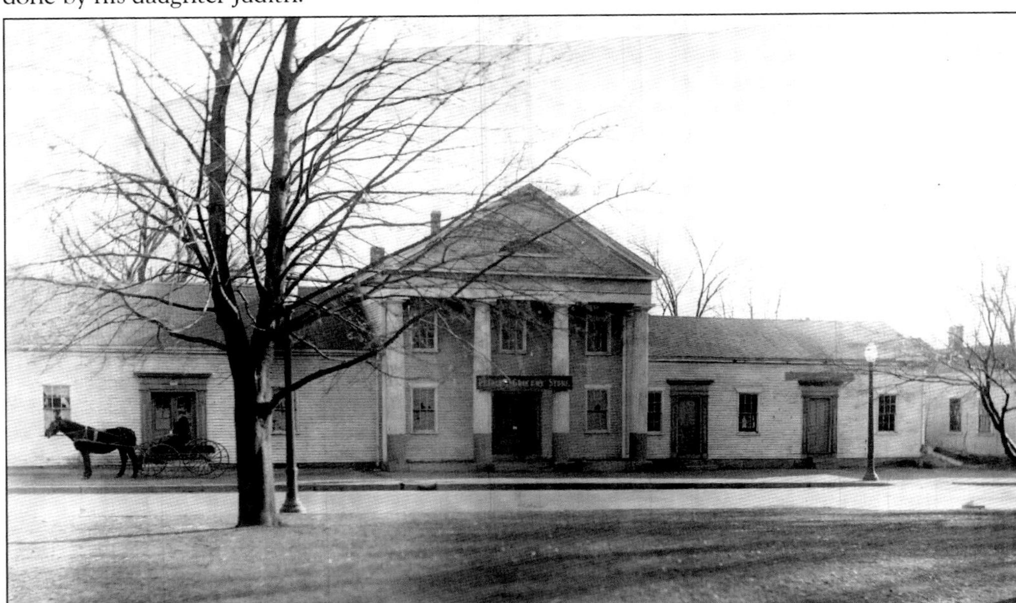

The building served for nearly a century as a grocery store and is seen here in its later days when it was operated by Herbert and Elton L. Pratt. Throughout the period, however, the firm continued to conduct business under the Peirce name, operating as P. H. Peirce and Company. In 1936, it was renovated for use by the Middleborough Police Department and Fourth District Court as a Public Works Administration project.

In 1936, this photograph of the abandoned Peirce store was captured. The curved counter and deep grain bins behind, as well as a distinctive four-partners desk, are now preserved in the collections of the Middleborough Historical Museum. The court remained in the refurbished store building until relocated to Wareham in the 1970s, but the Middleborough Police Department continues to occupy the building that remains a landmark in town.

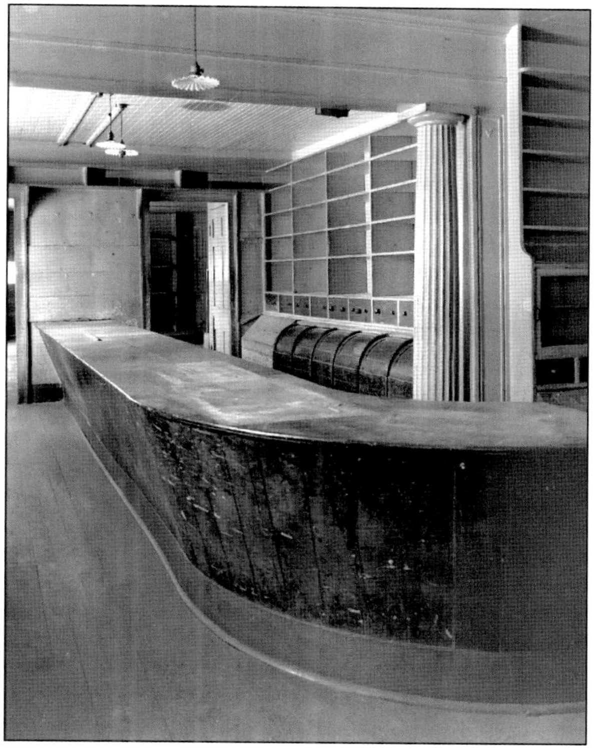

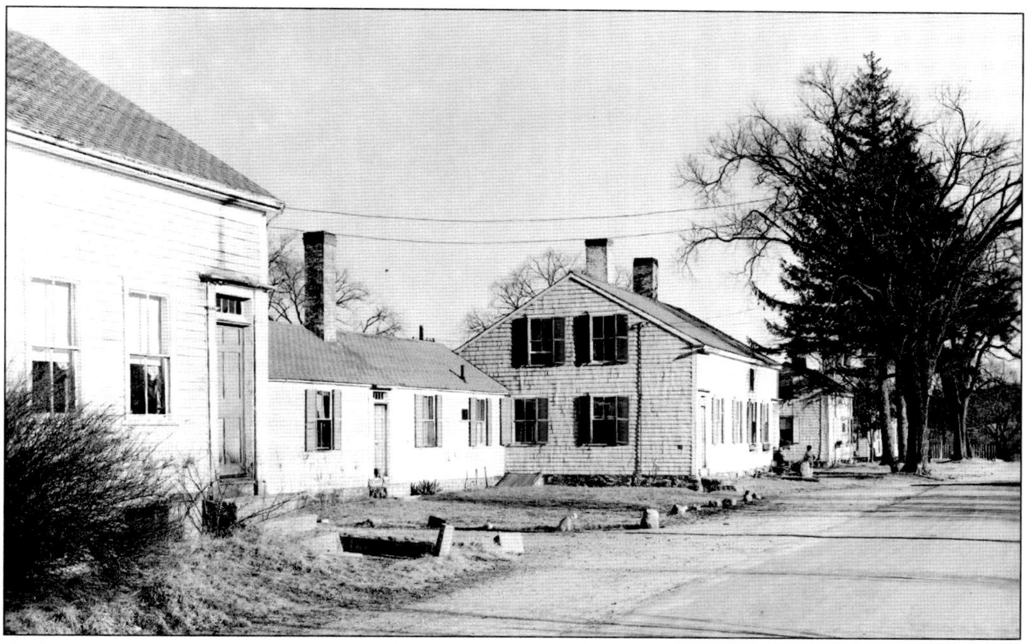

Although constructed to house families employed in the cotton mill and other industrial works on the Nemasket River below, these Jackson Street mill houses were later owned by Peirce and used as rental properties. All but two were demolished in the mid-20th century, and these now house the Middleborough Historical Museum.

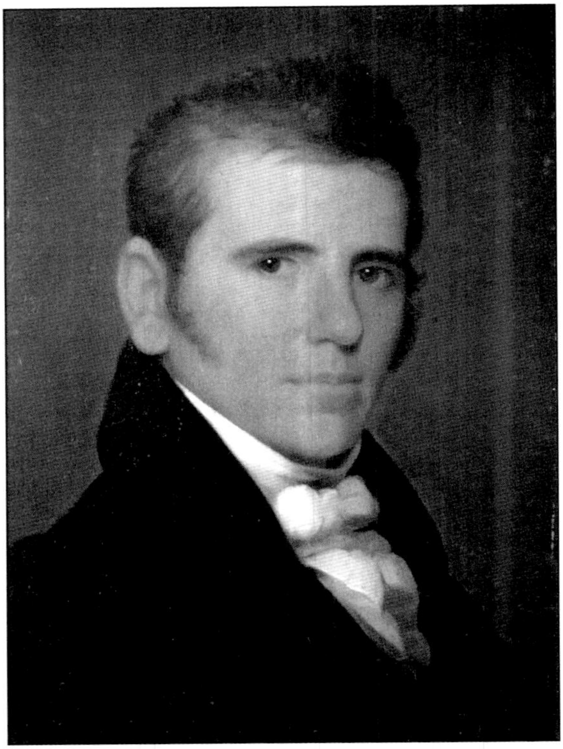

Dr. Arad Thompson (1786–1843) was one of Middleborough Four Corners's earliest professionals. A brother of noted Middleborough portraitist Cephas Thompson, the doctor established a wide practice. His wife, Mercy Bourne, was a member of the prominent Bourne family that had connections to the Peirces. The doctor served as an adjutant with the Fourth Regiment, the local militia, and for several years was Middleborough's town moderator.

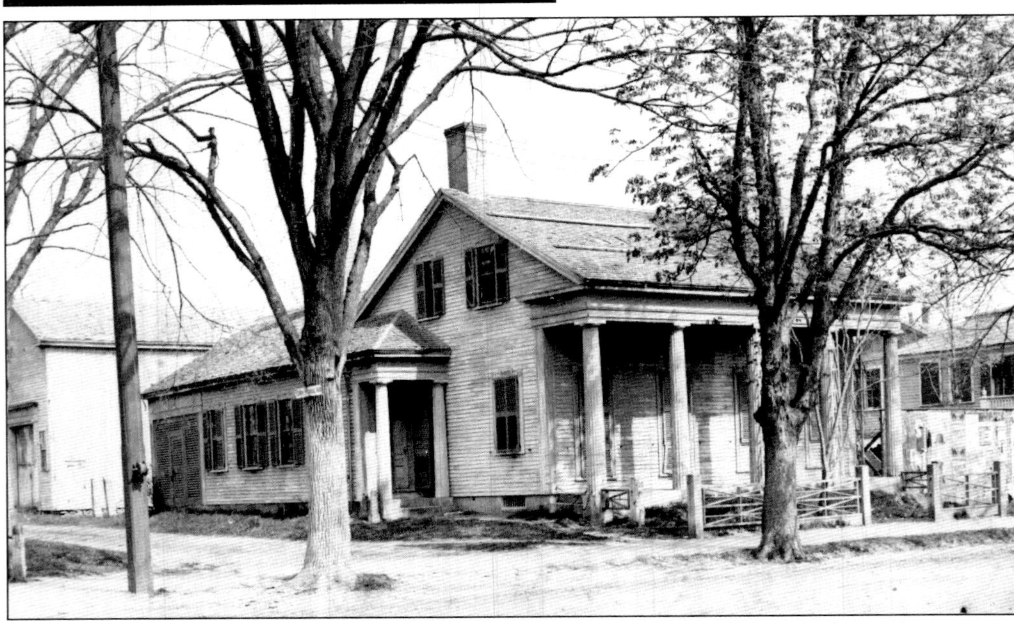

Dr. Arad Thompson constructed a beautiful Greek Revival style home befitting his position on South Main Street adjacent to that of Levi Peirce. Later occupied by the Parker family, it is seen shortly before its relocation to North Middleborough near Titicut Green in 1907. The dirt pathway to the left of the house is Temple Place, which was used as the approach to the Central Baptist Church from South Main Street.

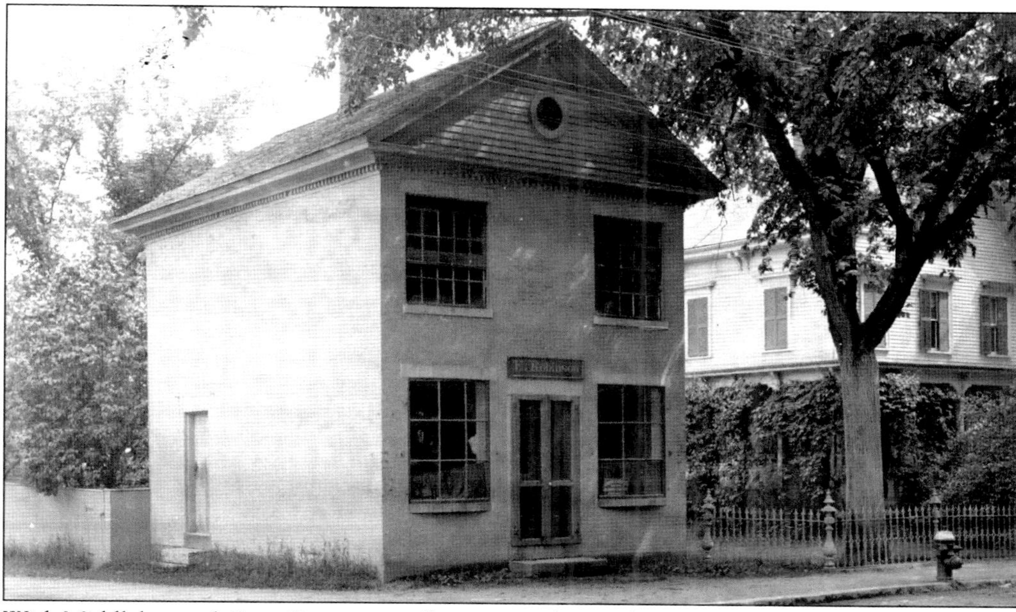

With Middleborough Four Corners rapidly growing during the second quarter of the 19th century under the guidance of the Peirce family and their associates, other entrepreneurs took notice. What was later the Robinson Law Office was constructed as a small commercial building, which was also used to manufacture straw baskets at one time. The house built for Maj. Ethan Earle, another of Peirce's sons-in-law, stands to the right.

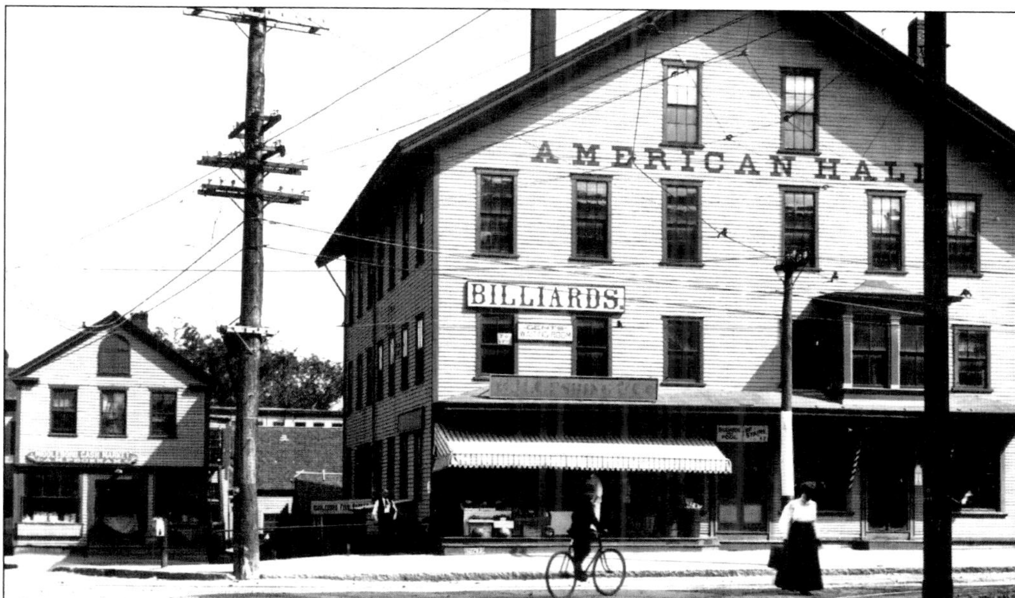

The largest commercial structure of the period, however, was the large American Hall on South Main Street, so named for the spacious hall that dominated its upper floor that became the center of Middleborough's social life following the building's construction about 1840. Lectures, concerts, and even church services were held on its upper floor while retail establishments occupied the street level. The view dates from the late 1800s.

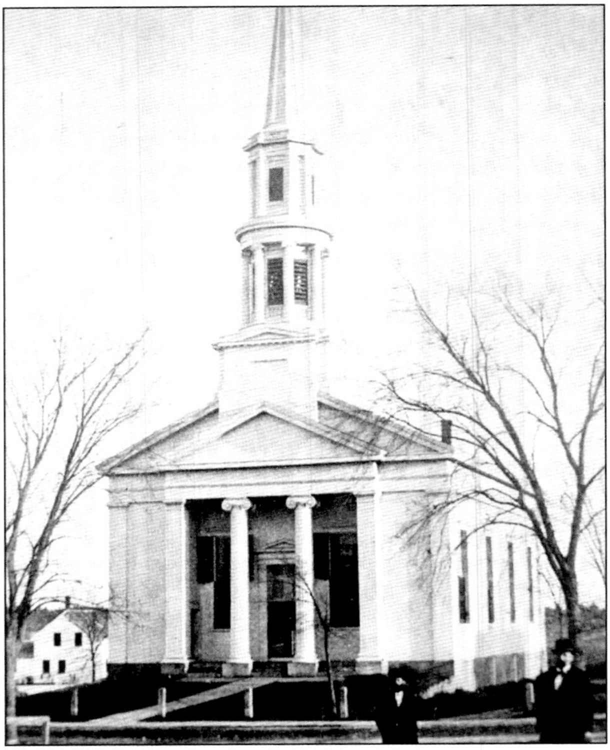

In 1848, the Baptists were joined at Middleborough Four Corners by the Congregationalists. Attracted by the area's growing prosperity, the Congregationalists became increasingly unwilling to travel to the green for weekly services, as it was inconveniently located from their new homes. As a consequence, a new parish and church, the Central Congregational Church, was raised on the corner of South Main and Webster Streets.

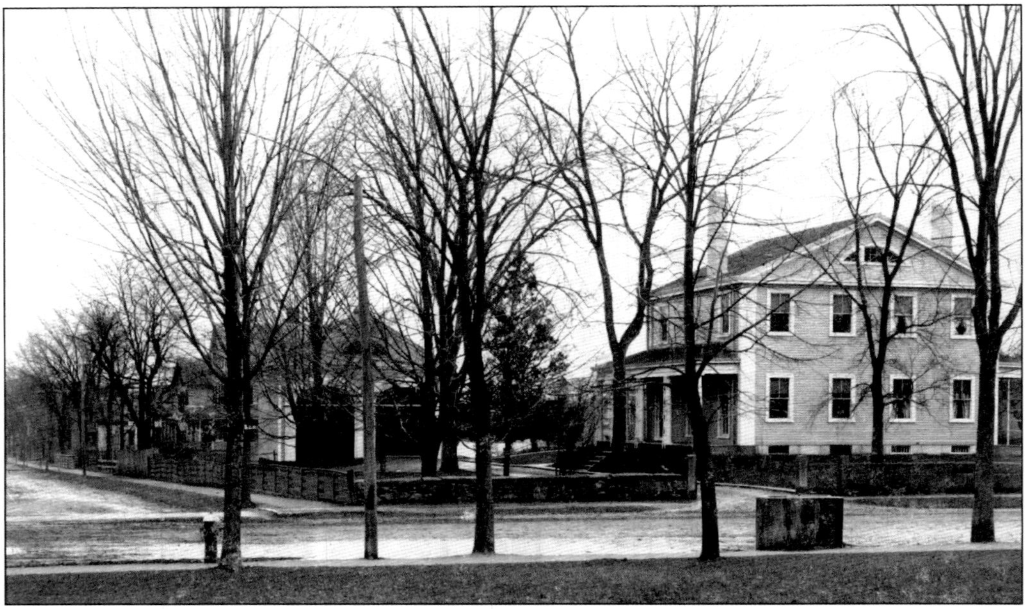

One of the supporters of the Central Congregational Church was Philander Washburn, who relocated from Muttock and constructed a comfortable Greek Revival–style home on South Main Street across Webster Street from the church. The house, later occupied by the Thatcher family and a funeral home, is now home to the Middleborough Gas and Electric Department. The photograph dates from the late 1890s and was taken by John Belden.

Residential growth about the four corners was fueled by the mid-century industrial and commercial expansion of the village and fostered by the Middleboro Loan and Fund Association, Middleborough's first formal mortgage lender, which was established in 1854. Alhough the association operated for only a brief time, the money it lent prospective home owners facilitated the expansion of middle-class housing in Middleborough, particularly on the West Side.

Fifth Annual Report of
The Middleboro Loan and Fund Association.

For the Year Ending September, 1859.

Receipts.		Expenditures.	
Cash brought from old account,	$1,014.22	Paid on 39 Shares Redeemed,	$11,239.00
Monthly Dues,	10,390.00	Paid on 5 Shares Withdrawn,	481.05
Fines,	261.87	Paid Expenses,	276.52
Interest,	1,567.67	Paid Interest on advance pay of Dues,	8.71
Transfer of Shares,	36.00	Cash on hand,	2,502.18
Rent of C. O. Smith's place,	52.00		
Mortgages Cancelled,	913.09		
Rent of E. H. Shaw's place,	72 61		
Cash of E. Stetson, on Account S. P. Brown Estate,	150.00		
Cash of E. Thompson on Acc't of J. Thomas,	50.00		
	$14,507.46		$14,507.46

Statement Showing the Net Assetts of the Association at the Present Time.

Amount due Association on Mortgages	$32,031.52	Deduct Dues paid in advance	$276.00	
Add Dues in arrears	884.00	Deduct Interest paid in advance	5.69	
Add Fines in arrears	219.35			281.67
Add Interest in arrears	357.25			
Add Cash on hand	2,502.18	Net Assetts of Association		$35,712.63
	$35,994 30			

Number of Shares subscribed for,	500	
Number of Reserved Shares taken,	46	
		546
Number of Shares Redeemed,	253	
Number of Shares Cancelled,	57	
		310
Number of Shares now unredeemed,		236

Which makes the present Value of the Shares, $151.32.

ELISHA PEIRCE,
E. W. WILBUR,
SYLVANUS W. REED, } Finance Committee.

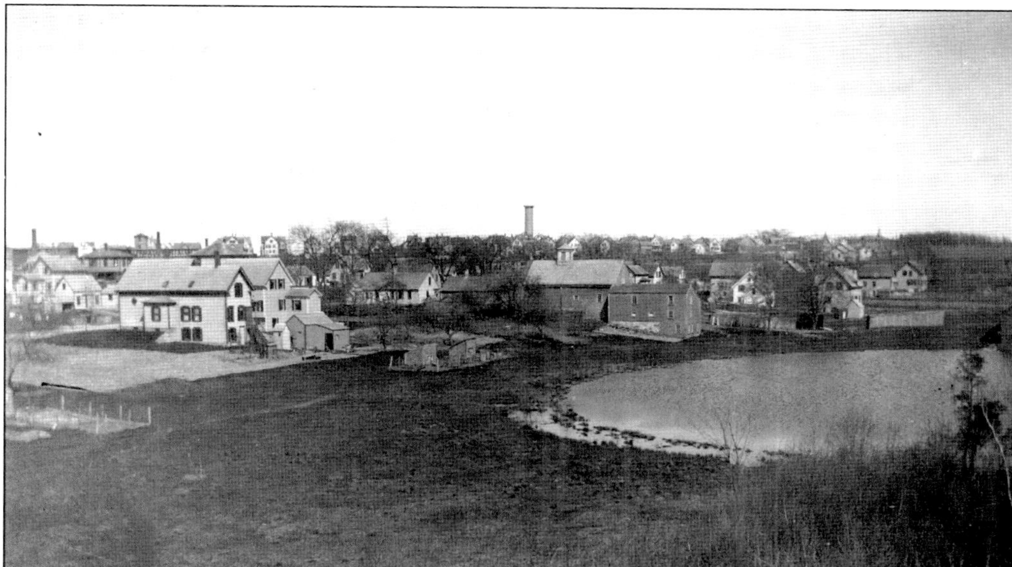

The growth of the West Side, which was named for its geographic location relative to the Old Colony Railroad line, was driven by industries along Vine and Cambridge Streets. Other new residential districts, including the West End (around Everett Square), Peaseville (Forest and Everett Streets), and the Star Mill neighborhood (East Main Street) accommodated the numerous operatives in local manufactories. The West Side is seen here with Nevertouch Pond at right.

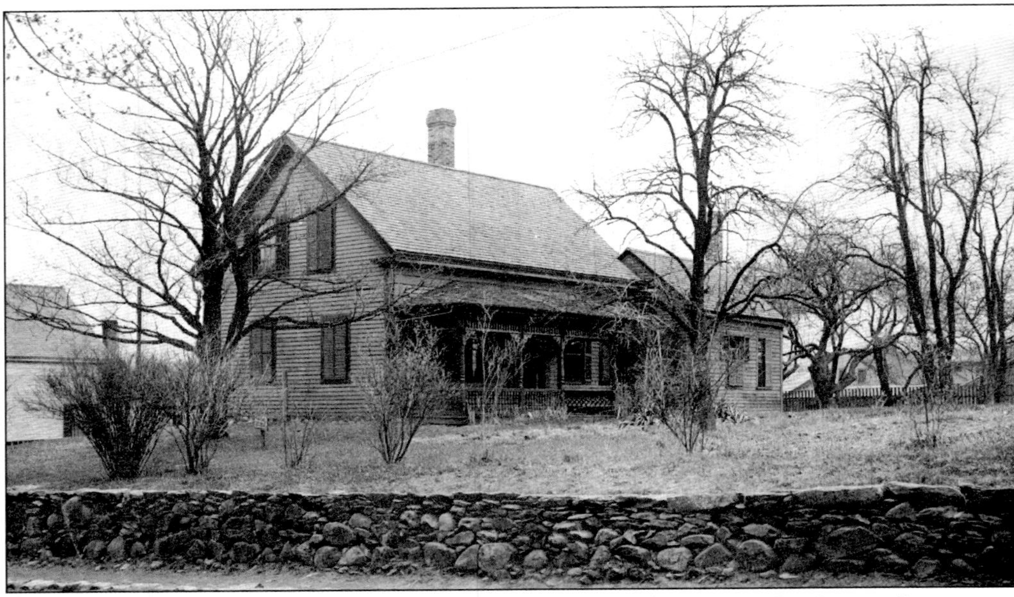

Typical of the new workers' homes was the William S. Hines house on West Street. Constructed during the initial phase of development on the West Side, the house stood near May Street in the rear of the LeBaron Foundry at which Hines was employed. At a time when transportation was limited, workers frequently lived close to their place of employment, a circumstance that promoted the growth of residential areas like the West Side.

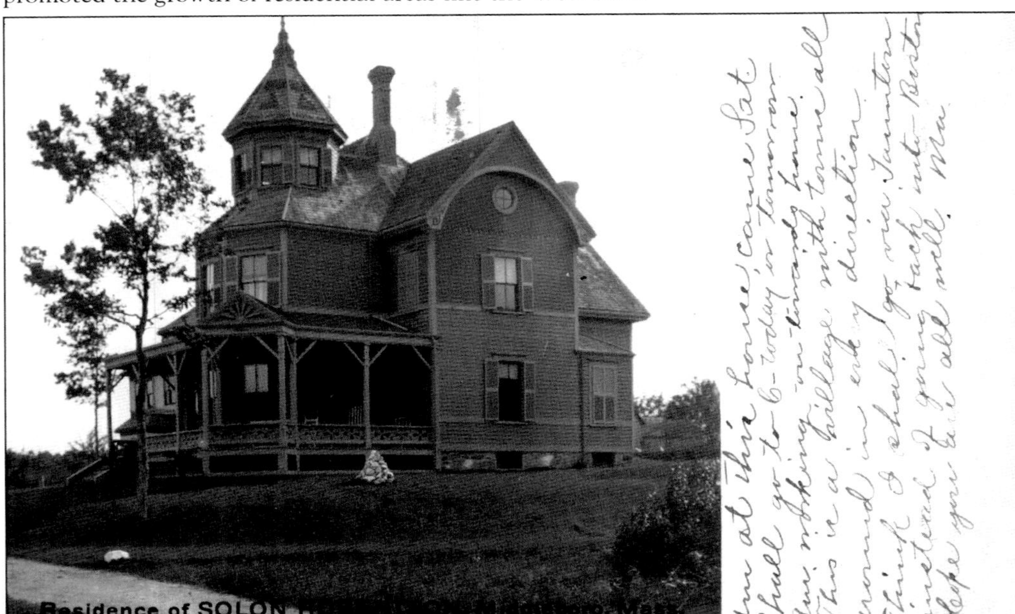

Although the West Side remained predominately a working-class neighborhood, some more elaborate homes were built. The stick-style Solon Robertson house was built on West End Avenue facing Nevertouch Pond and was the home of Robertson, a Civil War veteran active in veterans' issues. The house, now owned by the Griswold family, still stands next to the former West Side School. (Author's collection.)

Five

FROM AGRICULTURE TO INDUSTRY

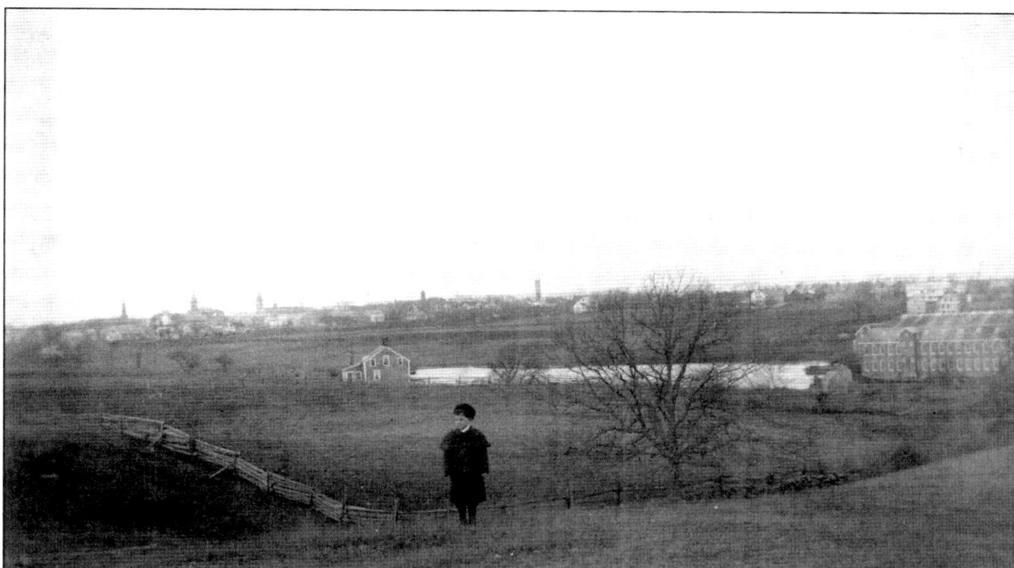

The initial basis for the prosperity of Middleborough had been agriculture, but by the early 1800s, the Industrial Revolution reached full flood locally at Middleborough center. Manufacturing output accelerated rapidly following 1846, tied to national expansions in the mid-1850s and mid-1870s. Yet, as this photograph of a solitary child on Indian Hill at the rear of the Star Mill attests, agriculture and industry coexisted for much of Middleborough's history.

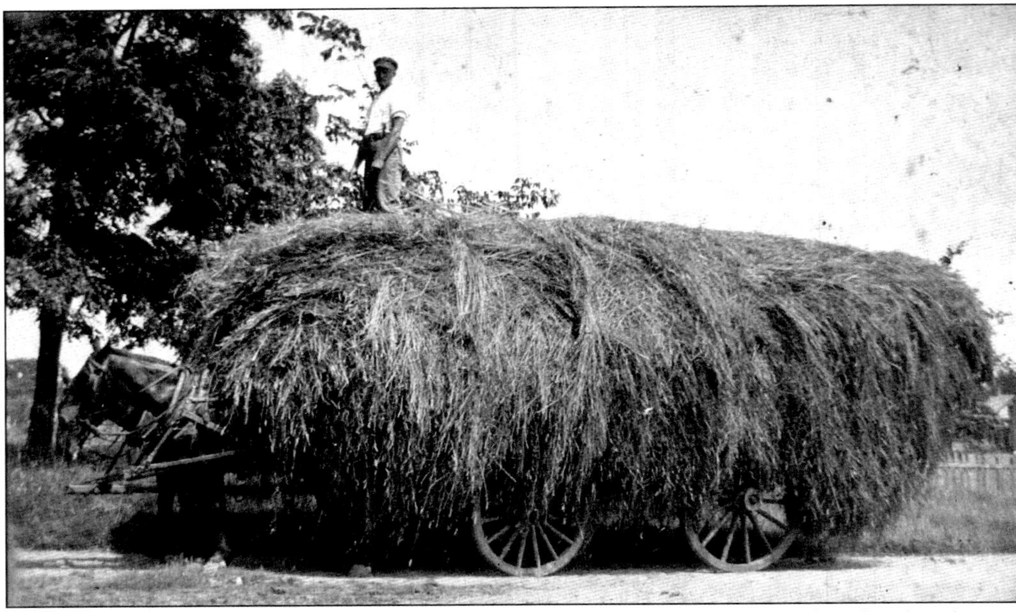

Such scenes of bursting hay wagons were common during late June and early July when haying was typically done. In 1855, the town produced over 3,000 tons of English and swale hay and had 3,000 acres devoted to mowing. One of the products easily grown in Middleborough's soil, hay was much in demand as fodder for livestock, particularly following the 1880s when the number of dairy cattle increased dramatically.

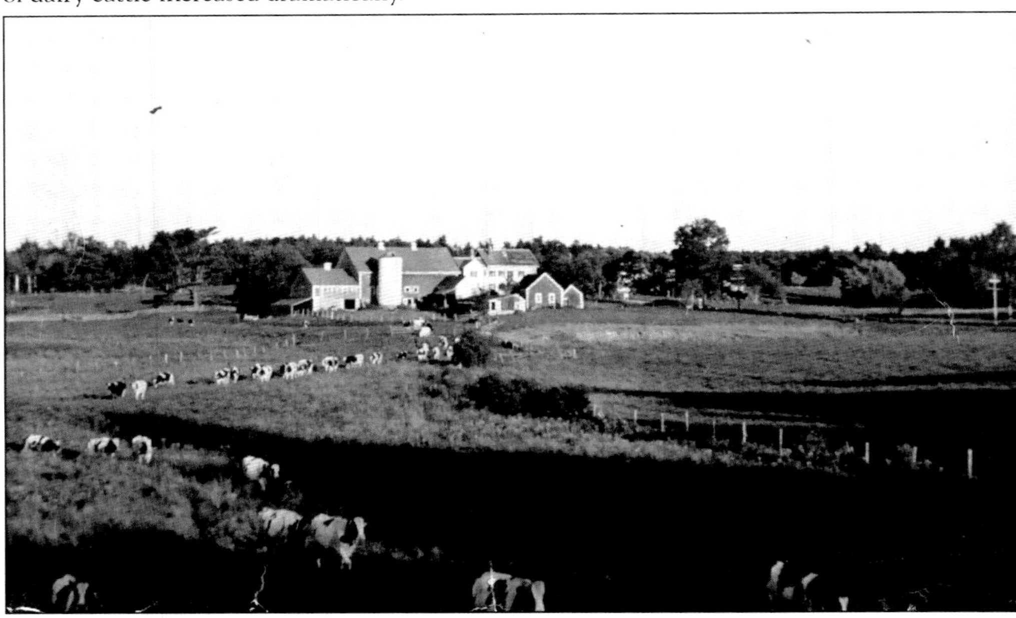

Among the many dairy farms established during the post-Civil War expansion of the local dairy industry was that of Augustus Soule on Soule Street. Under the ownership of Albert Deane and later Colombo and Donald Guidaboni, the farm remained active until the 1980s. It now operates as the Soule Homestead Education Center. Here, the Guidaboni Holsteins dutifully parade single file to evening pasture. (Courtesy of Donald and Mary Guidaboni.)

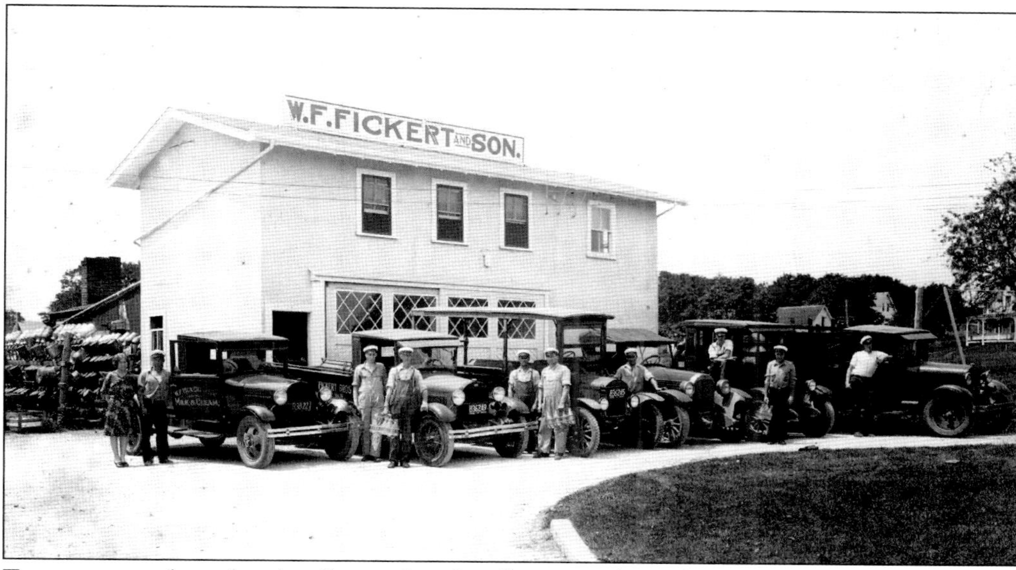

To process and market locally produced milk, a number of family run dairies, including Kinsman Brothers on Thompson Street, were established. Another was W. F. Fickert and Son, which was founded in 1912 and operated this dairy on Montello Street. Pictured from left to right are bookkeeper Olive (Chamberlain) McLaughlin, Norman Rudolph, Ernie Fickert, Frank Maddigan, Walter Rudolph, Bill Fickert, Phil Joncas, Chet Lewis, Albert Rudolph, and Charlie Rumpohl.

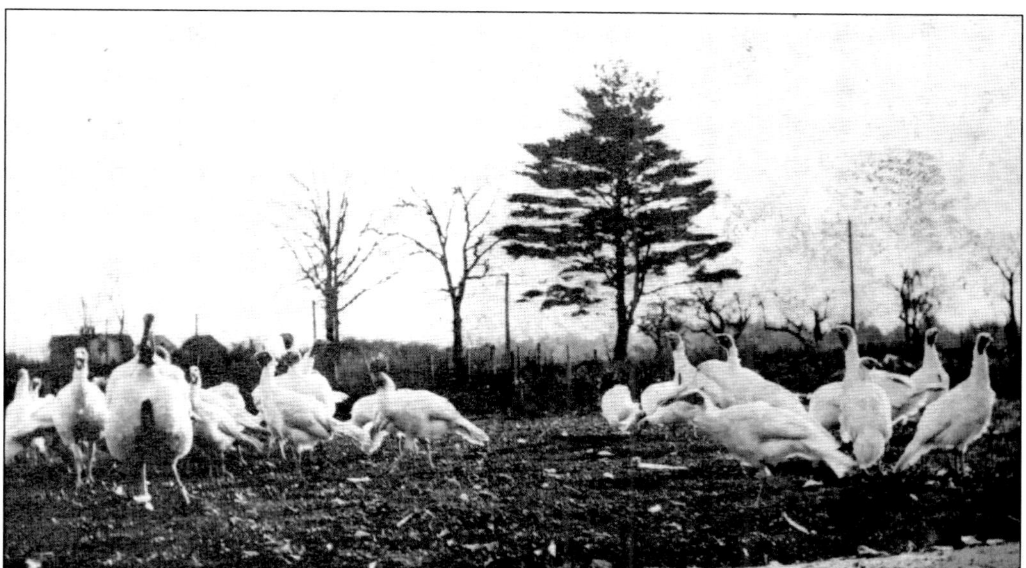

The rearing of poultry, like the turkeys seen above, became an important field of agriculture locally in the early 1900s. While many families kept a small number of chickens, larger operations raised the birds on a much more extensive scale. One industry associated with this development was the C. P. Washburn Grain Mill, known principally for producing animal feed in its Cambridge Street mill. (Courtesy of James G. MacDonald III.)

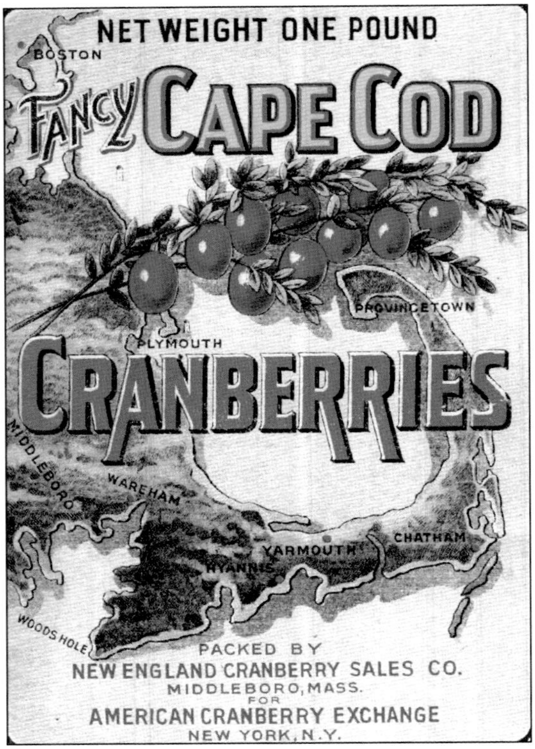

In the late 1800s, cranberry cultivation spread from Cape Cod and became a viable agricultural pursuit in Middleborough due to the large expanses of bog and sandy soil that covered much of the town. Anchoring Middleborough's self-proclaimed position as "cranberry capital of the world" was the location of the New England Cranberry Sales Company, an early grower's cooperative headquartered at Everett Square following 1907. (Author's collection.)

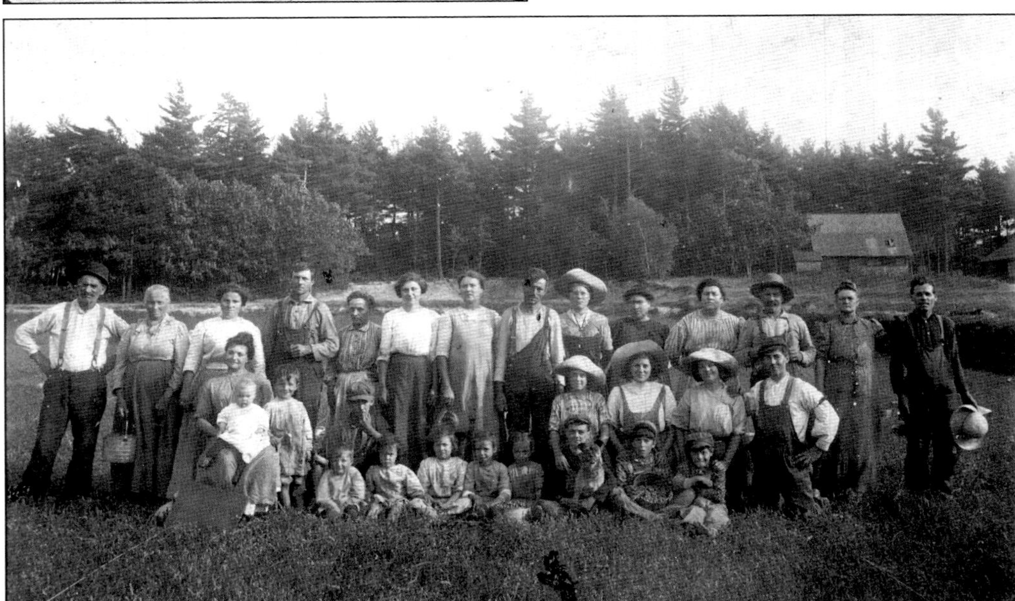

The annual autumn cranberry harvest drew hordes of workers to the bogs to help pick berries, including Finnish and Cape Verdean immigrants who settled in the area. Typically, so great was the need for workers that schoolchildren in places like South Middleborough were absented from school in order to help with the harvest. Here, a group of pickers pose with some of the children displaying full pails.

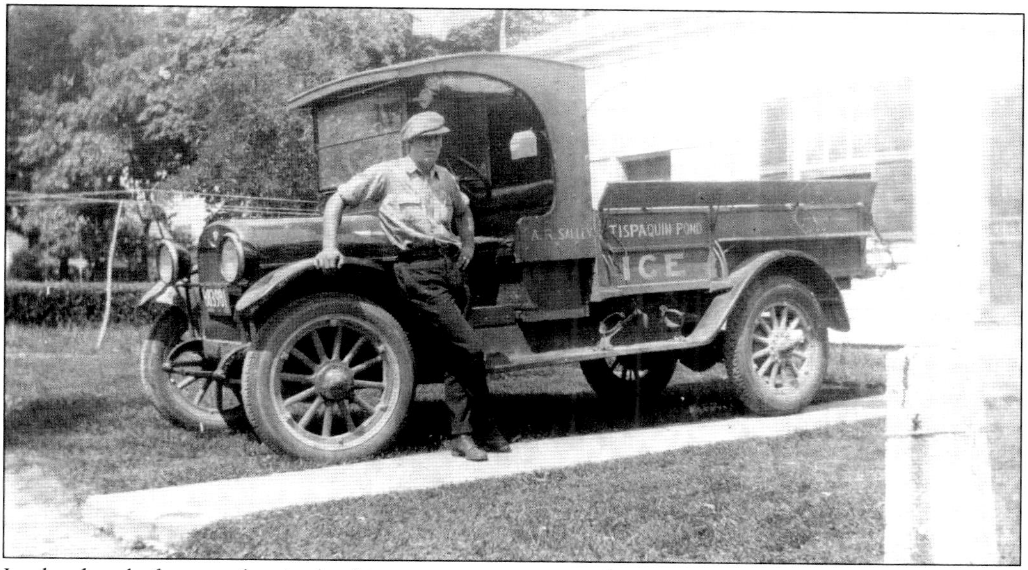

In the days before mechanical refrigeration, ice was another important crop for Middleborough. Although large ice dealers, including the LeBaron family and Ernest S. Pratt, were the most noted and operated extensive delivery routes about town, smaller dealers, including Arnold R. Salley (above), provided the community with ice throughout the warm summer months. Salley began business in the early 1920s and cut his ice on Tispaquin Pond.

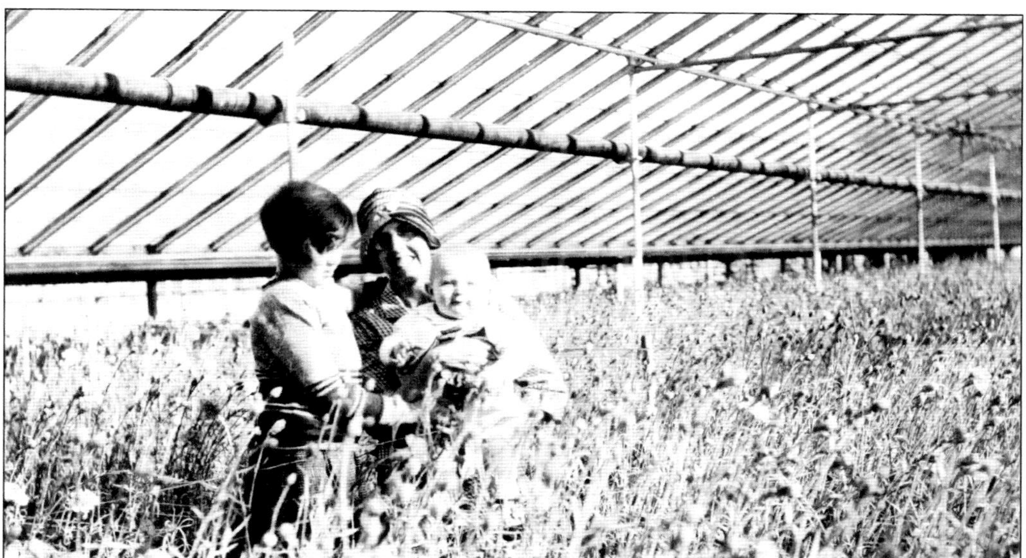

Following the Civil War, horticultural firms became prominent. Noted nurserymen included C. D. Kingman, Levi Thatcher, and Timothy F. Creedon. Later, in 1915, the Leland Carnation Company was established on Cherry Street with a store on South Main Street. Marian Leland and her children Shirley and Carlon appear above surrounded by the company's namesake product in one of the firm's Cherry Street greenhouses in February 1930.

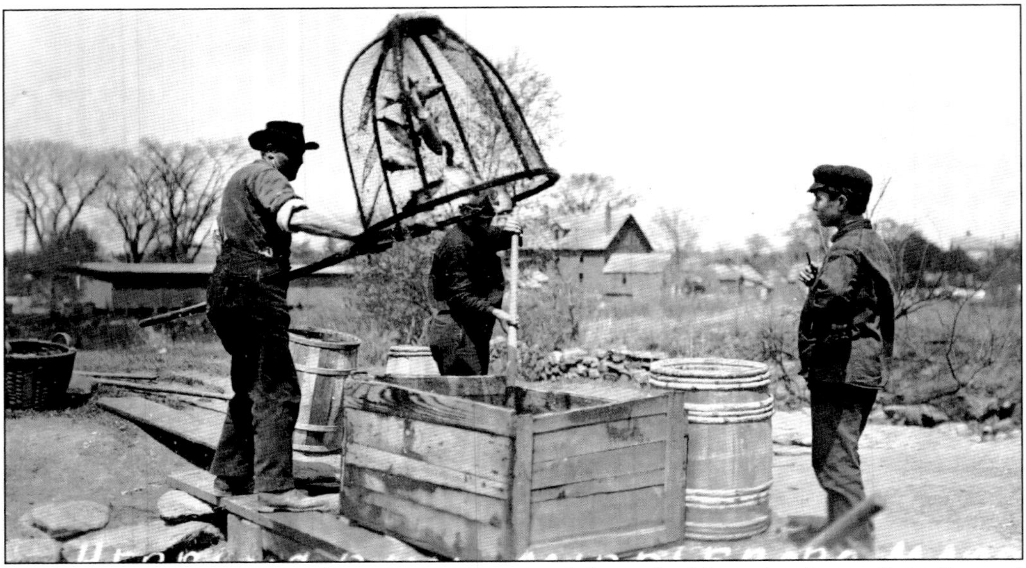

For generations, herring or alewives were harvested from the Nemasket River. Initially used to fertilize colonial corn hills, the fish were later avidly consumed by old-time Yankees as a succulent springtime treat. Many were also shipped to the West Indies where they were an important food staple. In the spring of 1910, George Morse captured the manual nature of the harvest at the rear of the Star Mill.

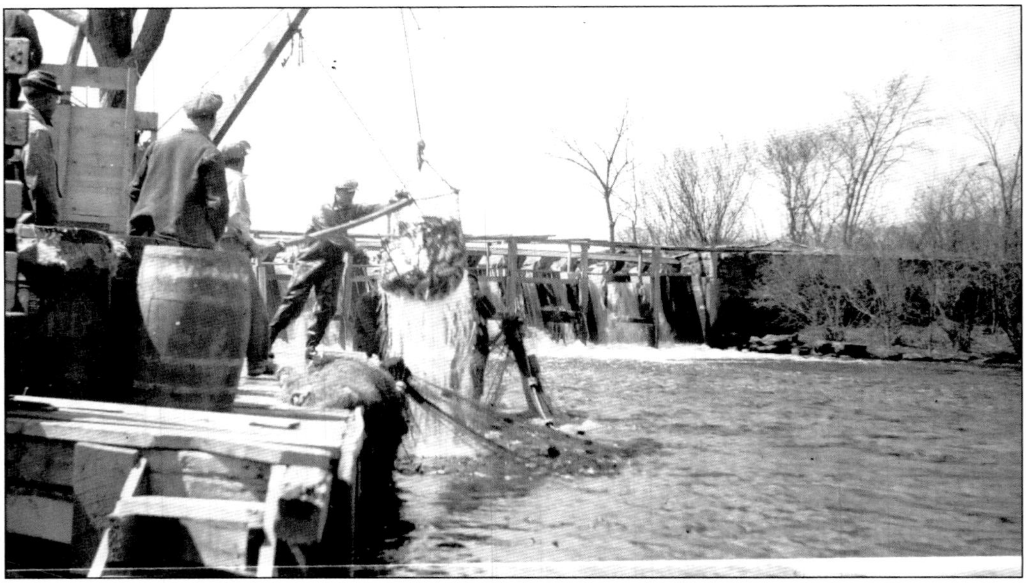

By the 1940s, when the above photograph was taken in front of the Star Mill dam, the process of capturing herring had been mechanized, and large nets were placed across the river to facilitate the taking. Large, outside companies also began acquiring the rights to take the fish, which they processed into cat food, fertilizer, and fish bait. Herring rights were last sold at auction in 1965.

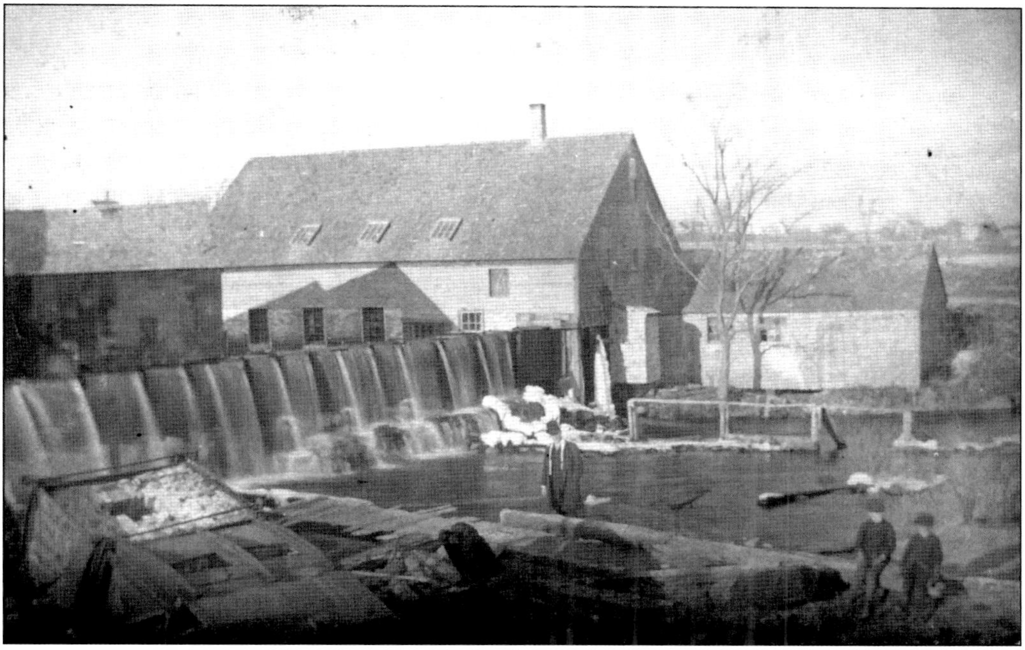

The Nemasket River also provided the motive power for Middleborough's first industries, including gristmills, cider mills, sawmills, and fulling mills. One of the earliest nonagricultural-related operations was iron works along the Nemasket River at what is now Wareham Street. By the early 1800s, this operation had evolved into an industry producing shovels. The shovel works, pictured here, stood upon the dam until 1883.

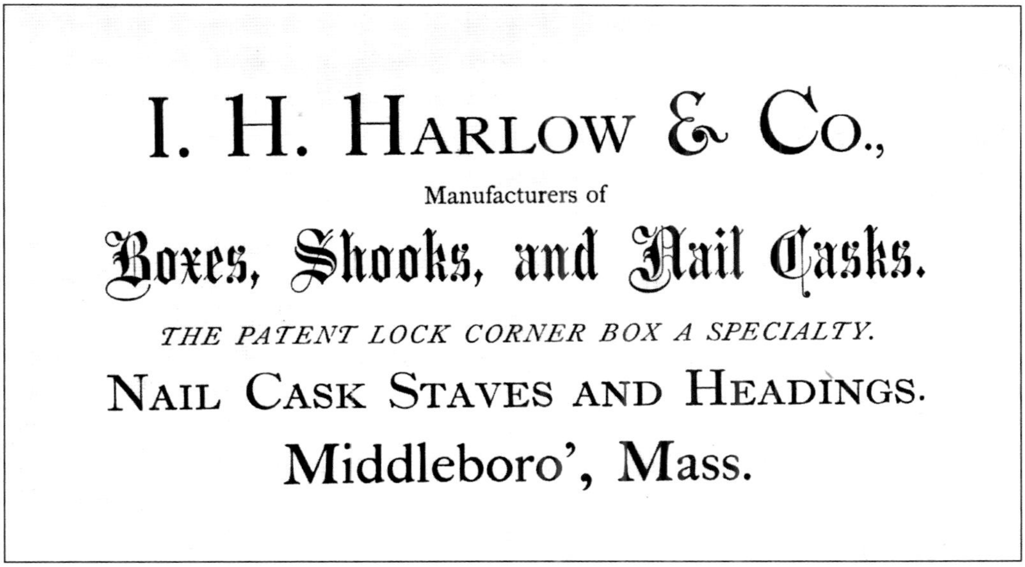

With the application of steam-power technology to manufacturing purposes in the 1850s, industry was no longer wedded to sites along the Nemasket River. The first local manufacturer to operate wholly by steam was the Middleboro' Steam Mill Company, founded in 1855 on Vine Street. A successor of the Steam Mill Company, I. H. Harlow and Company produced milled lumber and building materials, as well as packing boxes, crates, and barrels.

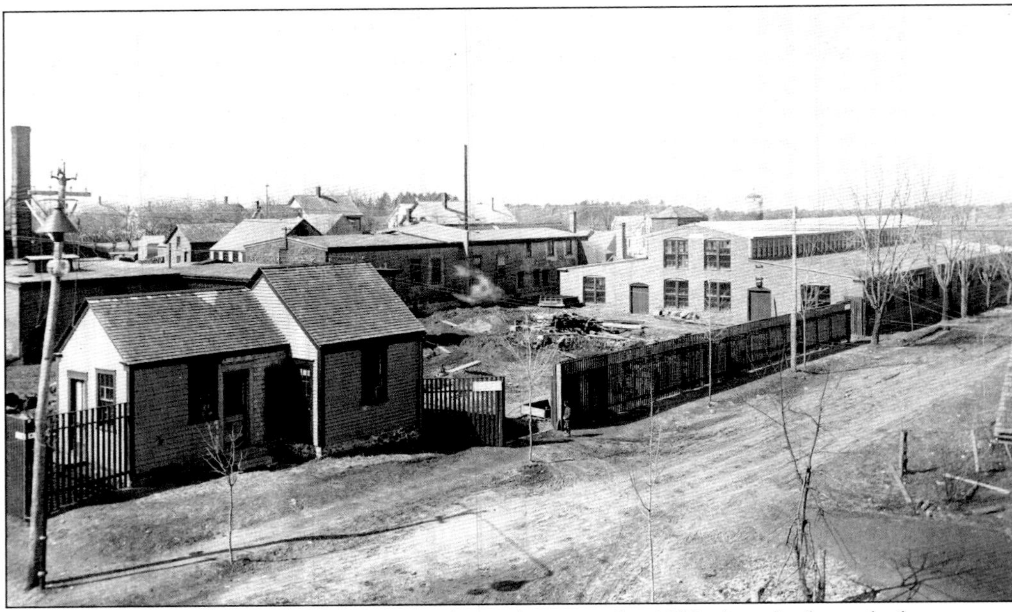

Vine Street developed as an important industrial area in the 1850s, largely through the presence of the Middleboro' Steam Mill Company, which was formed for the "purposes of Sawing, Planing and Manufacturing Lumber, and grinding Grain." In 1856, the mill established an iron foundry "on a somewhat large scale," seen here on the west side of Vine Street, and immediately leased it to John B. LeBaron and Samuel Tinkham.

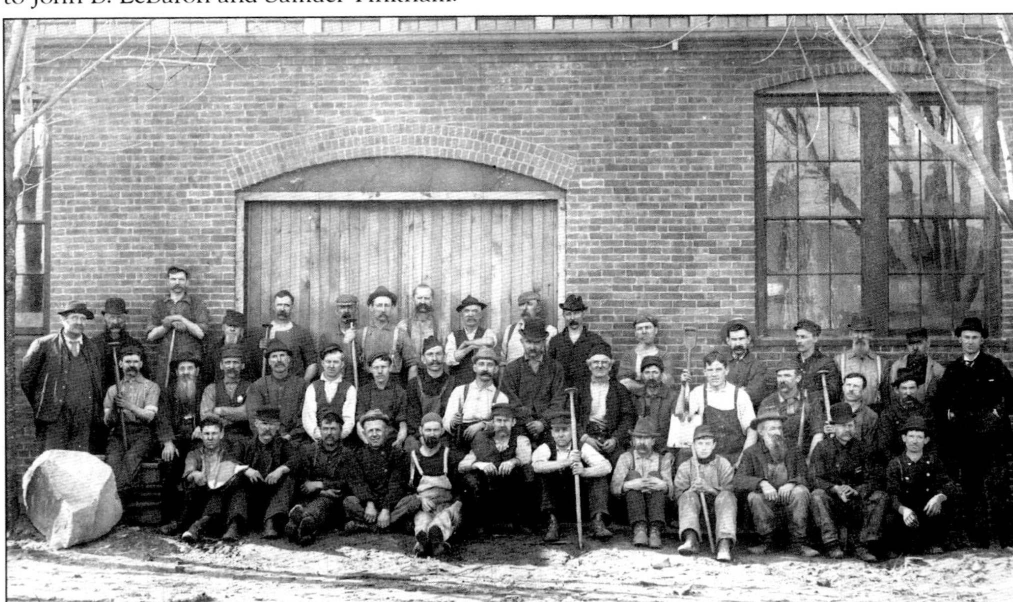

Initially, the foundry produced sash weights but later added a wide range of cast-iron products, including iron fencing and skate irons. Following 1864, the foundry was owned exclusively by the Lebaron family, operating in Middleborough until 1911 when the possibility of better transportation facilities lured it to Brockton. The Middleborough plant subsequently housed Colonial Brass. Here foundrymen during the LeBaron era pose for a formal photograph.

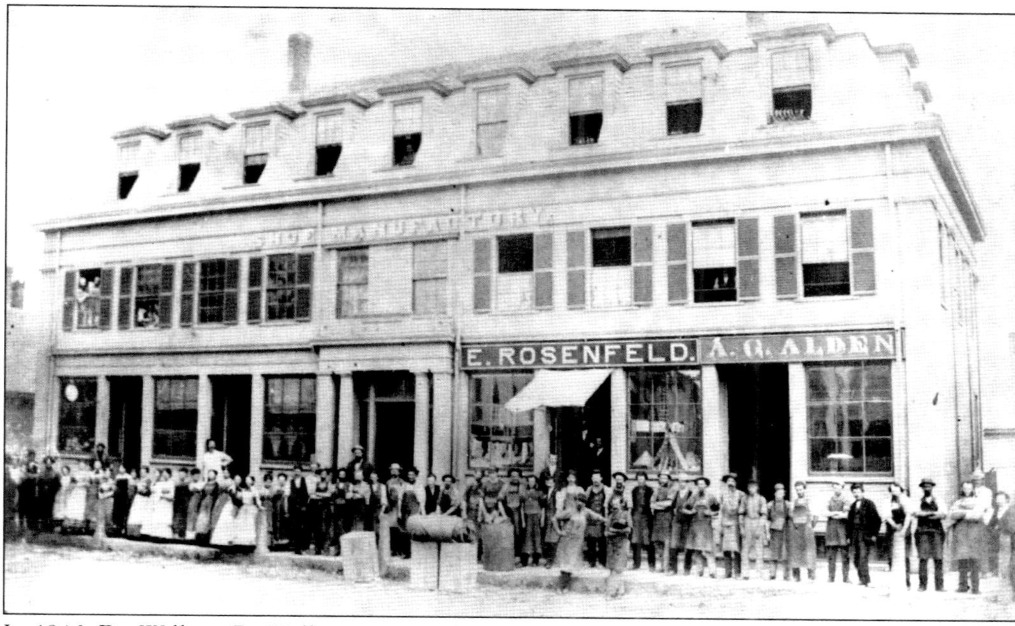

In 1846, Dr. William R. Wells constructed a large business block on North Main Street (where the Middleboro House of Pizza now stands), which was designed for both commercial and industrial purposes. The second floor was occupied by Leonard and Barrows shoe manufacturers, whose workers have assembled for an informal portrait sometime in the 1850s. Rosenfeld and Alden were dry goods merchants occupying adjoining stores.

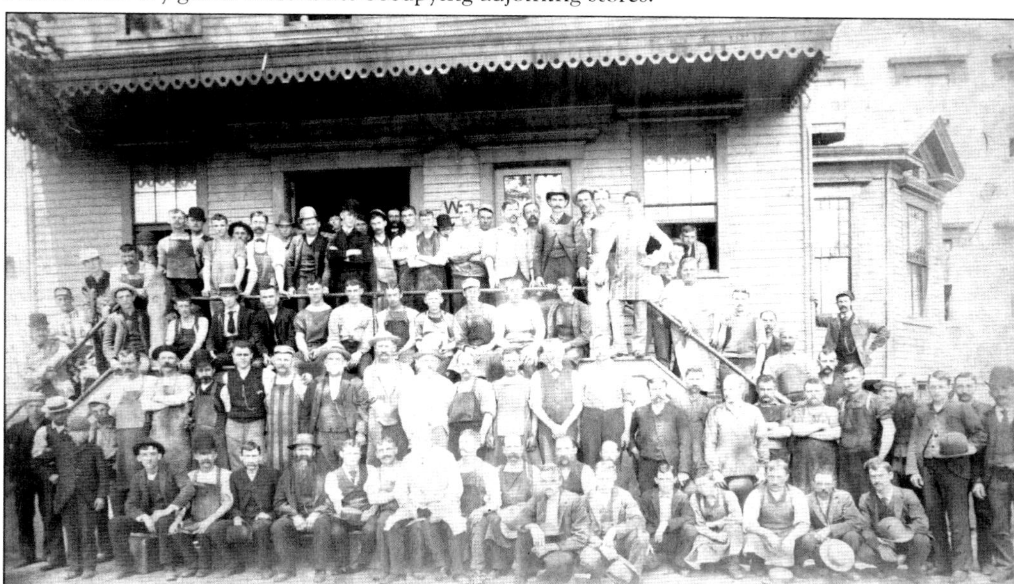

Leonard and Barrows workers pose for a photograph in front of a new factory built at Center and Pearl Streets in 1874. The group represented above is likely the factory's force of cutters, a process that required great manual strength, which explains the absence of female operatives from this view. The factory passed through a number of subsequent owners and was last known for making Earth Shoes in the 1970s.

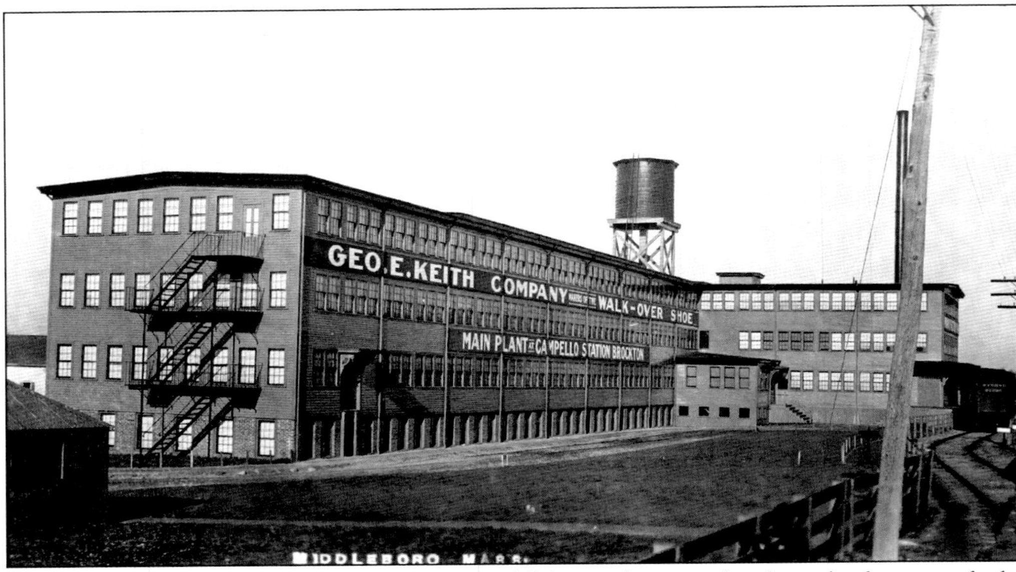

The largest of all shoe operations at Middleborough was the branch factory of the Brockton-based George E. Keith Company, which was erected on Sumner Avenue in 1905 and 1906. The factory was acquired by the Plymouth Shoe Company in 1956 but remained long vacant following the collapse of the shoe industry. Amid proposals to find a reuse for it, the factory was destroyed in a spectacular fire in December 1974.

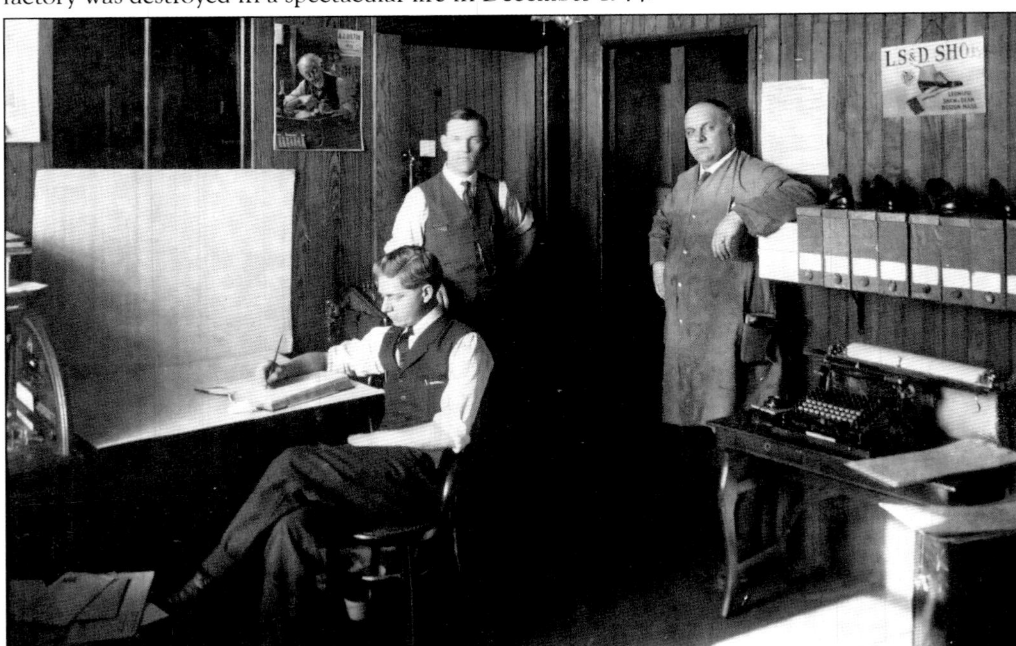

The management staff of Leonard, Shaw and Dean on Peirce Street pose momentarily for the photographer in the small but sunny factory office. Founded in 1892, the shoe-manufacturing firm was acquired in 1933 by the John E. Lucey Shoe Company, which had earlier purchased Leonard and Barrows. The Leonard, Shaw and Dean plant was later occupied by Winthrop-Atkins. Note the company advertisement pinned to the wall.

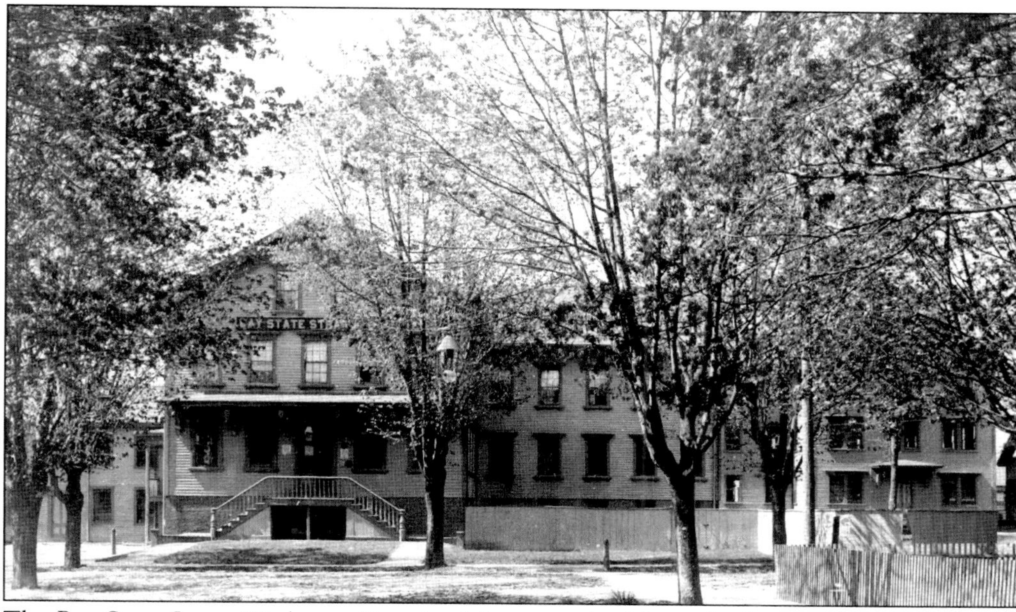

The Bay State Straw Works on Courtland Street evolved from the local industry of braiding straw, which was begun about 1835 by Ebenezer Briggs and developed by the Pickens Brothers. Following 1858, under the aegis of Albert Alden, the straw works became the town's largest employer for a time, as well as the world's largest manufacturer of straw hats and goods after 1876.

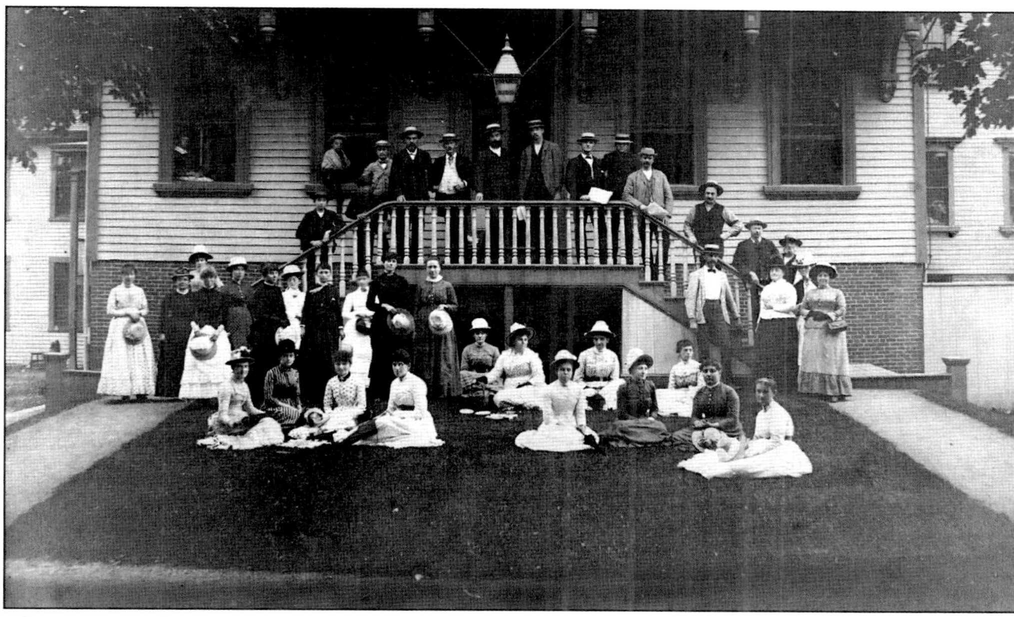

The straw works was also Middleborough's largest employer of female workers, a group who is posed for this 1880s summertime portrait outside the factory. The fact that nearly all those pictured wear straw hats indicates the reasons for the concern's success. The eventual decline in the popularity of straw headwear, however, led to the decline of the business, which closed in 1896.

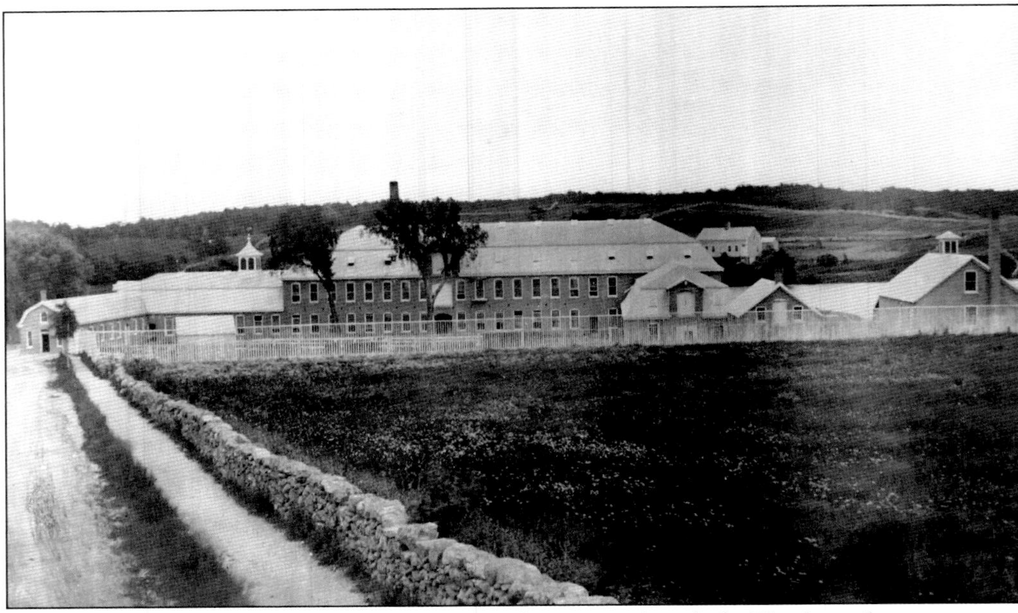

The Star Mill was established in 1863 to manufacture woolen cloth. The large factory, erected upon the site of an earlier cotton mill on East Main Street, employed local residents and newly arrived immigrants and gave its name to the neighborhood in which it was situated. This view, taken shortly after the mill's construction, looks down Star Mill Hill, the scene of 20th-century soapbox derbies.

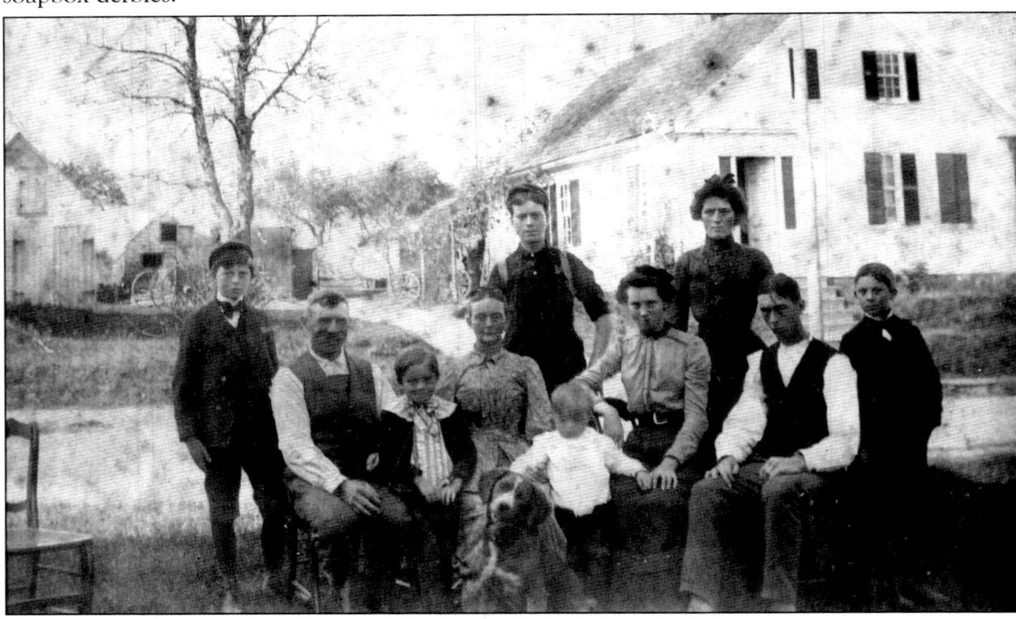

Attracted to the Star Mill were both Irish and French Canadian immigrants. The family of Michael J. Maddigan was typical of those that resided in the Star Mill neighborhood. Maddigan was engaged as a fireman and night watchman for the Star Mill in the early 1900s, while in 1900, his son John was working as a wool carder and his daughter Jane was employed in the finishing department. (Author's collection.)

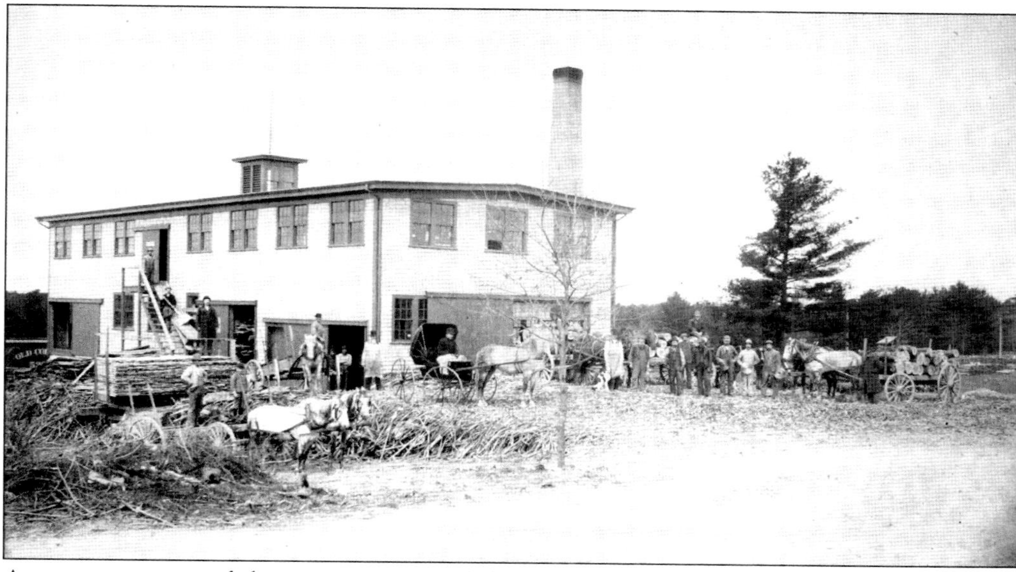

As a consequence of the growing national demand for lumber and packing materials in the mid-19th century, lumber milling and the associated industries of trunk, packing crate, and box board manufacturing became an important occupation in Middleborough, as farmers turned much of their wasteland into forested tracts. The Clark and Cole mill, built in 1889 on Cambridge Street, was the largest of Middleborough's several lumber mills.

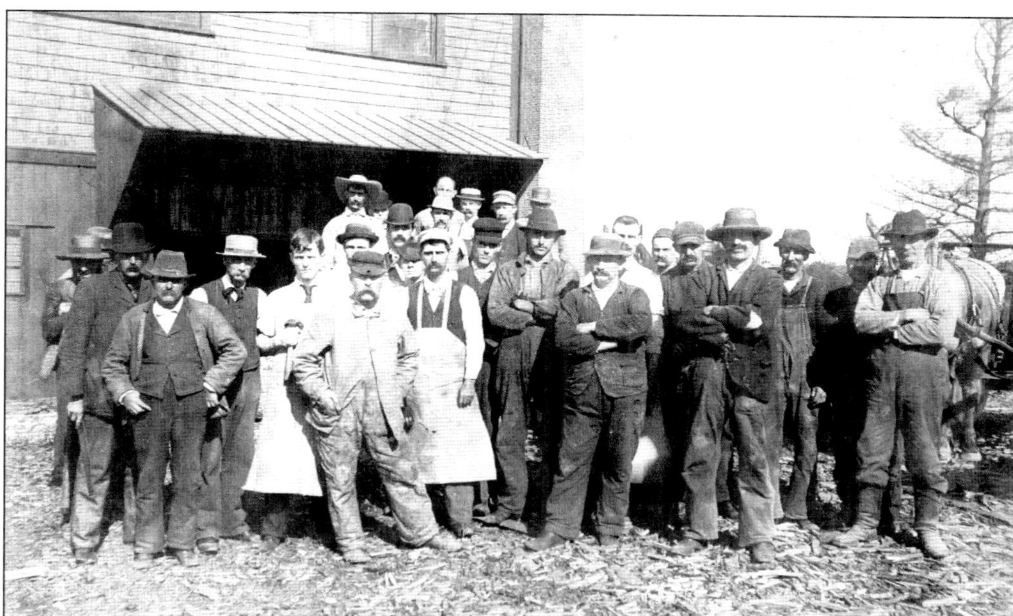

Clark and Cole, which was established in 1888, employed men such as these to harvest timber from throughout the region and process it in one of its two mills, either at Middleborough or at Darby in Plymouth. In 1909, Clark and Cole was bankrupted by the dubious activities of its junior partner, and its collapse led to the failure of a number of local milling concerns.

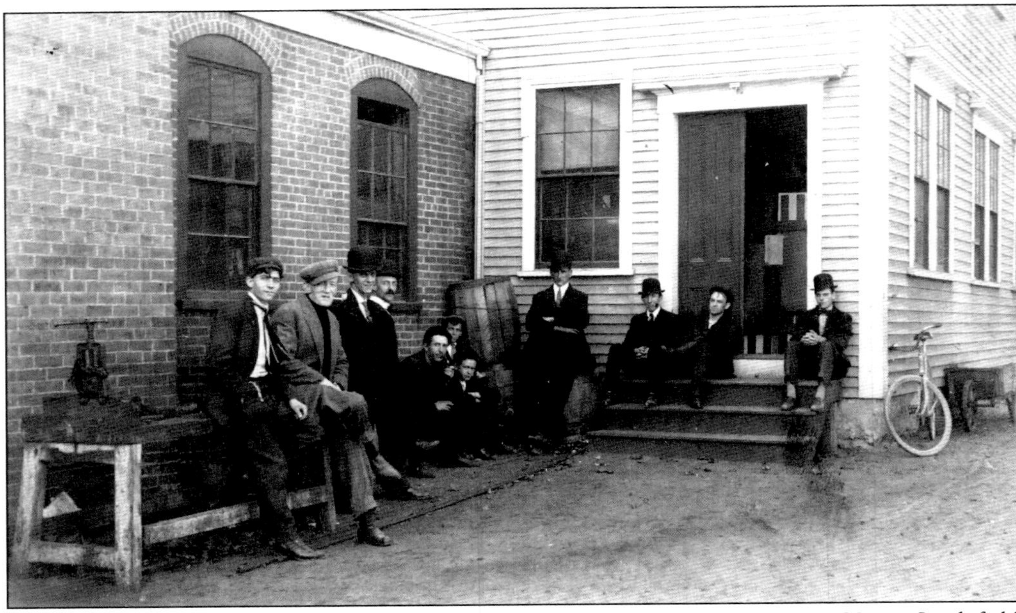

Nattily dressed employees of A. H. Alger and Company, including Louis Gay, Henry Littlefield, Frank Stickney, Jack Shaw, Glen Perkins, Pat Canavan, Ray Wright, and Henry Peirce, take a break from their work in the early 1900s. The Alden Street paper box manufactory was established in a portion of the former Bay State Straw Works plant in 1901 and was destroyed by fire in April 1928. It was not rebuilt.

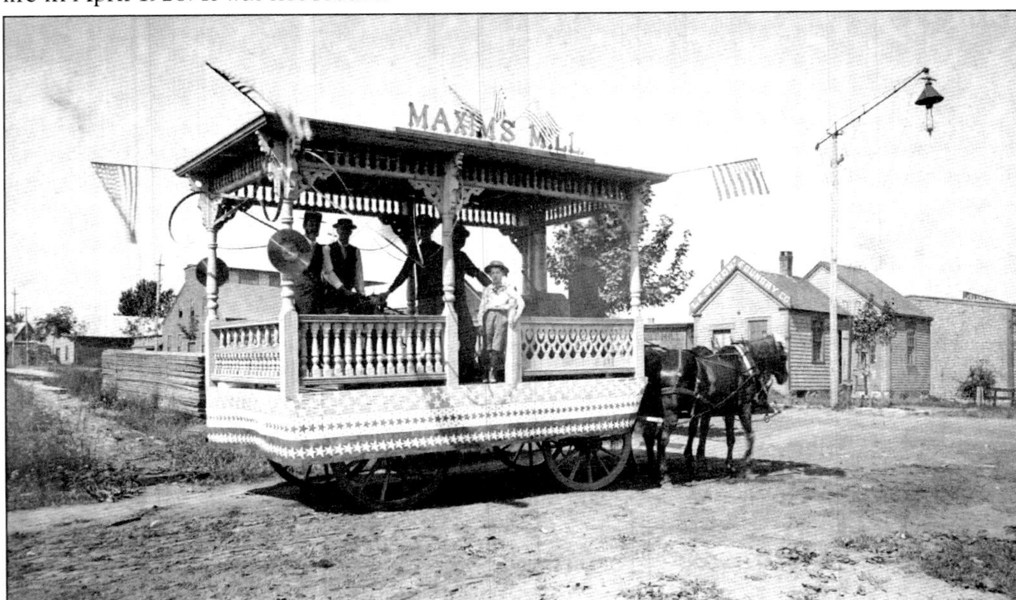

In 1888, Carlton W. Maxim relocated his woodworking business to Vine Street before relocating to a much larger mill on Cambridge Street the following year. Here, the craftsmanship of the Maxim mill is demonstrated through means of a unique parade float. It was Maxim's production of fire ladders in particular, that lead to the foundation of the fire apparatus industry in Middleborough following 1914.

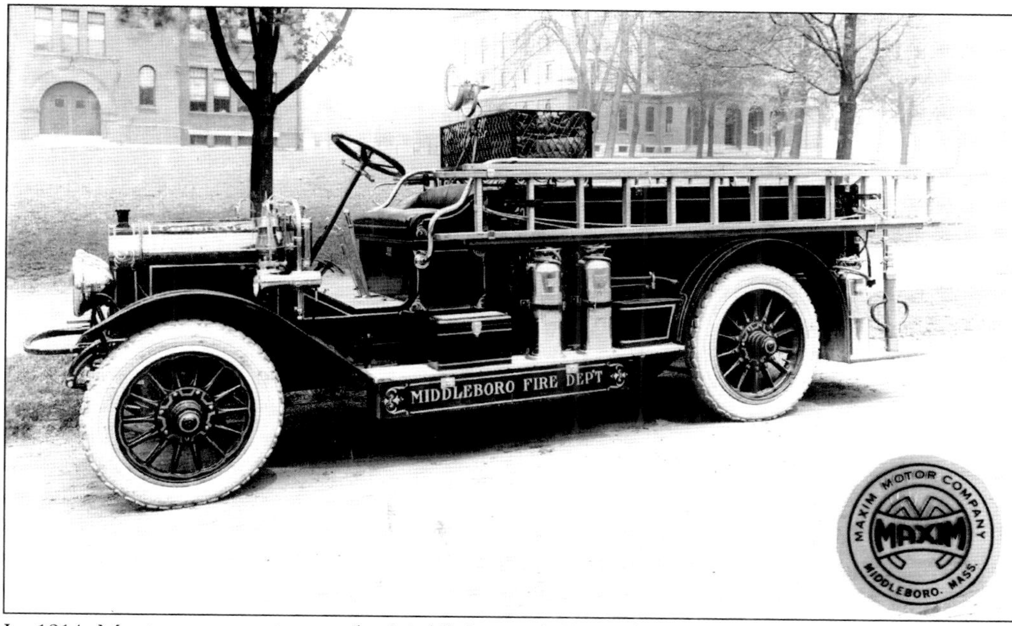

In 1914, Maxim was serving as the Middleborough Fire Chief as well as leasing and repairing automobiles through the Middleboro Auto Exchange. In response to his dissatisfaction with engines produced by other manufacturers for the local department, Maxim built his own, the Model F Combination (above), which became the first locally manufactured fire engine. Soon afterwards, the Maxim Motor Company was formed to manufacture fire apparatus.

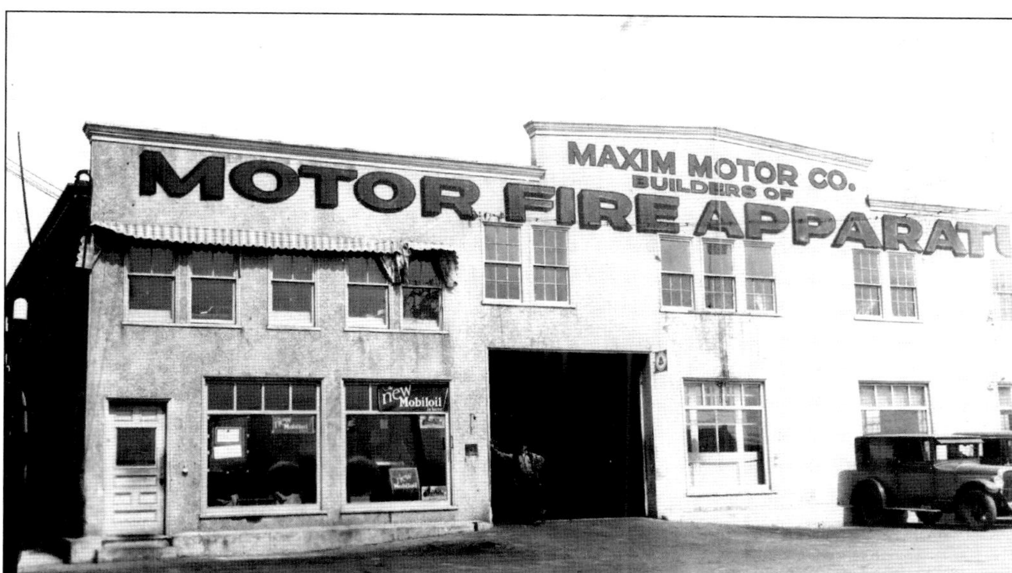

Maxim Motor Company operated in a cavernous building at the corner of Wareham and Lincoln Streets that was built in 1906 as a trolley car barn and later housed Maxim's own Middleboro Auto Exchange. From this modest plant, Maxim Motors produced engines that built for it a national reputation. The last fire engine built in Middleborough was made in 1986, appropriately for the local fire department.

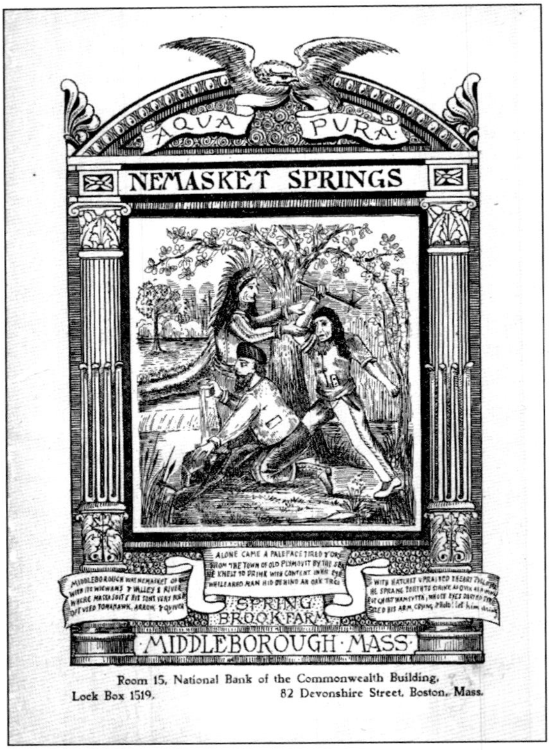

Long known for the medicinal value of its waters, the Nemasket Spring was tapped commercially in the late 1800s by Thomas C. Fielding, who commissioned this wildly inaccurate depiction of the spring. Only after 1920, however, when the Kayajan Brothers added carbonation and syrup, did the water achieve regional notice. The Kayajan's firm marketed a wide range of Nemasket tonics and sodas, as well as bottling Coca-Cola at its Plymouth Street plant.

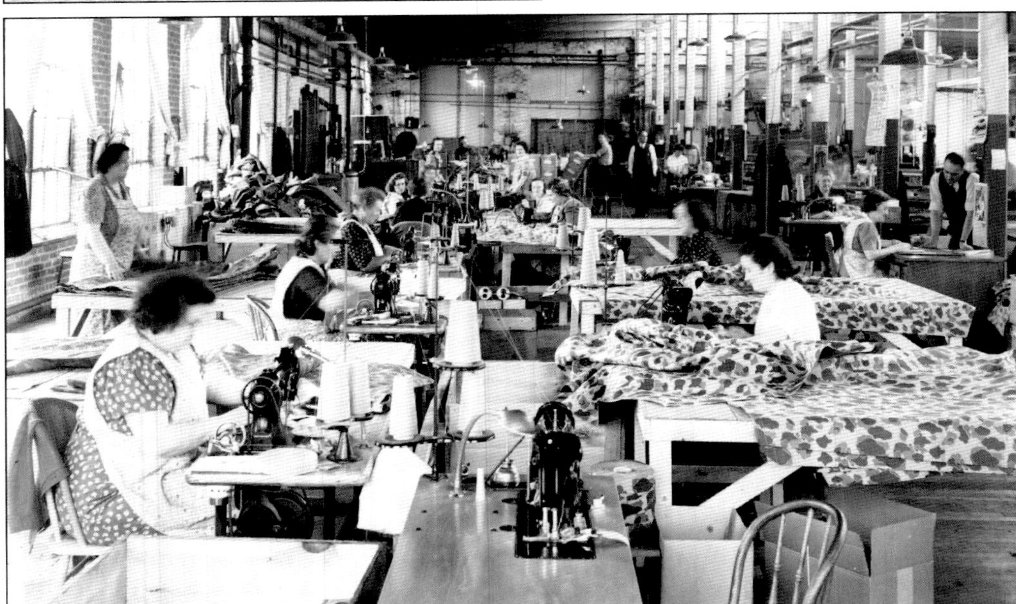

Female operatives of the Walker Company on East Main Street prepare various products, including heating pads and ice bags in the late 1940s. Despite the manual nature of much of the work, the Walker Company was one of the largest manufacturers of these products; a surprising outcome given the firm was founded in 1918 in David R. Walker's South Main Street barn. (Author's collection.)

Six

MUNICIPAL IMPROVEMENTS

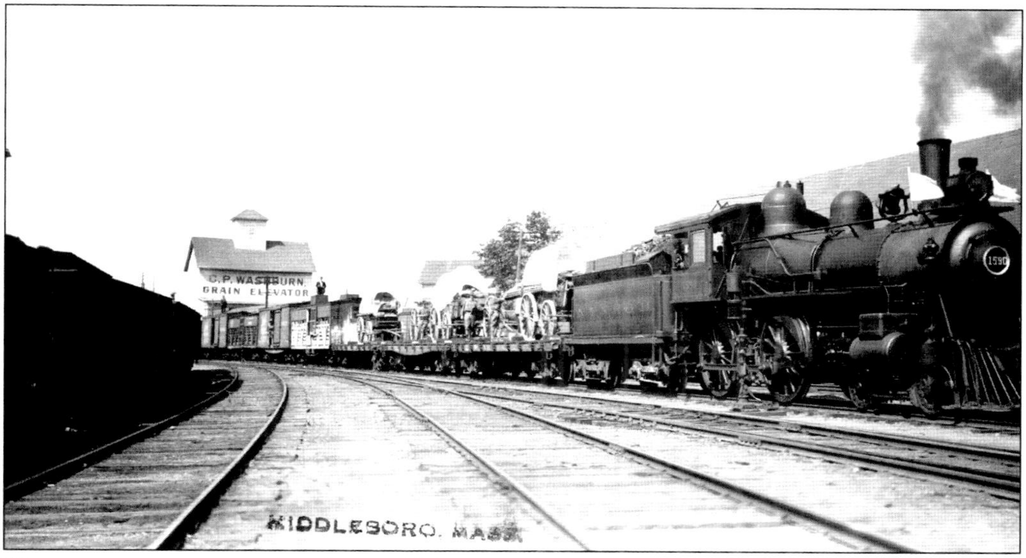

The most important catalyst for the 19th-century growth of Middleborough was the arrival of the railroad in 1846. The latter half of the 1800s similarly witnessed a host of other technological advances that remade the community, including transportation innovations, modern municipal services, and improvements in communications. Here, the New York, New Haven and Hartford's steam locomotive No. 1590 pulls into the Middleborough rail yard about 1910.

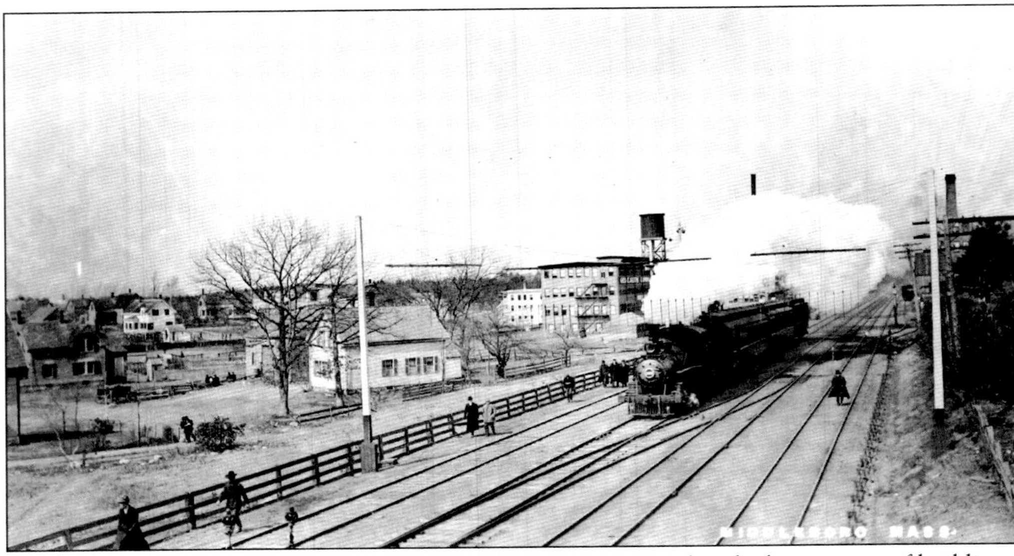

In April 1846, the Cape Cod Branch Railroad was incorporated with the purpose of building a separate rail line from Middleborough to Sandwich. The line effectively secured Middleborough's role as an important railway junction, as all traffic and freight destined for and bound from Cape Cod passed through the Middleborough rail yard. The locomotive seen here is headed into Middleborough's station. In the rear is the George E. Keith plant.

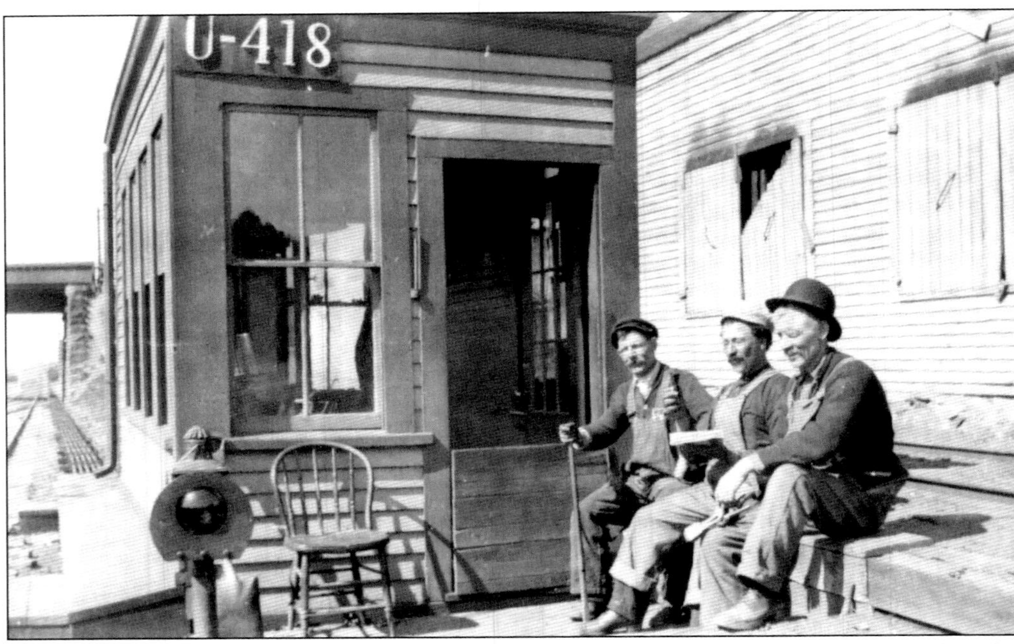

Old-timers such as these had years of experience working on the railroads. This trio of unidentified gentlemen takes a break outside what appears to be the signal house at the south end of the busy Middleborough rail yard. "The facilities for transportation from this place are becoming so great as to make it a most desirable business location," argued the *Nemasket Gazette* in 1856, explaining the community's post-railroad expansion.

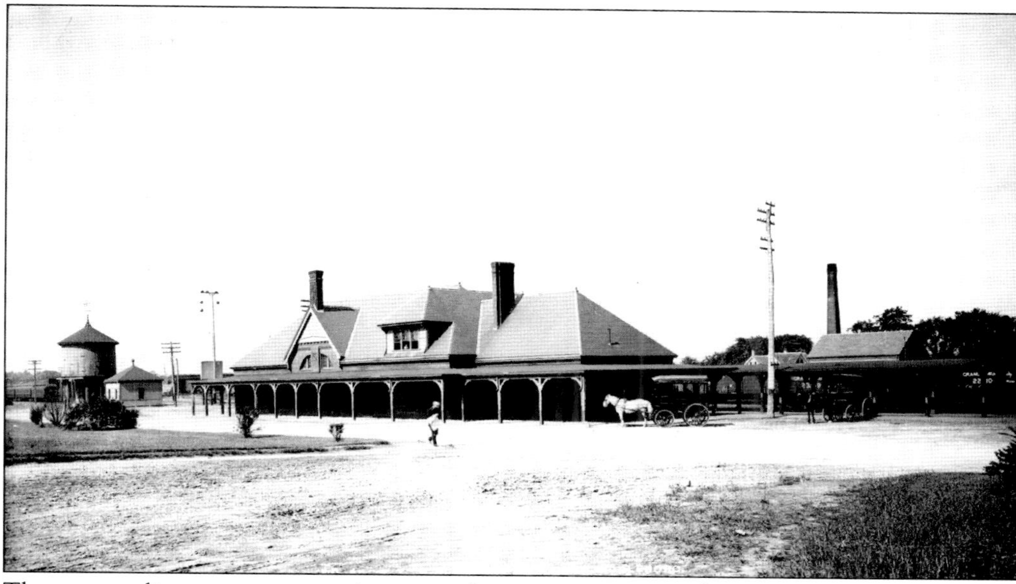

The commodious passenger station seen above was constructed in 1887 by the Old Colony Railroad and featured amenities including a lunch room and carefully landscaped grounds. Expansive roofed platforms protected passengers during inclement weather and provided a welcome greeting to returning residents. Here, too, were located the town's telegraph office and express agency.

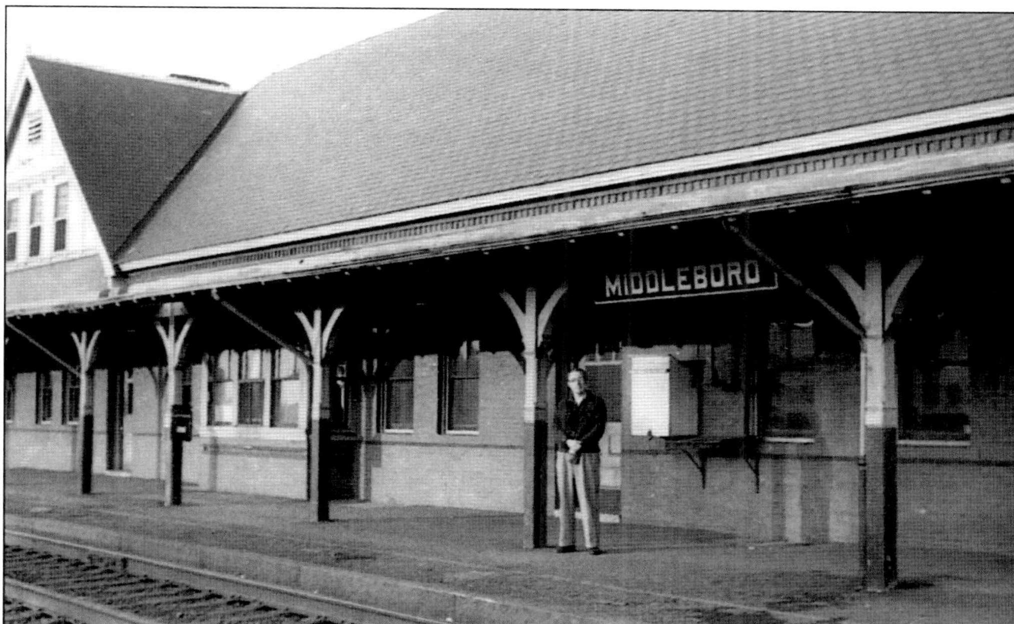

In addition to the regular passenger and freight service that passed through Middleborough, there were a number of special trains. The Fall River boat train connected with the passenger steamers of the Fall River line for New York, while the so-called "Dude Train" carried wealthy Boston businessmen on an express route to the summer resorts on Cape Cod. Passenger service was discontinued in 1959 and the station demolished in the 1990s.

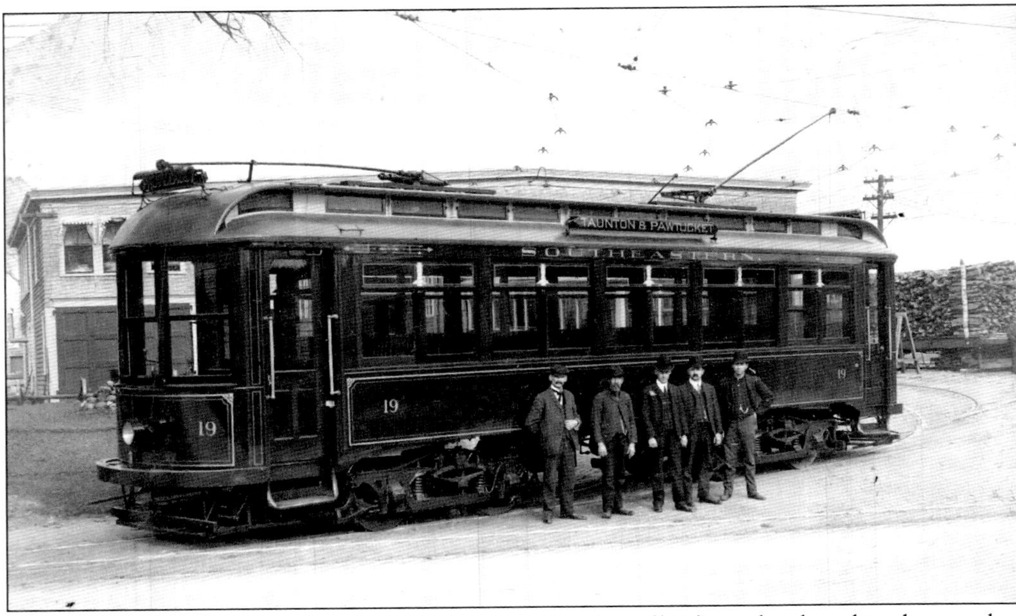

To supplement the steam railroads, long-distance electric trolley lines developed in the very late 1890s. Following 1899, Middleborough was ultimately serviced by several such lines, including the Taunton and Pawtucket, one of whose cars is seen outside the Wareham Street trolley barn (later Maxim Motor Company). Not confined to Middleborough, electric trolleys linked the community to the wider world, including Brockton, Taunton, New Bedford, and Cape Cod.

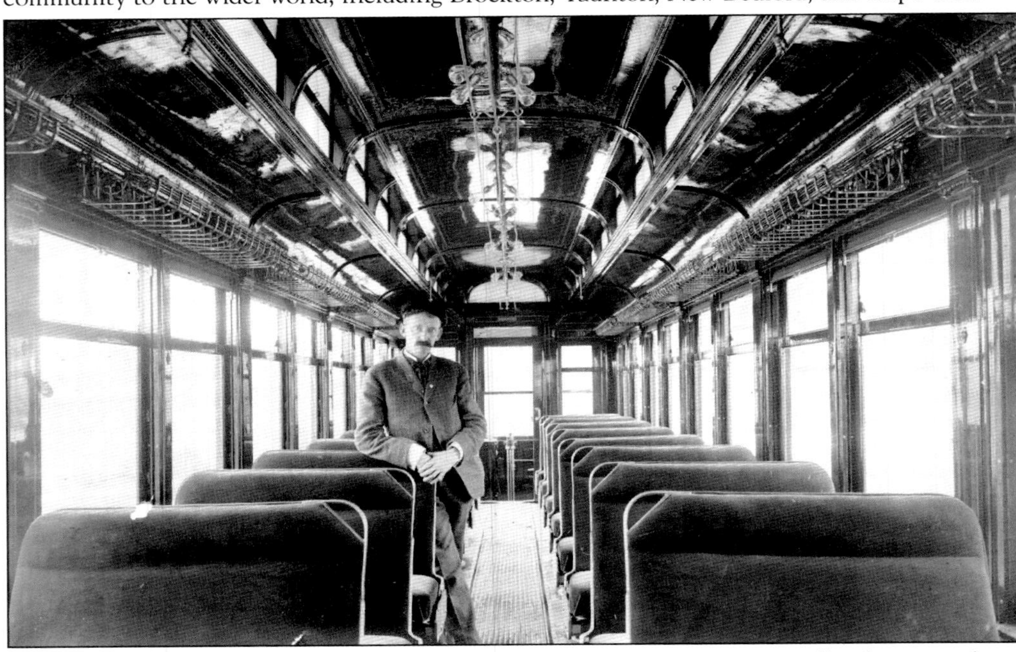

To compete with the older, more-established steam railroads, the new trolley lines sought to provide a high level of comfort coupled with more frequent service. Electric lighting and heat made the interior of the trolley car agreeable, even in the foulest weather. Here a local trolley conductor poses inside one of the cars that once serviced Middleborough.

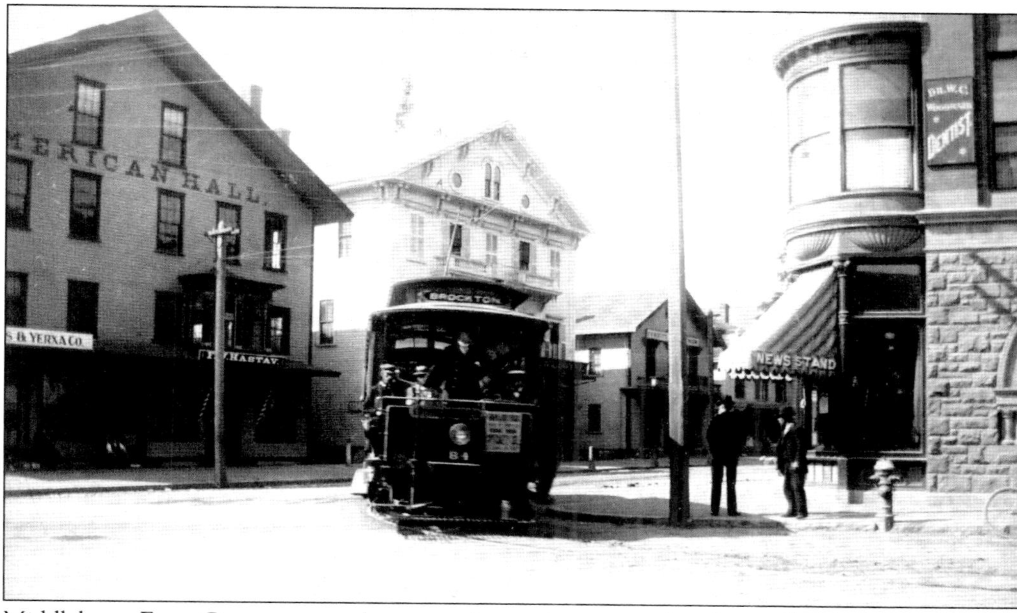

Middleboro Four Corners was the natural meeting point for the trolley lines that served Middleborough. Here, a Brockton-bound trolley on the New Bedford, Middleboro and Brockton Street Railway turns from South Main Street onto Center Street. The Brockton line was the first in Middleborough, opening in 1899. Nearby, Tripp's Candy Kitchen on Center Street served as a convenient waiting room for trolley passengers.

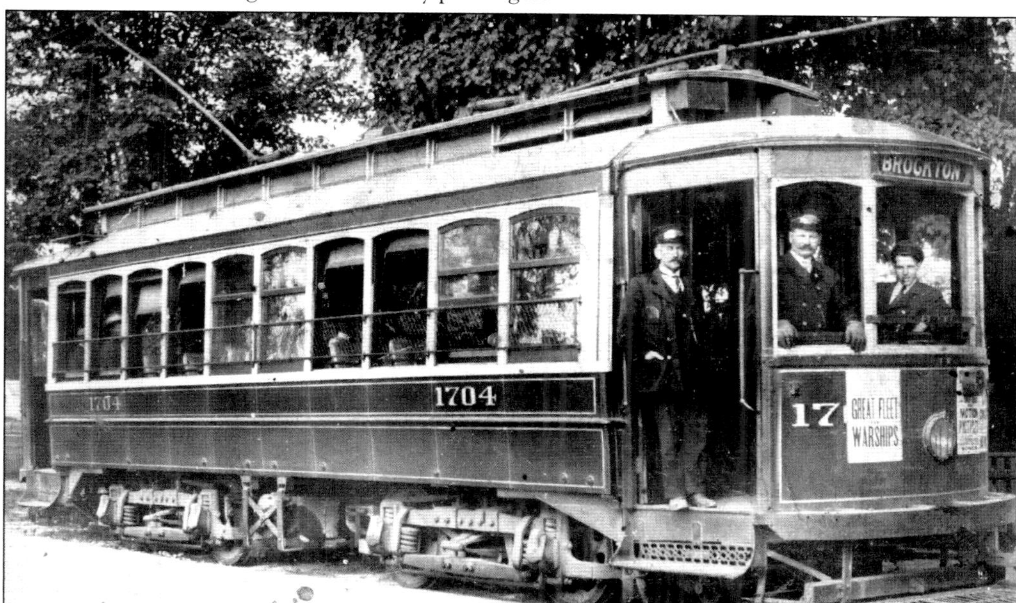

Yet another New Bedford, Middleboro and Brockton Street Railway trolley, No. 1704, passes through Middleborough en route to Brockton. A sign on the front advertises the "Great Fleet of Warships." Frequently, trolley companies advertised excursions to see such sites as a means of increasing business. Some even built their own parks along their lines. For Middleborough residents, the trolleys offered inexpensive fares and convenient transportation.

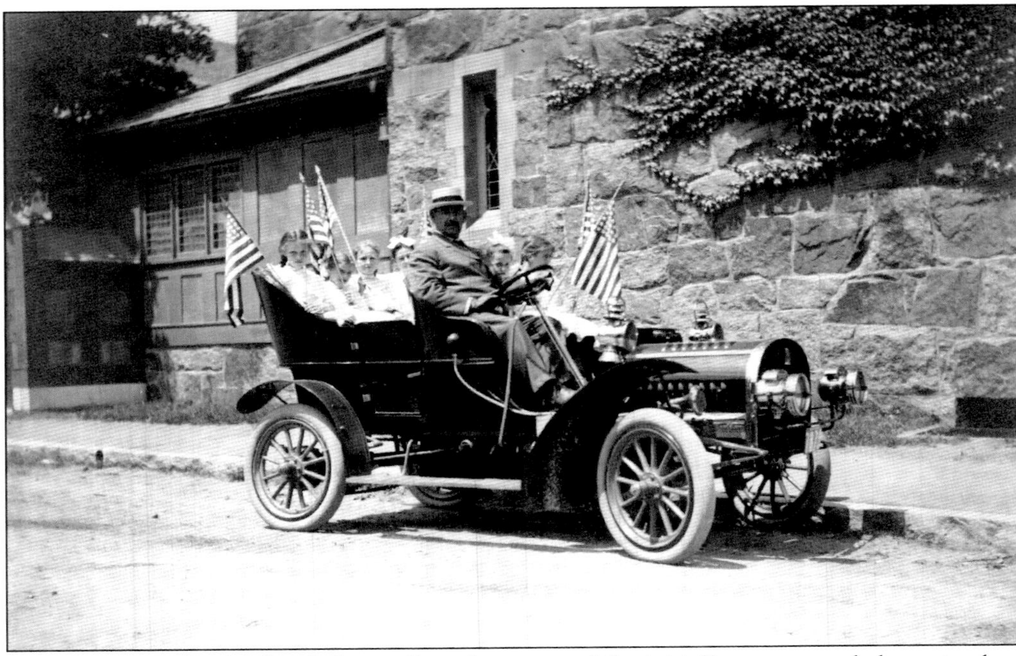

Coming upon the heels of the trolley, the automobile initially was regarded as simply a recreational vehicle for the wealthy, used for jaunts in the countryside or for outings like that of James F. Casey and friends who halted on Union Street in 1906 long enough to accommodate the photographer. As the number of automobiles proliferated, however, improvements were made to many of the town's roads, further facilitating the automobile's growth.

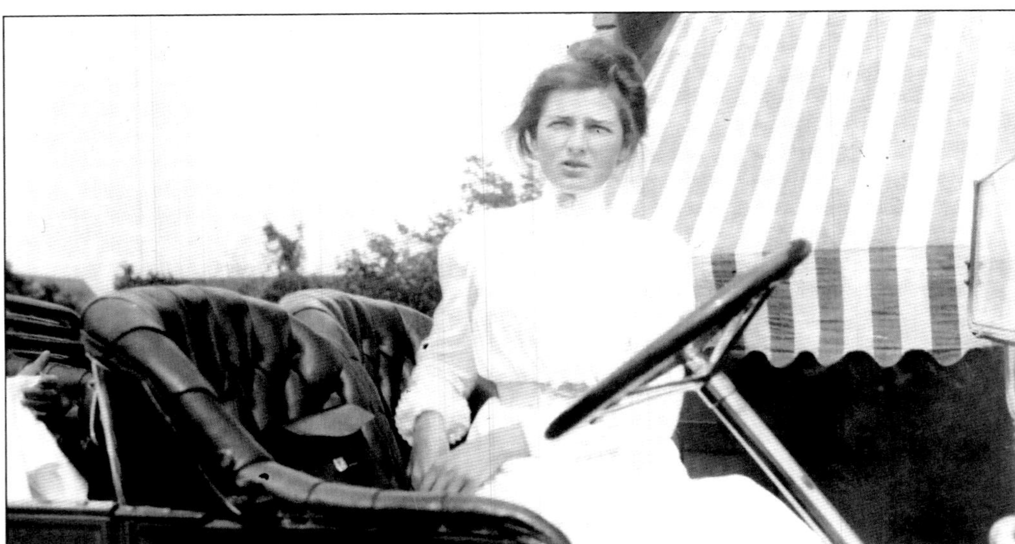

The first automobile owned in Middleborough was acquired by sports enthusiast Fletcher L. Barrows, a partner in the Leonard and Barrows shoe-manufacturing firm. In time, Barrows owned a number of machines. Few restrictions were placed on early automobilists. The first woman licensed to drive in Middleborough was Myra (Andrews) Shaw, who was just 14 when her father, shoe retailer and cranberry grower William A. Andrews, taught her to drive.

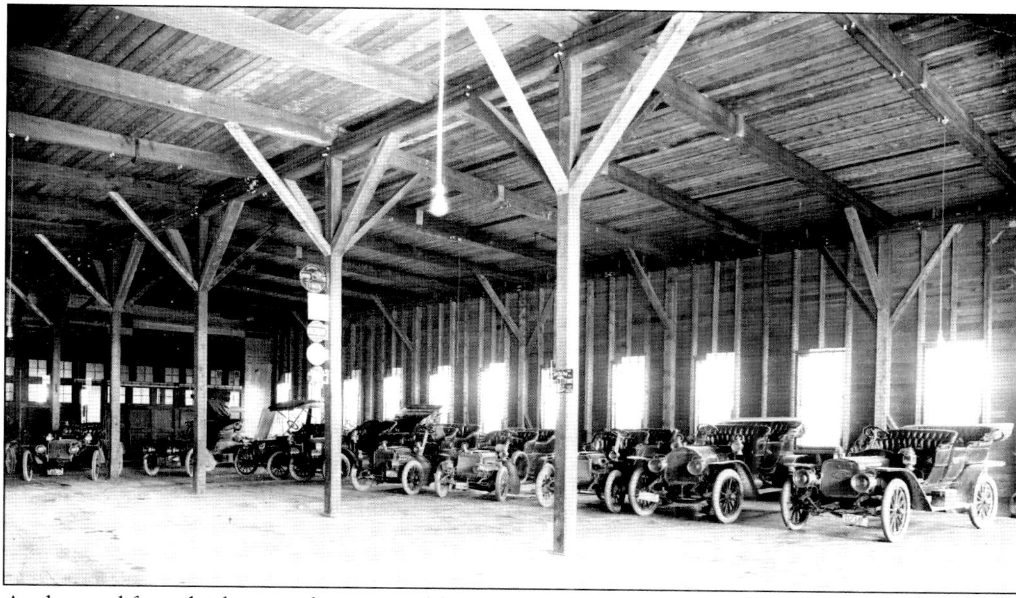

As demand for vehicles rose, businesses like the Middleboro Auto Exchange on Wareham Street were established. Operating on the principle of the livery stable, the exchange leased automobiles to customers for short-term periods, thereby inaugurating the car rental business. The exchange was housed in a building that had previously served as a trolley car barn and was later occupied by Maxim Motor Company.

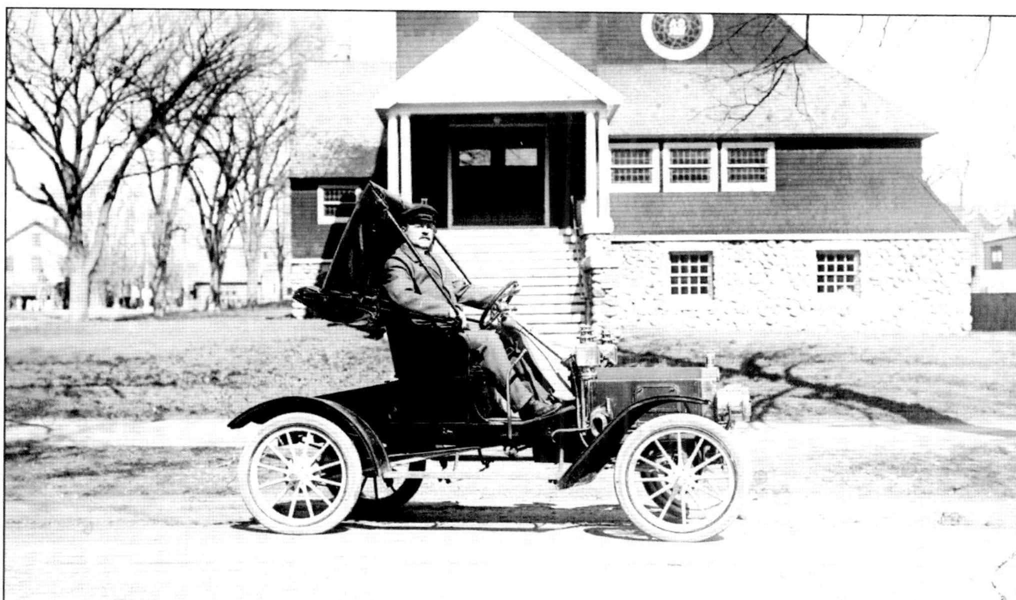

Although World War II was a long way off when this driver posed outside the Unitarian church, following that war, automobiles came to be considered a necessity for every family. The dramatic increase in automobile ownership hastened social changes, including suburban sprawl and the incumbent loss of identity for Middleborough's traditional villages and neighborhoods, including Middleboro Four Corners.

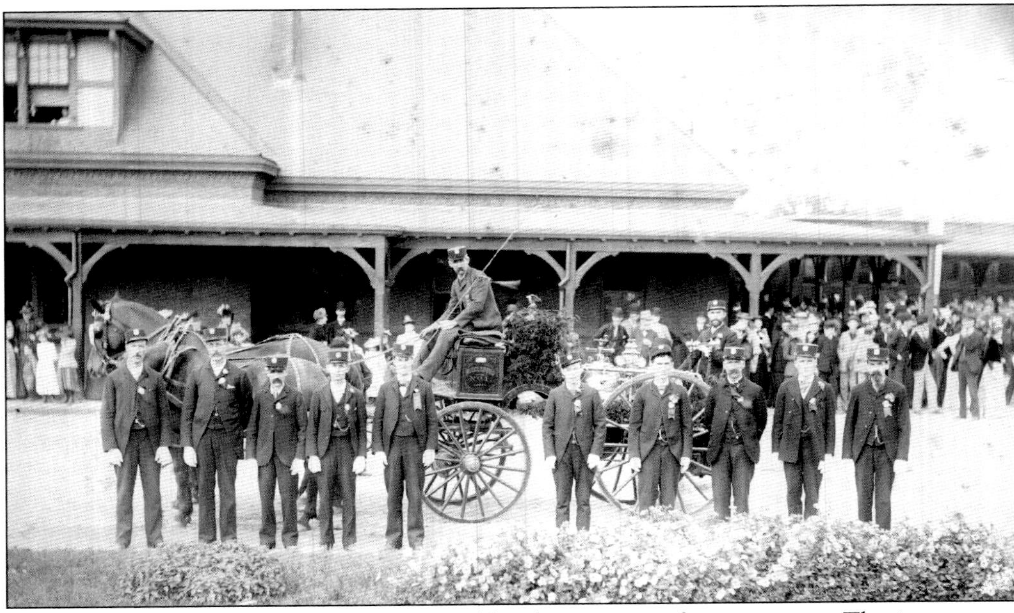

One of the first municipal services provided by the town was fire protection. The issue proved divisive, and a compromise solution was reached with the creation in 1852 of a fire district covering Middleborough Four Corners only, with fire companies like that pictured above protecting the center. Residents lying outside the pale of the district were left to their own devices, providing their own communal fire protection as in days past.

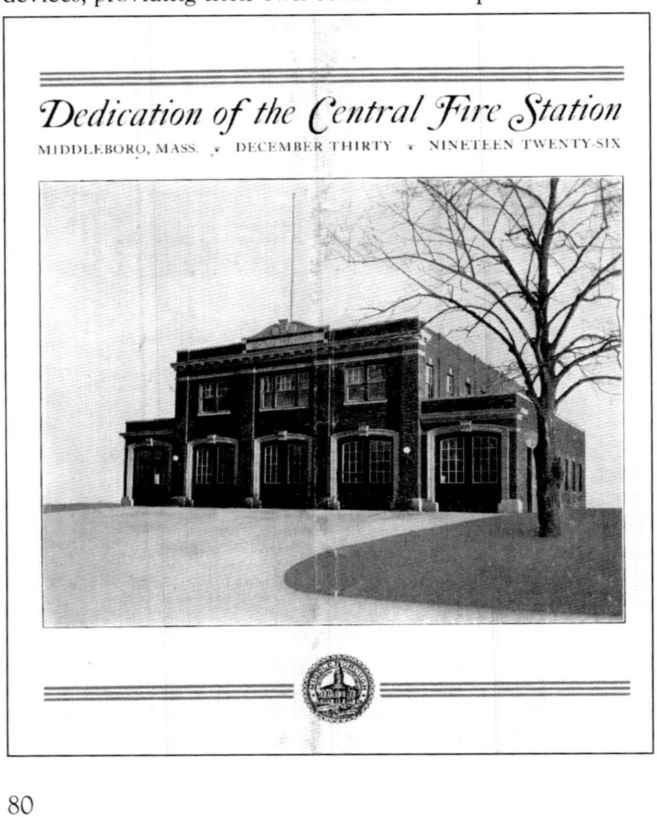

Middleborough's original central firehouse was a three-bay station constructed on School Street shortly following the establishment of the fire district. In 1926, it was succeeded by a modern station that was built on North Main Street. Like its predecessor, the 1926 station served an important role within the community until 2003 when it was replaced by the present facility. (Author's collection).

With the conclusion of the Civil War, Middleborough Four Corners entered a new period of growth and prosperity, driven by the expansion of its industrial base. The community's assurance of its own future was seen most tangibly with the construction of a new town house and memorial hall in 1872 and 1873. Designed by North Middleborough native Solomon K. Eaton, Middleborough Town Hall became the emblem of Victorian Middleborough's self-confidence.

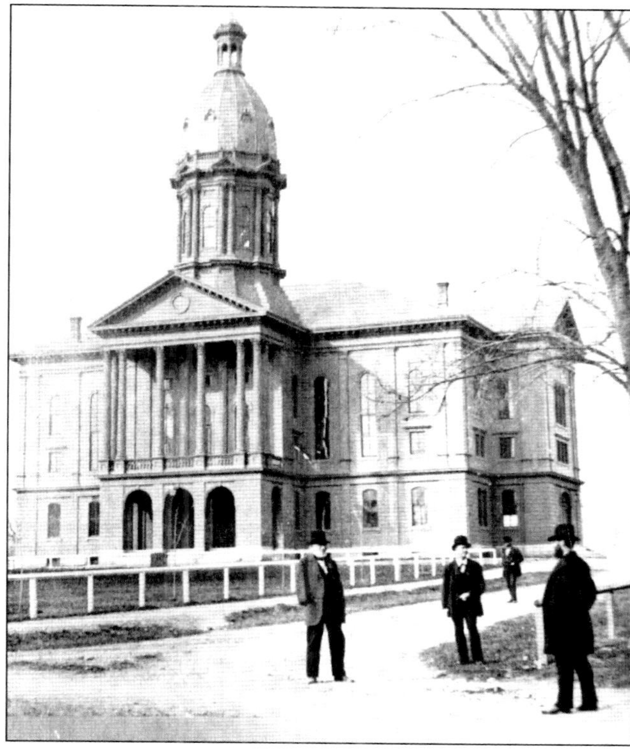

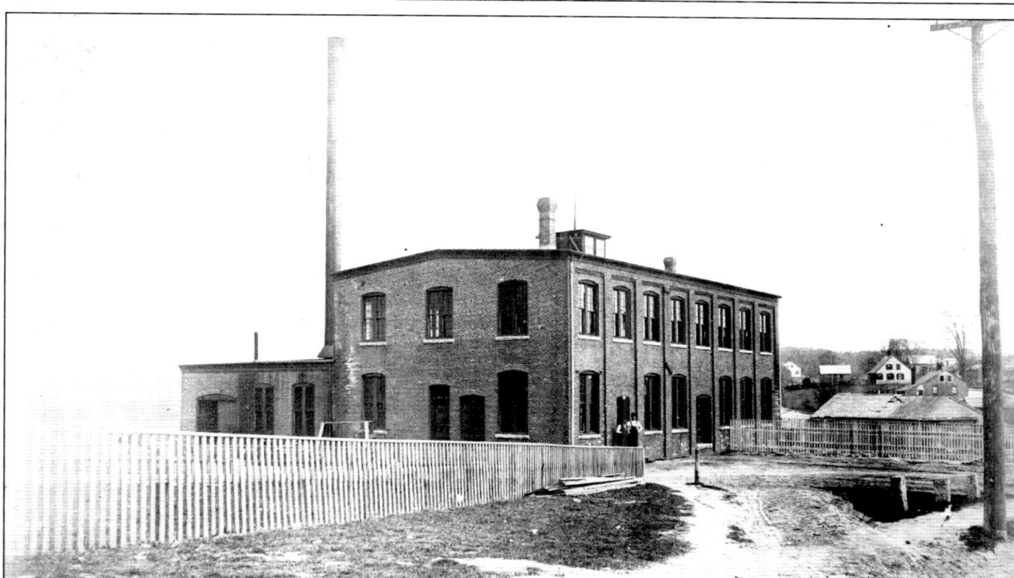

As the most industrialized and urbanized of Middleborough's several villages, Middleborough Four Corners became the seat for technological advances. In the 1880s, Middleborough moved to establish electrical lighting. The present Middleborough Municipal Electric Light Plant on Wareham Street at the Nemasket River was erected in 1889 by the Middleboro Electric Light and Power Company when it rushed to become the first company to provide electrical power to the community.

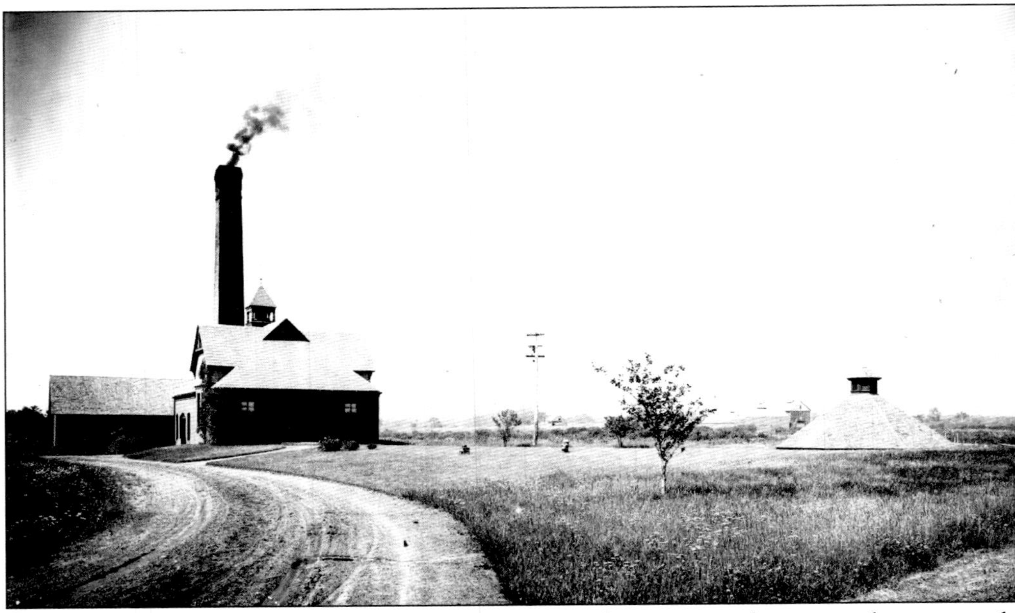

Yet another improvement was the establishment of a municipal waterworks system for Middleborough in 1884 and 1885. The system consisted of a pumping station and covered well (above) on East Grove Street and a standpipe on Forest Street. The introduction of pure water into the community marked the culmination of a decade of lobbying by local residents who advocated both the health and safety benefits of a public water supply.

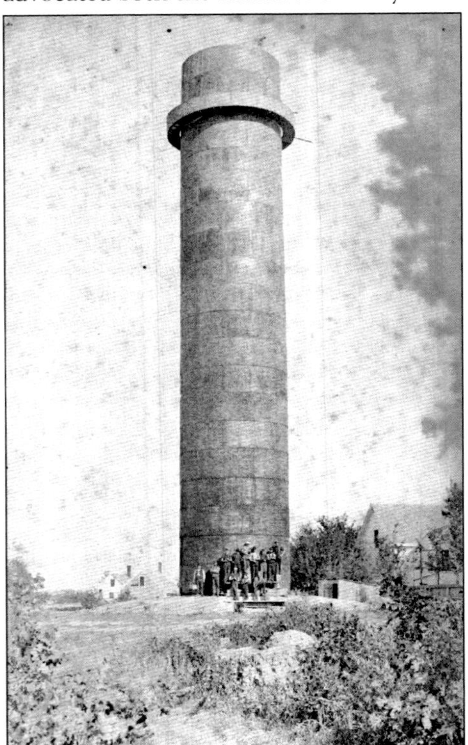

The supply itself was stored in a large standpipe that was constructed by Italian laborers on a site on Forest Street, selected as the highest point within the center of town. The standpipe was a prominent landmark until 1915 when it was replaced with a concrete water tower on Barden Hill. At that time, the standpipe was disassembled and sold, reputedly to make sugar cane syrup barrels in Puerto Rico.

Helping foster these Victorian-era improvements were the *Nemasket Gazette* (founded in 1852 and still serving the communities of Middleborough and Lakeville as the *Middleboro Gazette*) and its friendly rival, the *Middleboro News* (1881–1914). Middleborough developed a small but lively publishing community, and a number of newspapers and periodicals were produced in addition to the *Nemasket Gazette* and *Middleboro News*, including S. H. Sylvester's *Domestic Fashion Gazette* and F. B. Washburn's *Fireside Journal*.

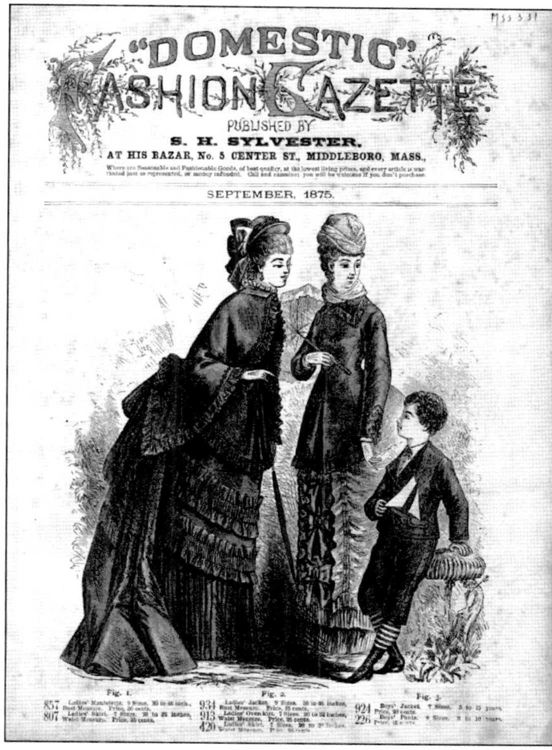

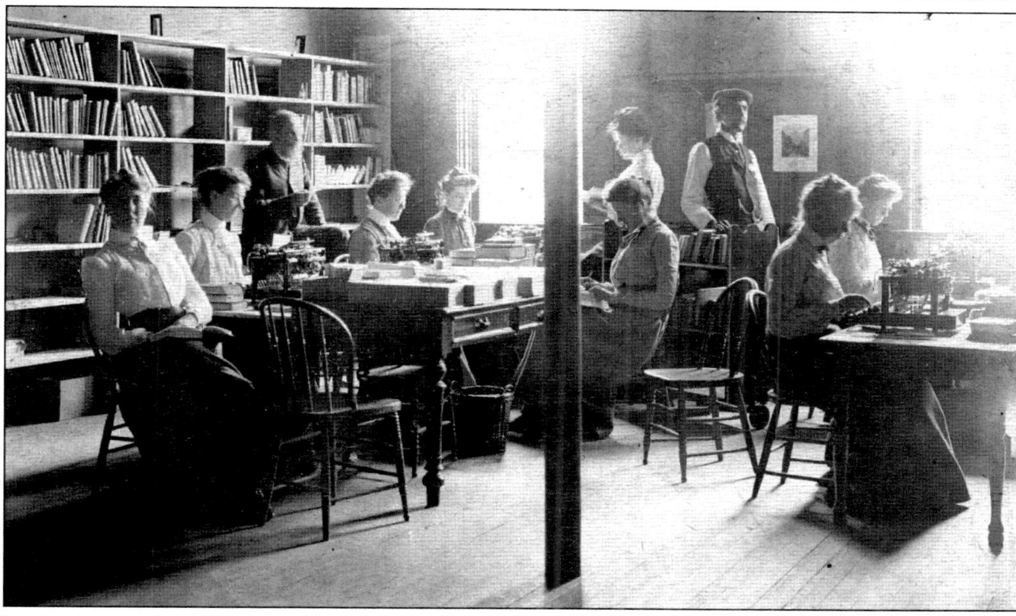

Middleborough's reading public also benefited from the Middleborough Public Library, which was established in 1874 and first housed in the town hall. Before the move to a new library building in 1903, the librarians recataloged and packed the books, a process pictured above. Library trustee Joseph E. Beals watches from the left while the unidentified gentleman in his shirtsleeves undoubtedly had the unenviable task of carting the books to their new home.

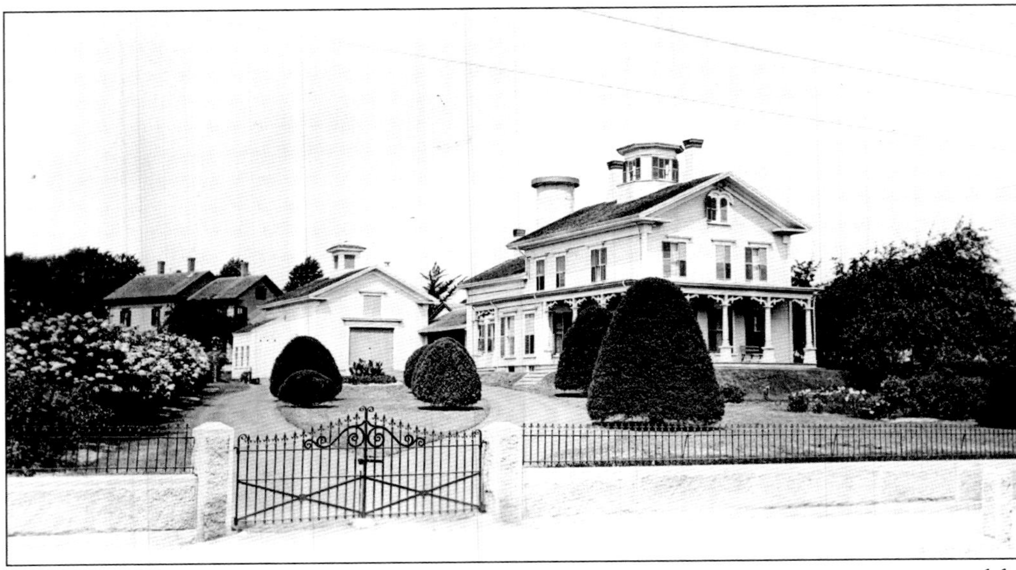

In 1920, the former Oak Street estate of shoe manufacturer Calvin D. Kingman was acquired for use as Middleborough's first formal hospital, known as St. Luke's Hospital, with facilities for the care of 18 patients. Named in accordance with the wishes of Peter H. Peirce's daughter-in-law Maria (Harlow) Peirce, whose $100,000 bequest made financially possible the institution's foundation, the hospital replaced the Kingman house in 1968 with a modern brick addition.

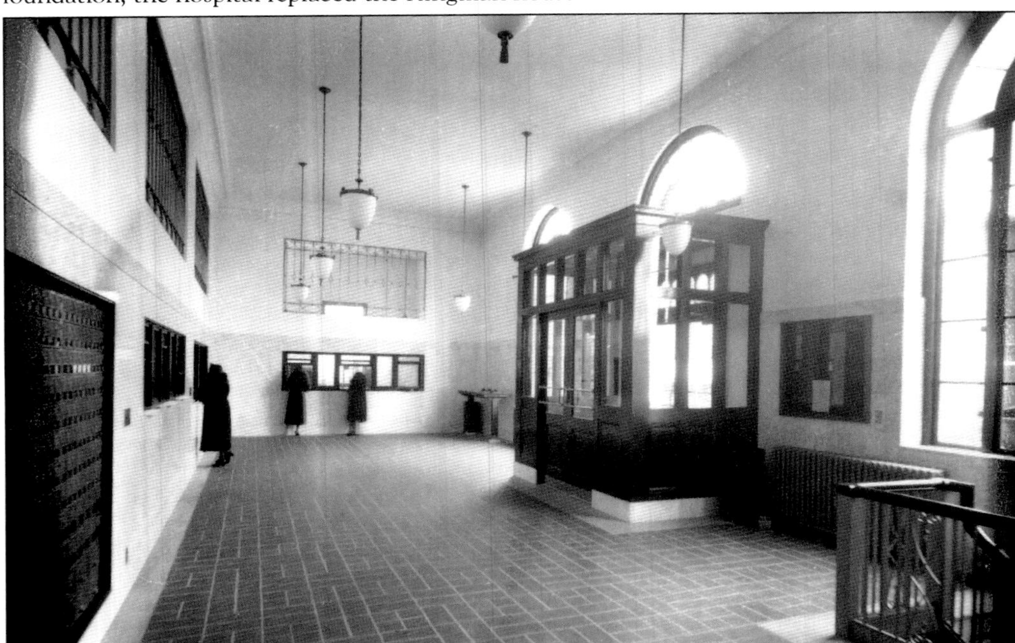

The demolition of Peirce Academy in 1932 for the construction of a new post office awakened the community's latent sense of historic preservation. While the destruction could not be halted, most agreed that the main hall of the new post office pictured here was a marked improvement upon the quarters of the previous post office that had been located in the Peirce Block at Middleboro Four Corners.

Seven

COMMERCE

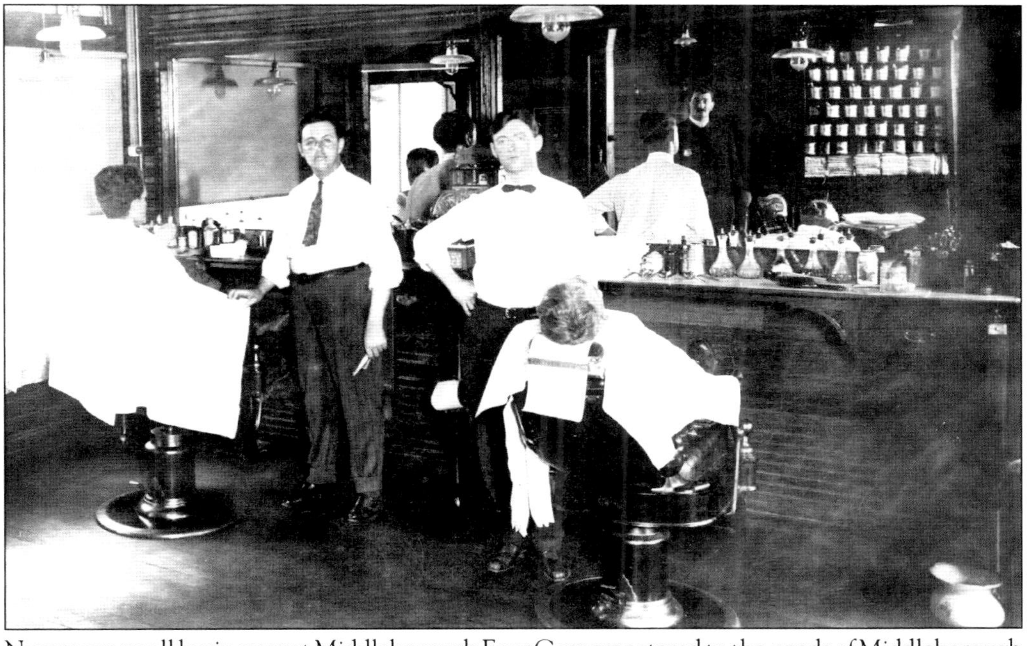

Numerous small businesses at Middleborough Four Corners catered to the needs of Middleborough residents and those from surrounding towns. The Thatcher's Row barbershop operated for over 100 years. Here owner Milt Sherrard (left) and Charles Gaskin momentarily interrupt their work to pose for the photographer. Notice the ceramic shaving mugs, each labeled for use by a specific regular customer reflected in the mirror.

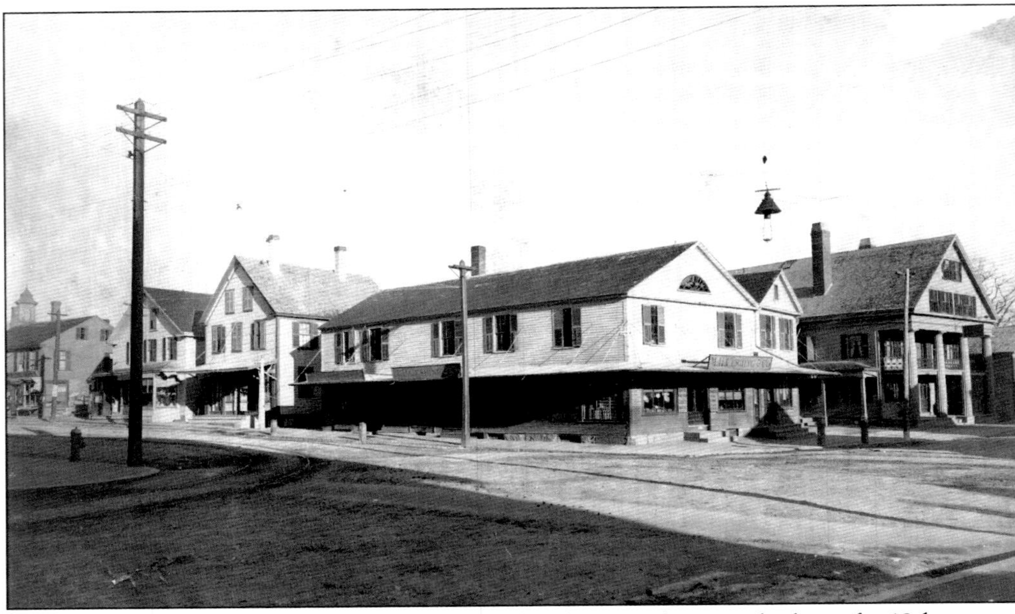

Middleboro Four Corners, the site of the Peirce family stores, became the locus for 19th century commercial development in Middleborough. This view shows the corner of Center and North Main Streets, the site now occupied by the Peirce Block, just before 1900. From left to right are the Lovell building, once home to the *Middleboro Gazette*; the Lincoln building; the Cushing Block, which housed the early Peirce store; and the Nemasket house.

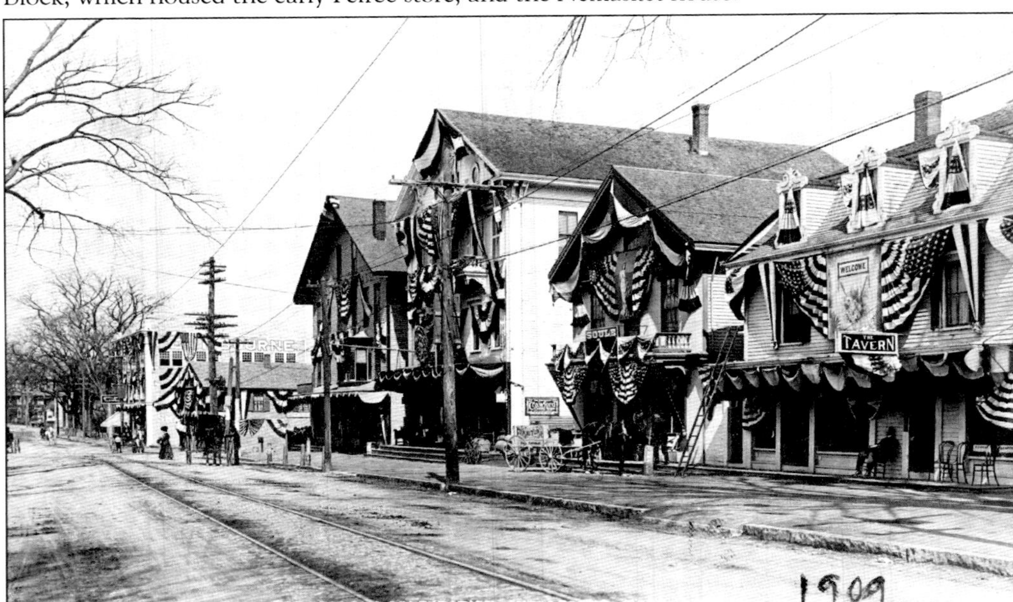

As the community grew, so too did the business district, extending along both North and South Main Streets (the latter of which is pictured here in 1909), as well as Wareham Street. To accommodate newer businesses, residences like the Drake house at the far right were renovated, and purpose-built structures, like the American Hall, Doane Block, and Soule Block, seen in the center from left to right, were constructed.

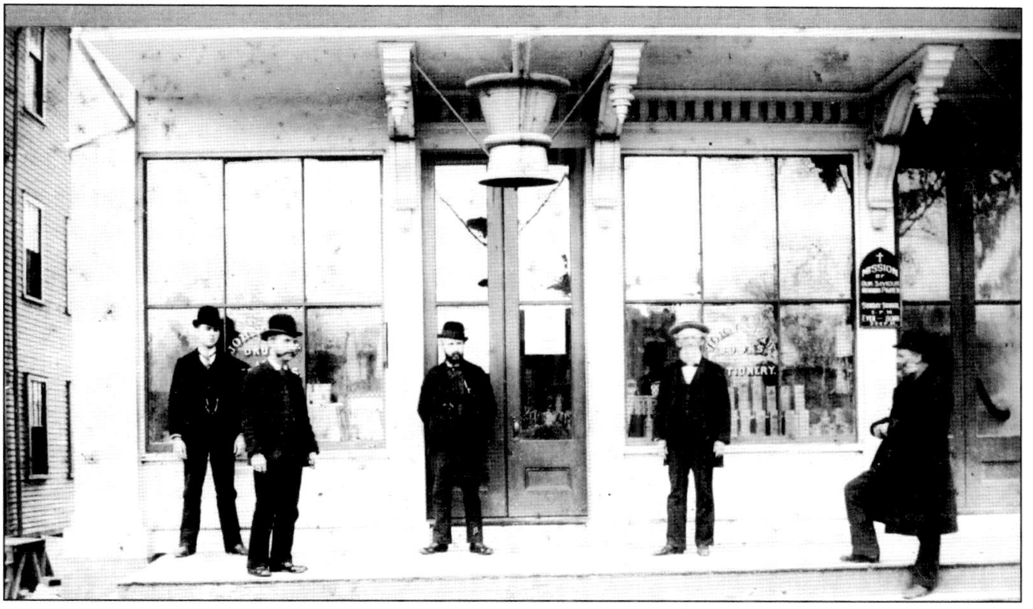

South Main Street merchants from the late 1800s pose in front of John Shaw's drug and stationery store, which was located in the Doane Block. The large display windows and bracketed overhang were designed to invite passersby to window-shop, a favorite pastime for many. Note the large mortar and pestle hanging over the entrance. Later residents remember the building as home to Faietti's Hardware.

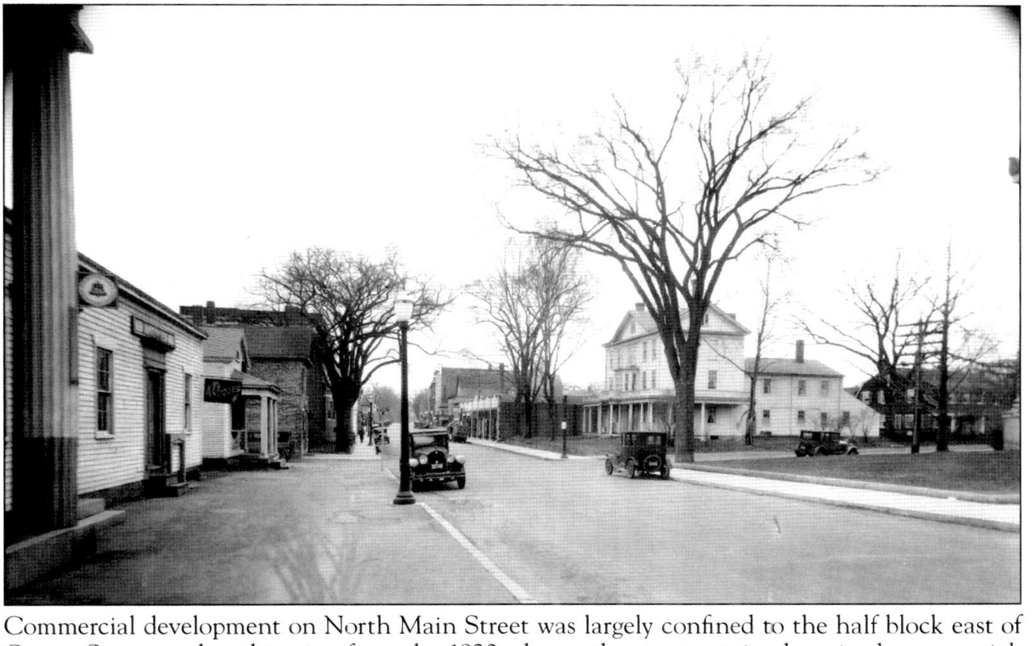

Commercial development on North Main Street was largely confined to the half block east of Center Street, and as this view from the 1920s shows, the street retained a mixed commercial, residential, and municipal use. The large house in the center is the Tucker-Jenks house, which was last known as the Martinique. It was demolished for the construction of a gasoline station in 1957.

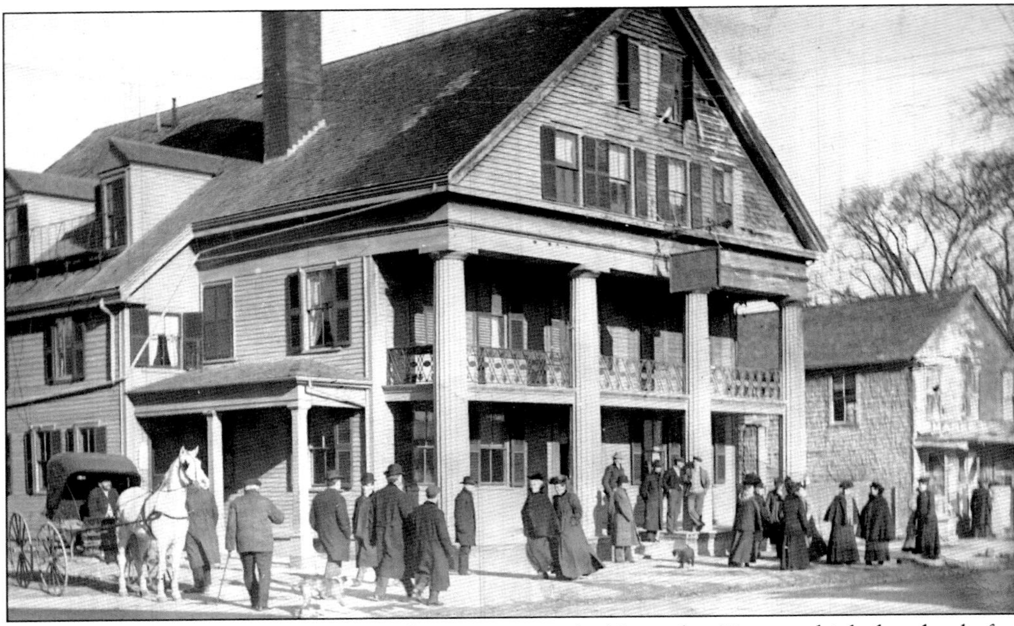

Prominent among North Main Street businesses was the Nemasket House, which dated to before the Civil War. The hotel was Middleborough's most noted, particularly among horse fanciers, and it stood next to the present Peirce Block. To the right of the picture is the Eaton, Leonard and Company shoe manufactory and retail store. The Nemasket House was demolished in 1939 to make way for a Shell gasoline station.

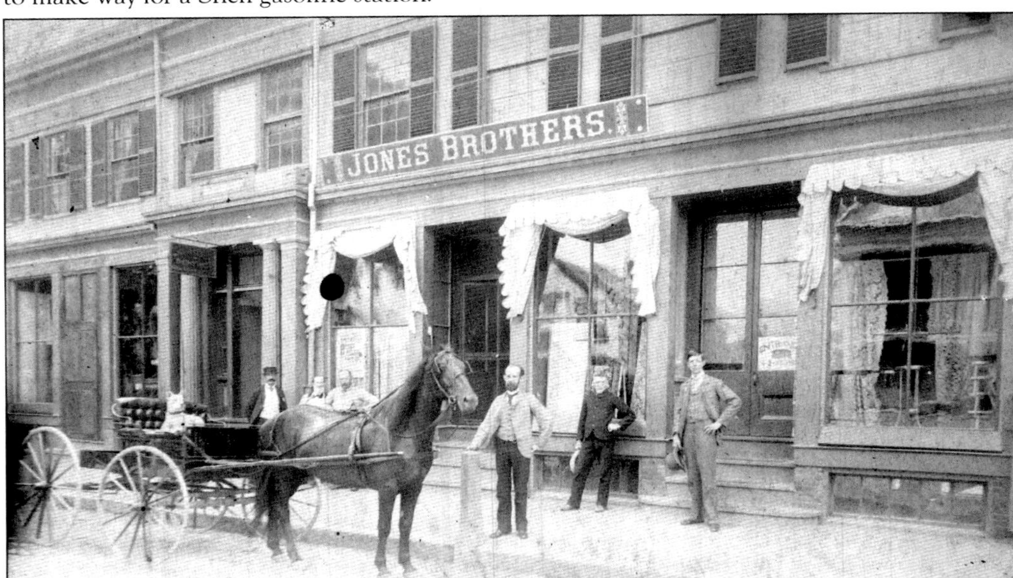

Opposite the Nemasket House stood the Wells Block, the bottom floor of which was occupied at the dawn of the 20th century by the Jones Brothers furniture store. Although many mercantile operations sold some furniture, Jones Brothers remained the most prominent in Middleborough. The building, including the store, was destroyed in a spectacular fire in December 1905. It was replaced by the block that later housed Cleverly's Market.

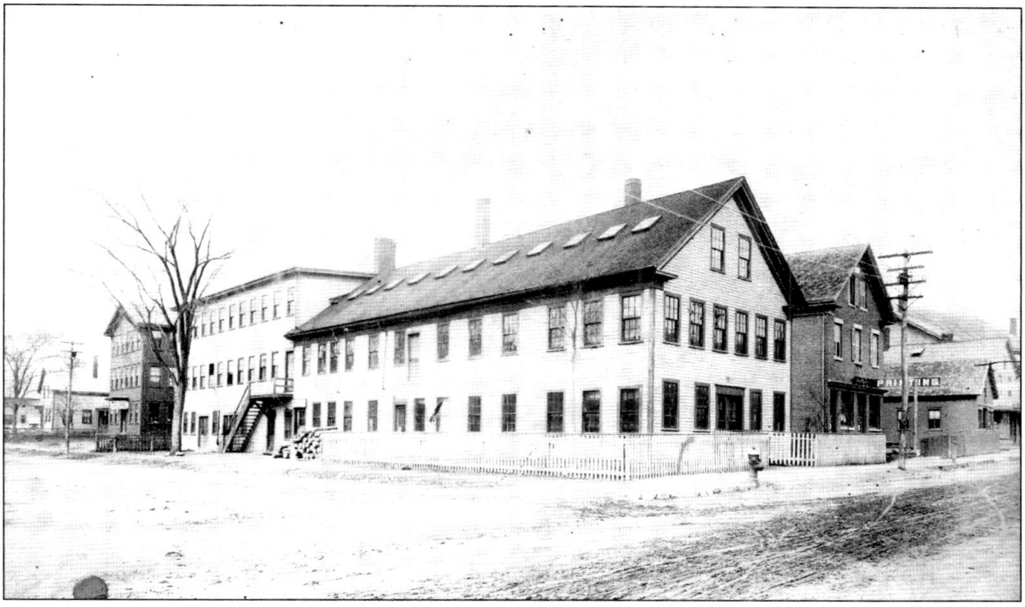

The upper portion of Wareham Street (known as Water Street until 1903) saw equal amounts of commercial and industrial development. The Jenks Machine Shop on the corner of Wareham and Clifford Streets is flanked by the brick Gazette building (1876) on Wareham Street and the Domestic Needle Works building on Clifford Street, which manufactured sewing needles for a brief period in the 1880s.

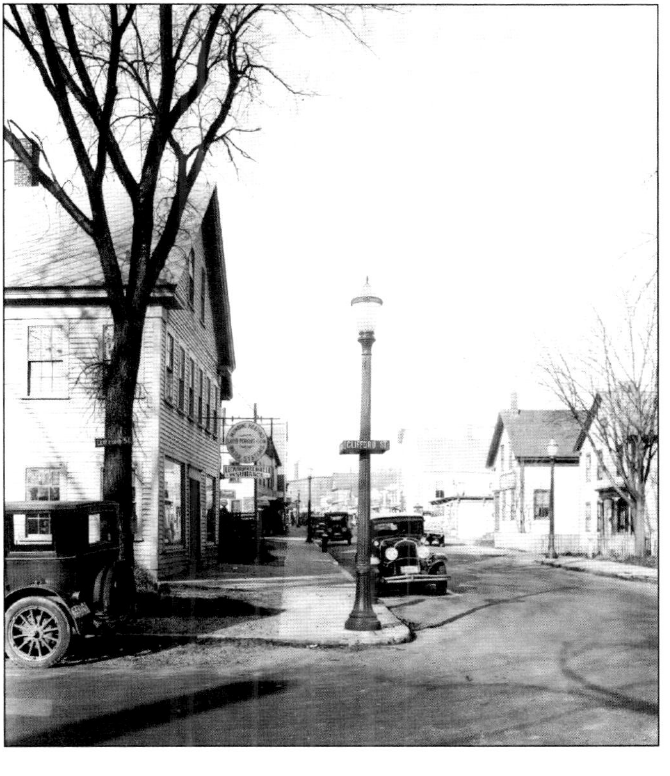

This view from about 1930 was taken from near the same corner and looks towards the four corners. During the intervening years, streets were paved, concrete sidewalks were constructed, and electric streetlights were installed. The lampposts were part of the "White Way," which was installed in 1928 amid great celebration locally, and "so pleased were merchants with this transformation from a dark and dingy main street to one brilliantly lighted," as quoted from a local newspaper.

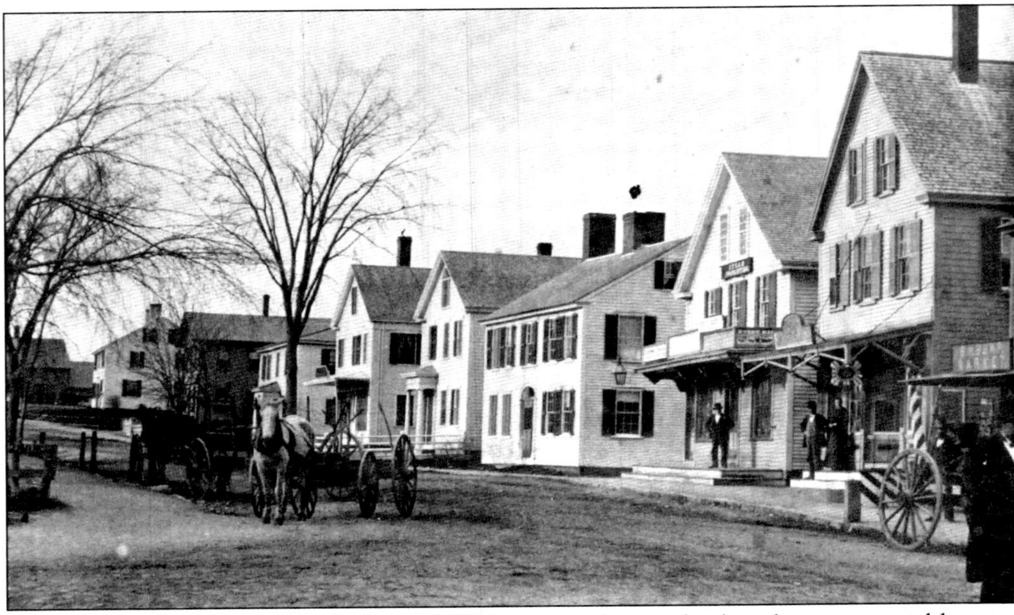

It was Center Street (seen here about 1870), however, that evolved as the commercial heart of Middleborough, particularly after the railroad opened in 1848. Following the 1850s, businesses spread northwards along the street towards the depot, encroaching upon previously residential areas. Only the fourth and fifth houses from the right survive today, and they appear as the two houses on the right in the photograph below.

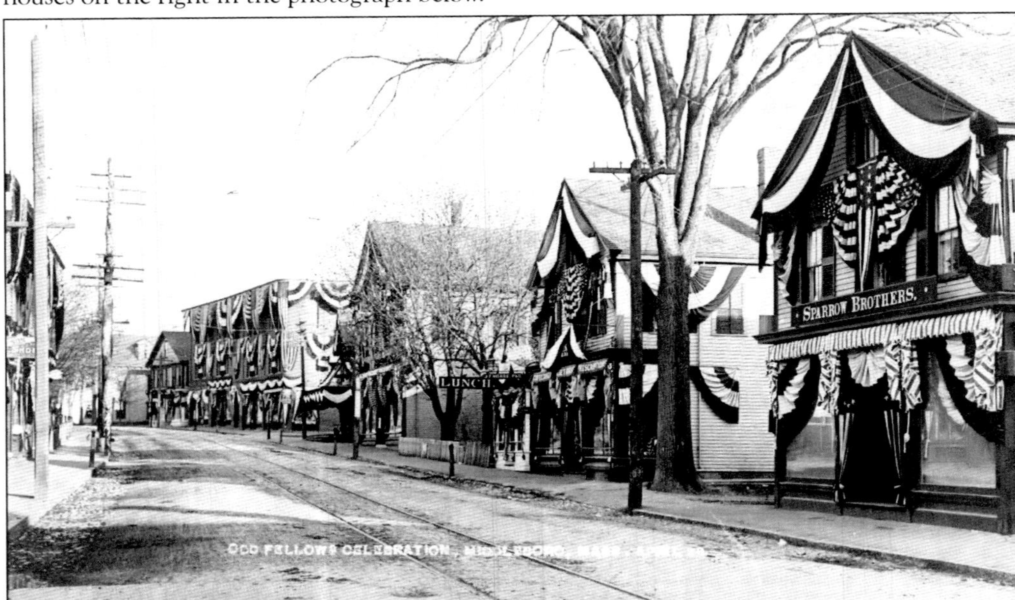

A similar 1901 view taken from a vantage point farther up the street demonstrates the changes that occurred in 30 years. Sparrow Brothers was a popular men's clothier, and the building later housed the local Sears and Roebuck office. The building to its left served as a pharmacy for nearly a century following 1875, housing Shaw and Child's, Morse's, LaForest's, and Craig's Pharmacy. The Glidden Building appears in the distance.

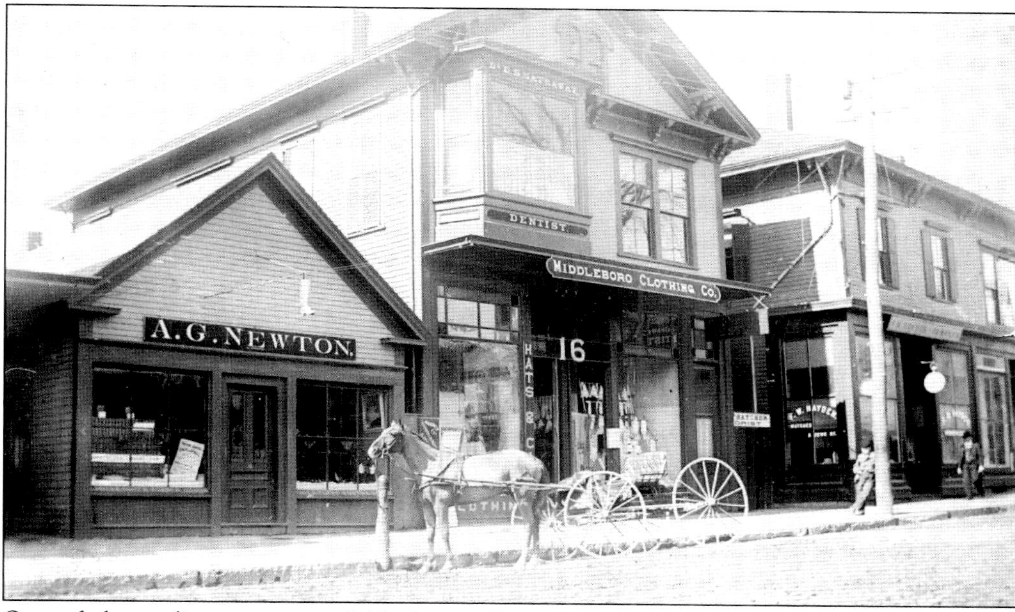

One of the earliest commercial blocks on Center Street was the Middleborough Clothing Company building, shown here in the center about 1890. Originally it housed Levi Thatcher's daguerreotype rooms. The unusual second-story bay window was installed to illuminate the dental offices of Edward S. Hathaway, which occupied the second floor. It is now an art gallery. To the left is A. G. Newton, a boot and shoe dealer.

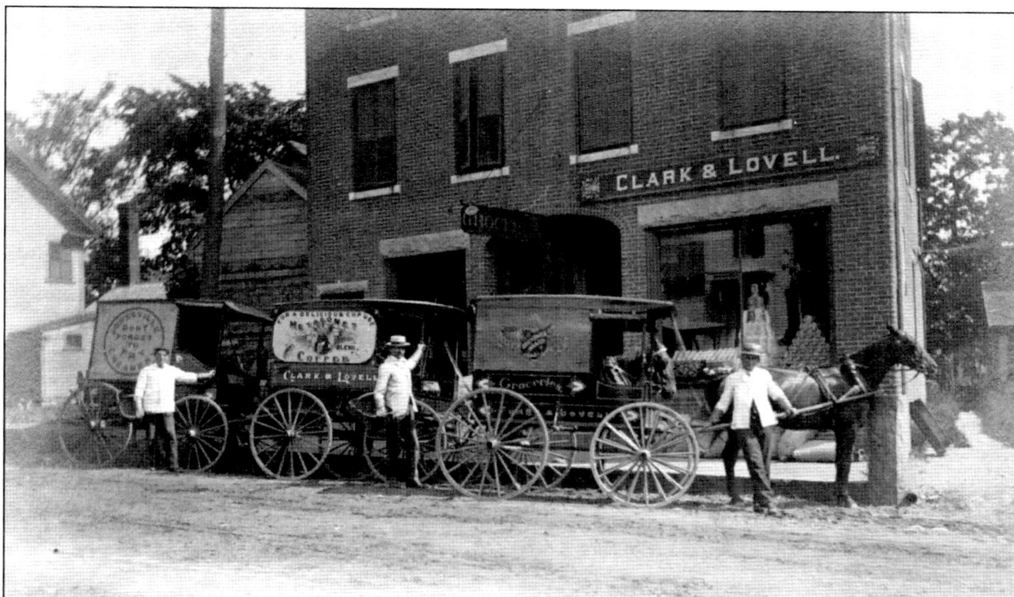

At the opposite end of Center Street (on what is now Center Avenue), Clark and Lovell operated a grocery store in a substantial brick block serving what was once known as the West End—the area immediately around Everett Square. Like other merchants who delivered groceries, baked goods, meat, fish, ice, coal, and milk, Clark and Lovell operated delivery routes, and their wagons are proudly displayed before the store.

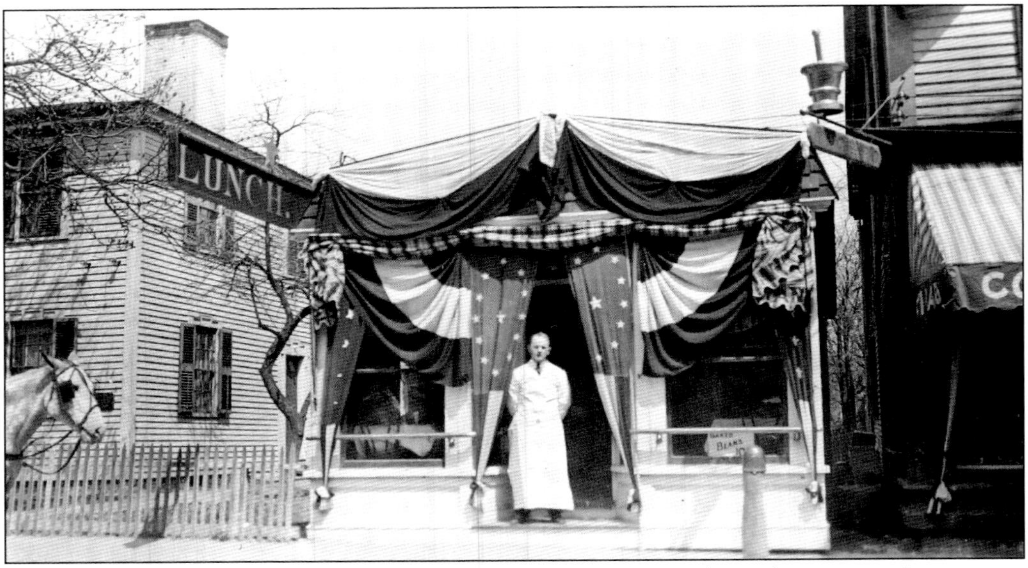

Numerous small restaurants and lunchrooms catered to the workers, shoppers, and visitors at Middleborough center, including Charlie Bourne's restaurant on Center Street, seen here in 1911. The sign in the window advertises the New England staple of baked beans for 10¢. Bourne's Restaurant and the Ryder House (left), which served as the Central Baptist Church's parsonage, were replaced by the Ryder Block in 1924.

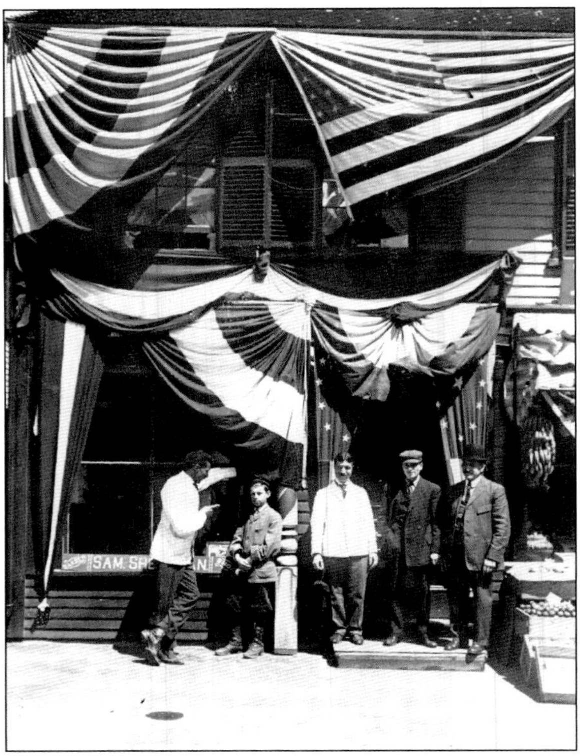

Sam Shellman operated a barbershop on Center Street between 1904 and 1911. Here he is seen admonishing a young boy, who is more interested in the cameraman than in what Shellman has to say. Oneto's Fruit Store (with its hanging bananas and sidewalk fruit stall) occupied the adjoining space, operating from 1898 until 1922. In 1927 and 1928, Woolworth's was constructed upon the site, which is now home to Reedy's Archery.

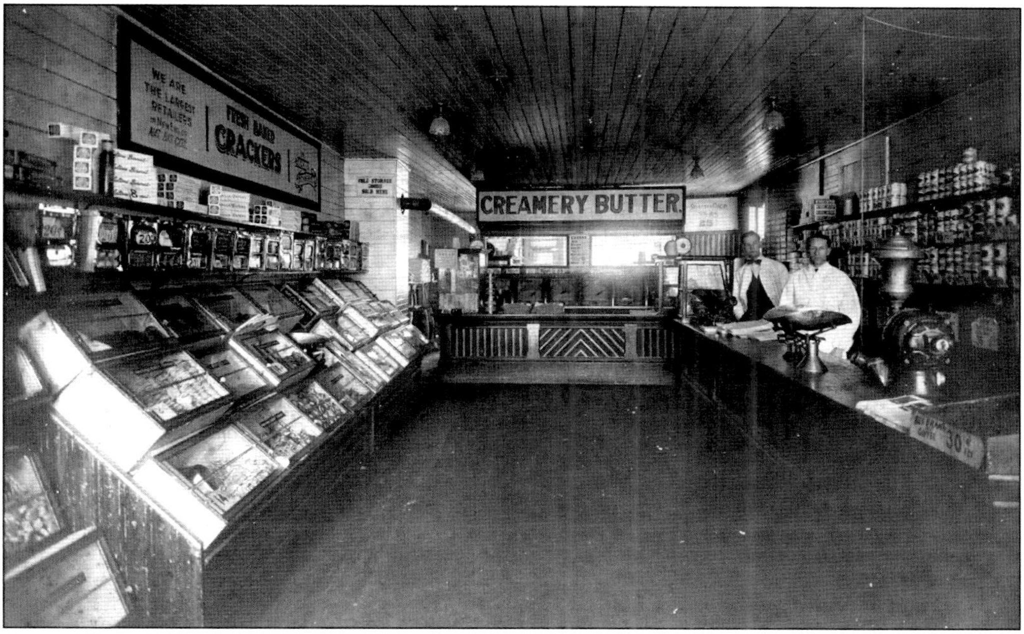

One of the town's first chain stores was the Cloverdale grocery store, which occupied a number of locations about Middleboro Four Corners. In the days prior to self-service shopping, clerks waited on customers individually. Here clerk Charles Naughton and manager William Wilder await their next patron. Wilder served as the local Cloverdale manager for 14 years.

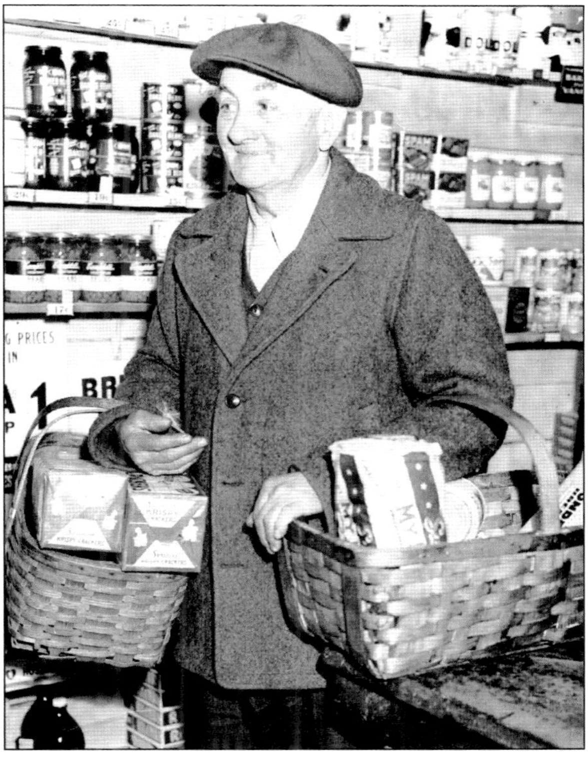

Middleborough merchant Foster Wade is captured inside the small local grocery store that he operated on School Street near North Street during the second quarter of the 20th century. Numerous small-scale groceries such as Wade's competed with larger national and regional chains, including the A&P and First National stores, which maintained branches at Middleborough Four Corners until the late 1950s when both built new modern supermarkets on the outskirts of downtown.

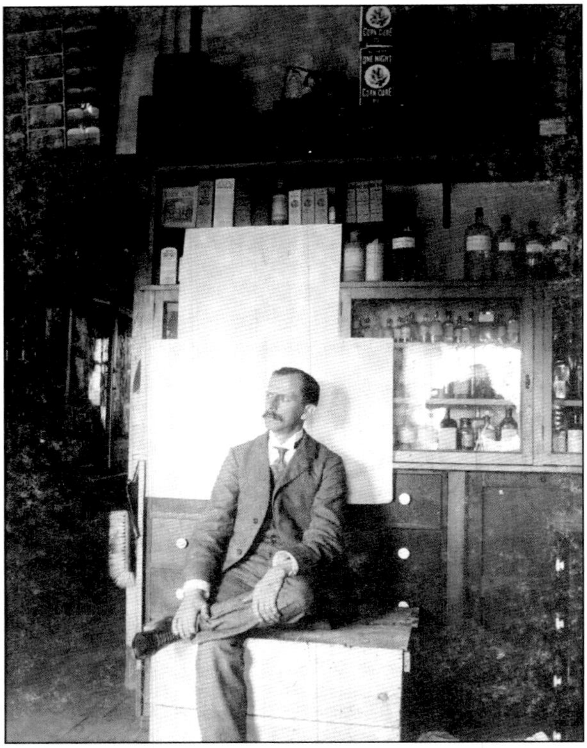

Among the several pharmacists plying their trade in Middleborough over the years was Clarence L. Hathaway. For years, the Smith and Hathaway drugstore occupied a prominent location at the corner of Center and South Main Streets in the Savings Bank Building. Here, Hathaway poses for an informal portrait by his employee, John Belden, who is reflected with his camera in the glass case behind Hathaway.

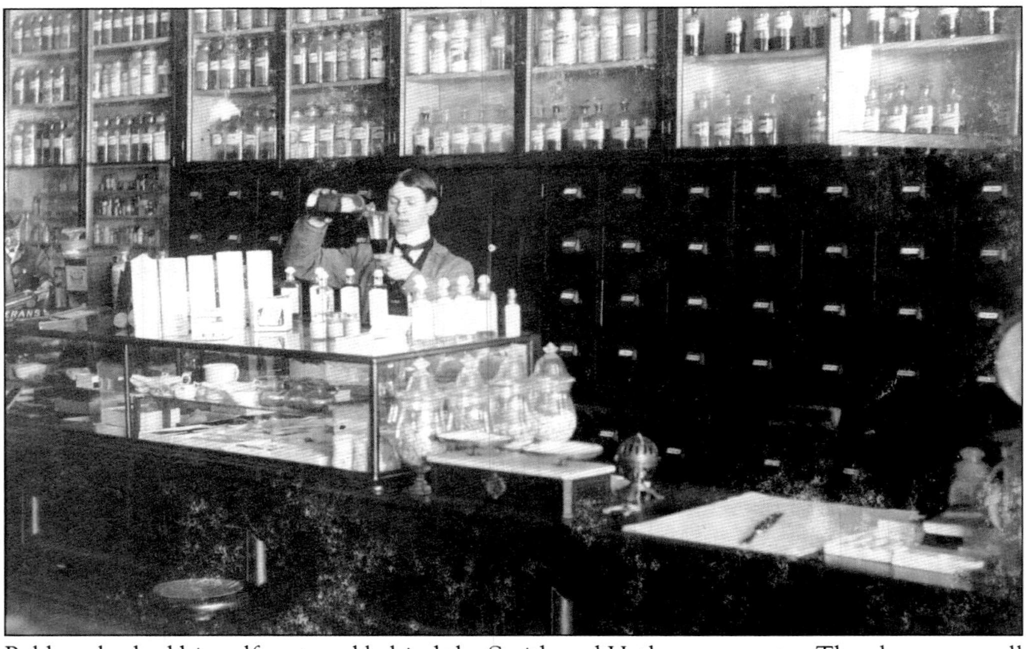

Belden also had himself captured behind the Smith and Hathaway counter. The pharmacy wall is lined with glass-filled drug bottles and drawers containing even more pharmaceuticals. In 1933, Hathaway sold the business to Malcolm Buck, whose corner drugstore (with its noted soda fountain) remained a local fixture until 1958 when it relocated to South Main Street.

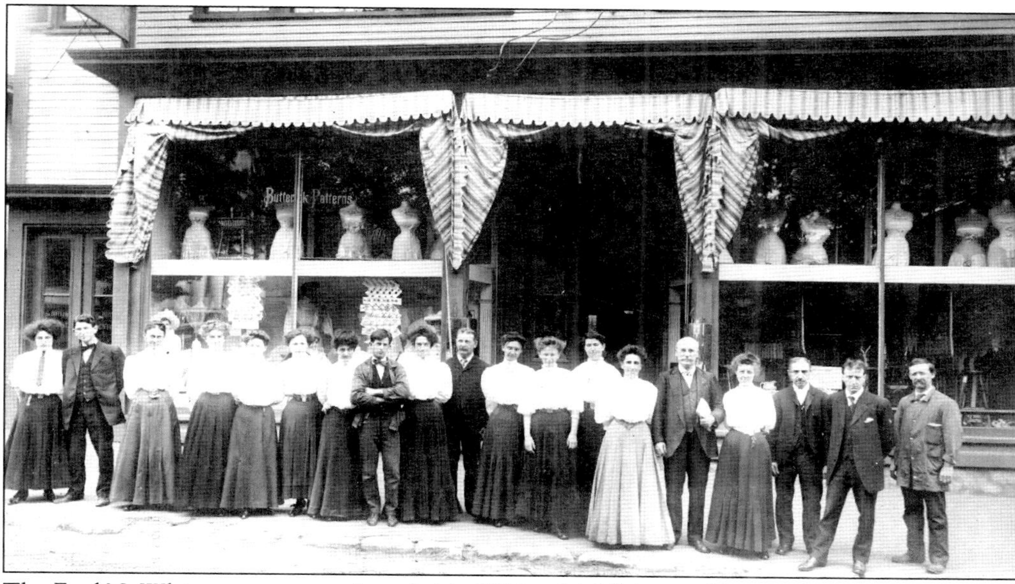

The Fred N. Whitman store was founded in 1894 as Middleborough's own department store and stood on the site of Sovereign Bank on Center Street. Pictured about 1910 from left to right are Lulu Shea, Walter Gillis, Abbie Brett, Lucy Crawshaw, Elizabeth Williams, Sara Levy, Nellie Drummond, Oliver Brett, Mary McDonald, George Tate, Emma Breach, Frances Purdon, Mary Shaw, Nellie Kelley, Alonzo Ryder, Lydia Holmes, Amasa Glidden, James McNeil, and Neil Harrington Sr.

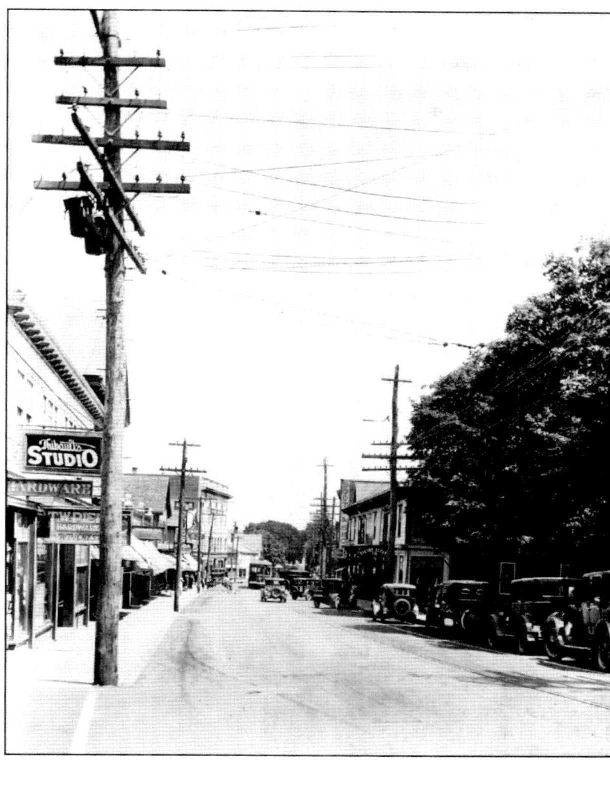

By the mid-1920s, when this photograph was taken looking from School Street towards the four corners, Center Street was a bustling thoroughfare crowded with automobiles, trolleys, and telephone poles. In 1927, the unsightly telephone poles were replaced with underground wires, and new streetlights were installed. William Thibault's photographic studio is at left above the T. W. Pierce hardware store on the site now occupied by Benny's.

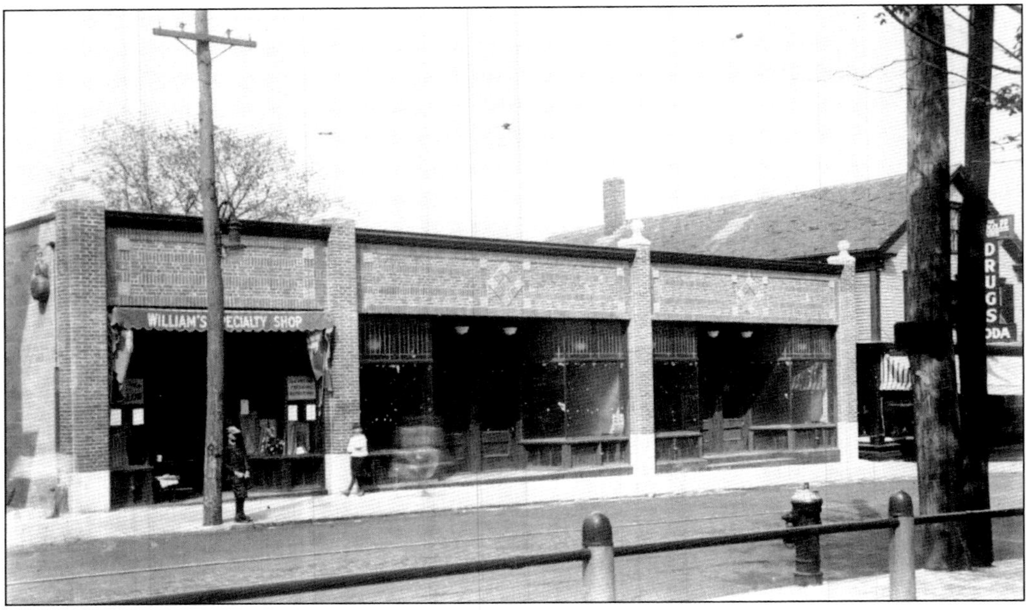

The Ryder Block next to Whitman's store was the first modern commercial block built on Center Street. It is pictured shortly after its construction in 1924. The vacant stores were occupied in 1927 by the First National grocery chain and W. T. Grant Company. It was best known as the last home of the Boston Store, a retailer of women's apparel. To the right is the Rexall drugstore operated by Jesse Morse.

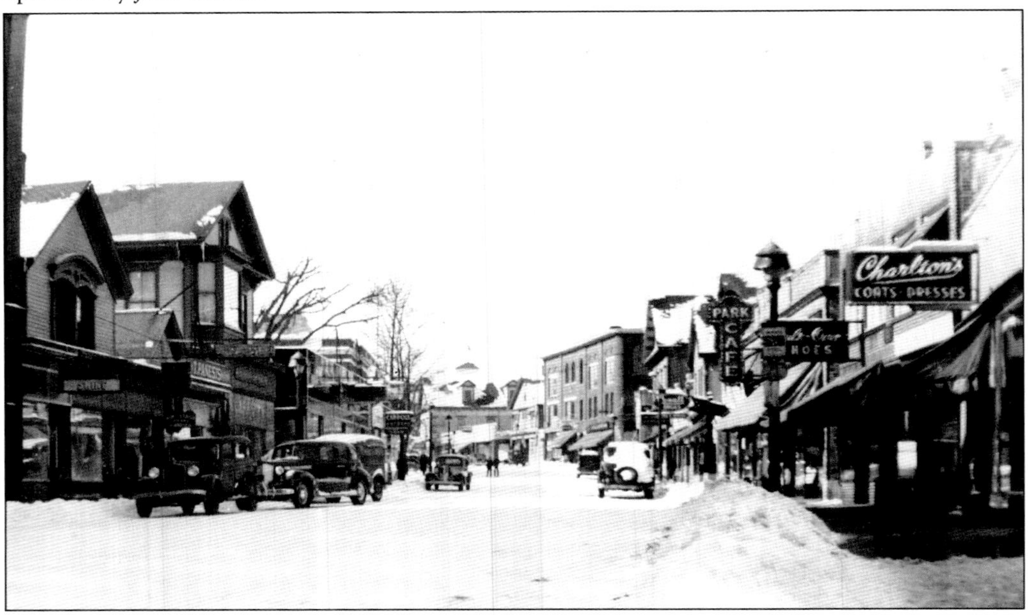

This shot from the 1940s depicts a commercially vibrant downtown, although heavy snow has temporarily halted business. National and regional chain stores such as Woolworth's, the First National, the A&P, and Grant's operated alongside numerous small, locally owned businesses like Panesis', the Park Café, and Charlton's. Downtown Middleborough remained a commercial hub for surrounding communities until the advent of regional shopping malls in the 1970s.

Eight

EDUCATION

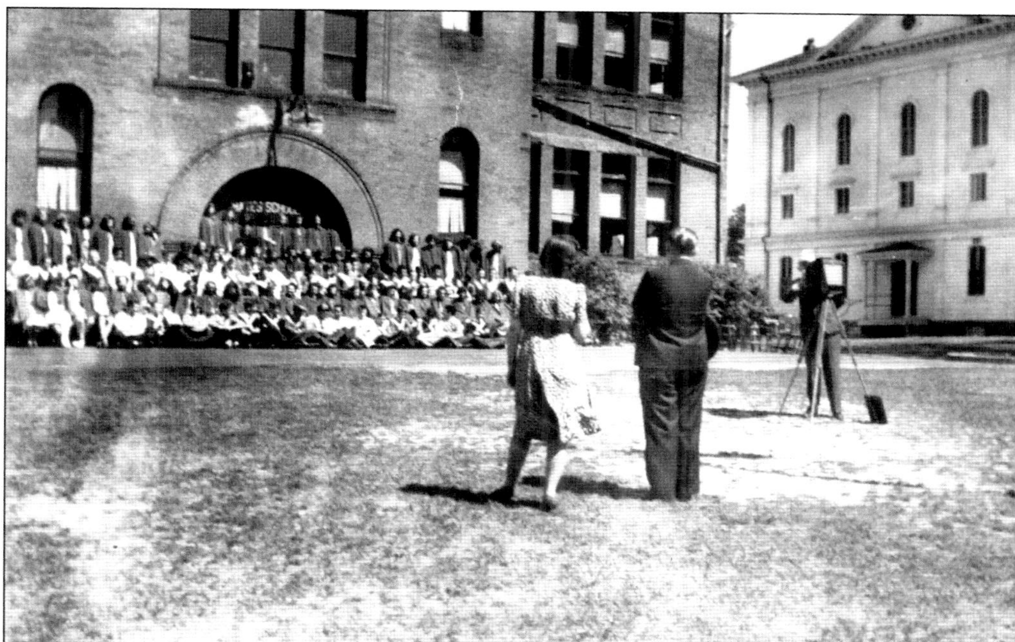

In this unusual photograph taken on June 10, 1942, Bates School children pose for their annual class portrait. Photographer William J. Thibault is at the camera, while principal Henry B. Burkland observes from the foreground. Built in 1887 as Middleborough's high school and first brick school building, it served as the town's central middle school between 1927 and 1954. The town hall is at the right.

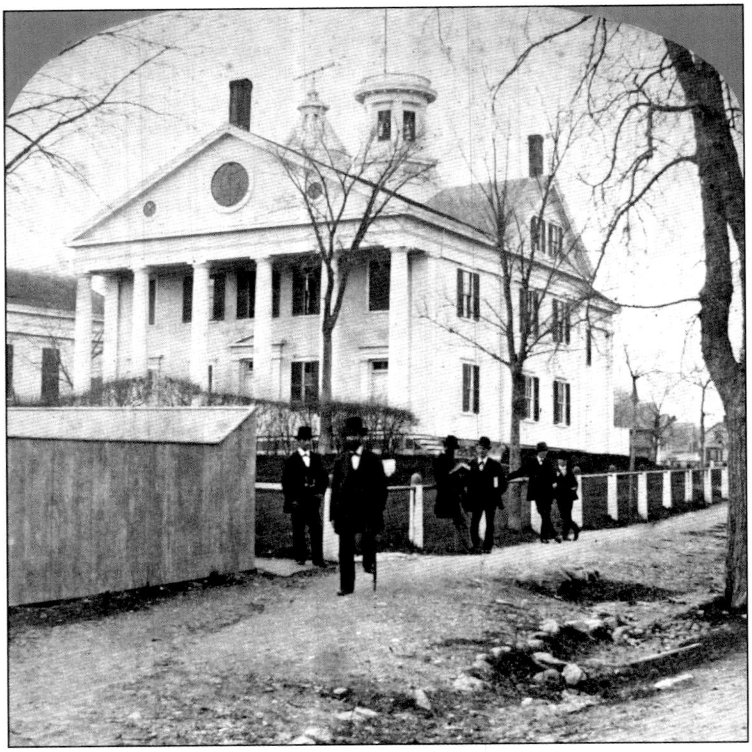

Peirce Academy, a private academic institution endowed by Levi Peirce, was originally founded upon Baptist principles but later became nondenominational and attracted pupils from across the nation. Well-dressed gentlemen loiter along the fence that separates Peirce Academy from Center Street in the late 1870s. The close-board fence on the left encloses the Thatcher property on which a business block was constructed in 1877.

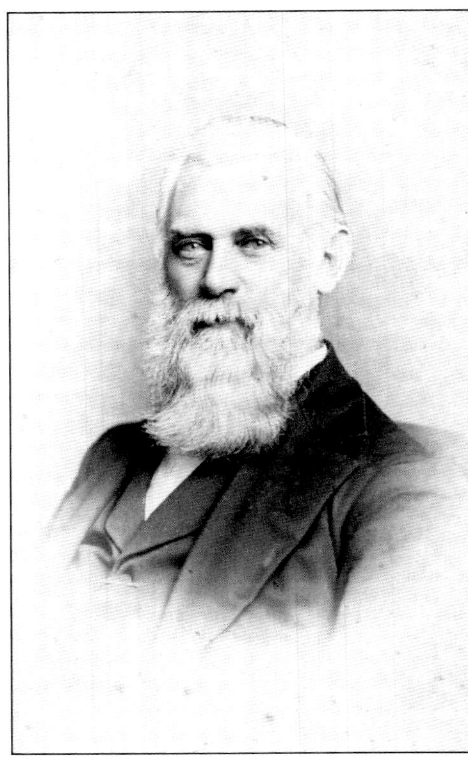

Under the direction of Elisha Tucker's son-in-law John Whipple Potter Jenks (1819–1894), Peirce Academy thrived and became a leading college-preparatory institution known throughout New England and beyond. Middleborough "is greatly indebted to him for what has been done through him, as an educator, as also to promote her civic, social, moral and religious interests," wrote one commentator upon Jenks's death in 1894.

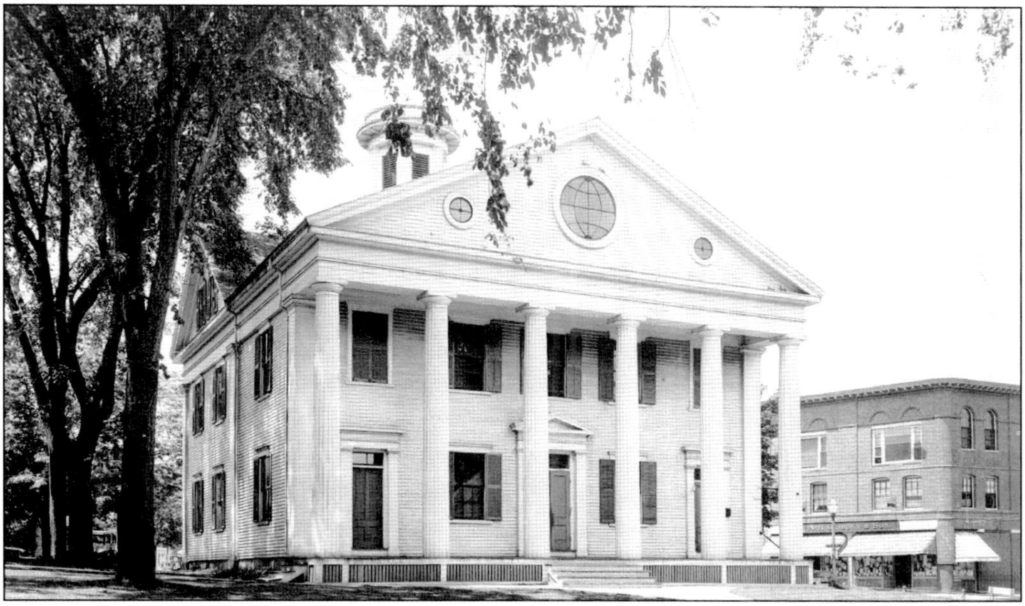

Peirce Academy in its later years still presented an imposing appearance, facing Thatcher's Row and what was once known as Academy Green. The building later housed the Middleborough police, the Fourth District Court, and the GAR veterans organization. Despite calls for its preservation, the building was demolished in 1932 to be replaced with the present post office. In the background is the Glidden Building on Center Street.

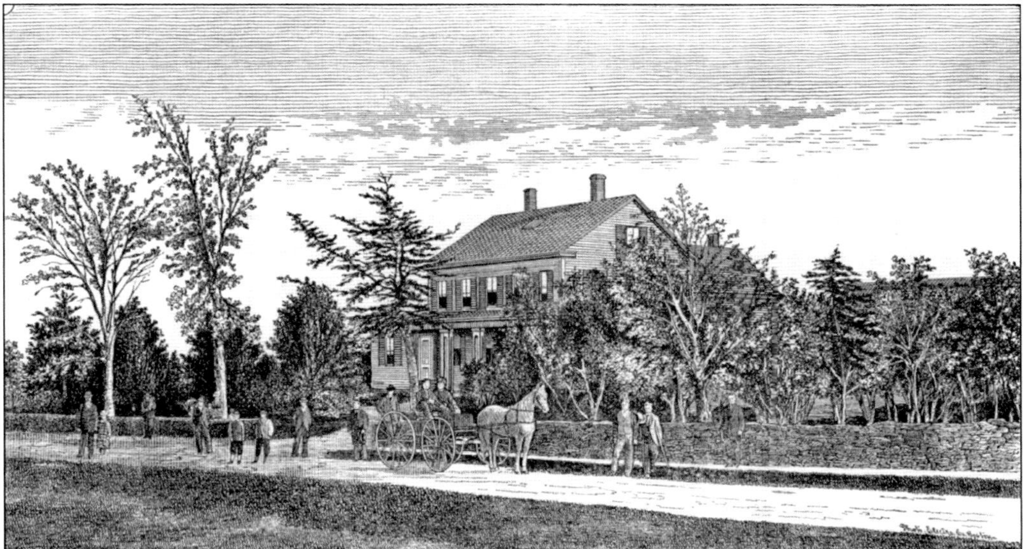

Succeeding Peirce Academy in prominence was the Eaton Family School, originally founded in 1854 as Marston's Family School. Under the ownership and management of Amos H. Eaton following 1874, the small, family oriented school prospered, offering not only college preparatory courses but also more practical courses like mathematics and bookkeeping, as well as vocational classes. The school closed in 1898, but the building remains on East Grove Street near Hannaford's supermarket.

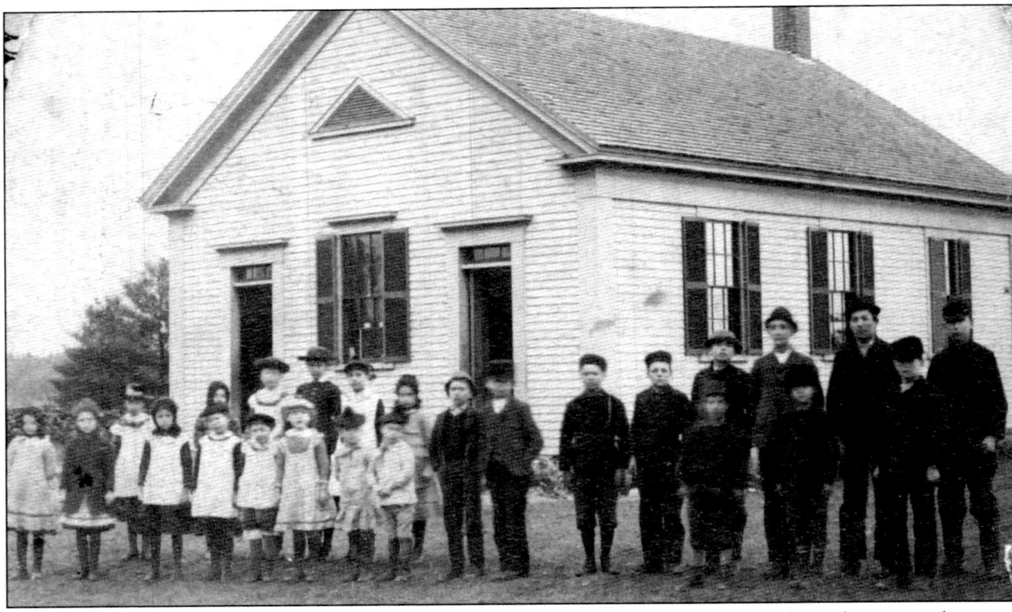

Despite the success of these private academic institutions, Middleborough's educational system remained dominated by the public one-room schoolhouse. Because of the town's geographical size, there were as many as 50 of these schools prior to 1853 when Lakeville became a separate town. Typical of these was the Fall Brook School built in 1872 by James P. Sparrow on Wareham Street near Sachem Street. Closed in 1923, it was demolished in 1946.

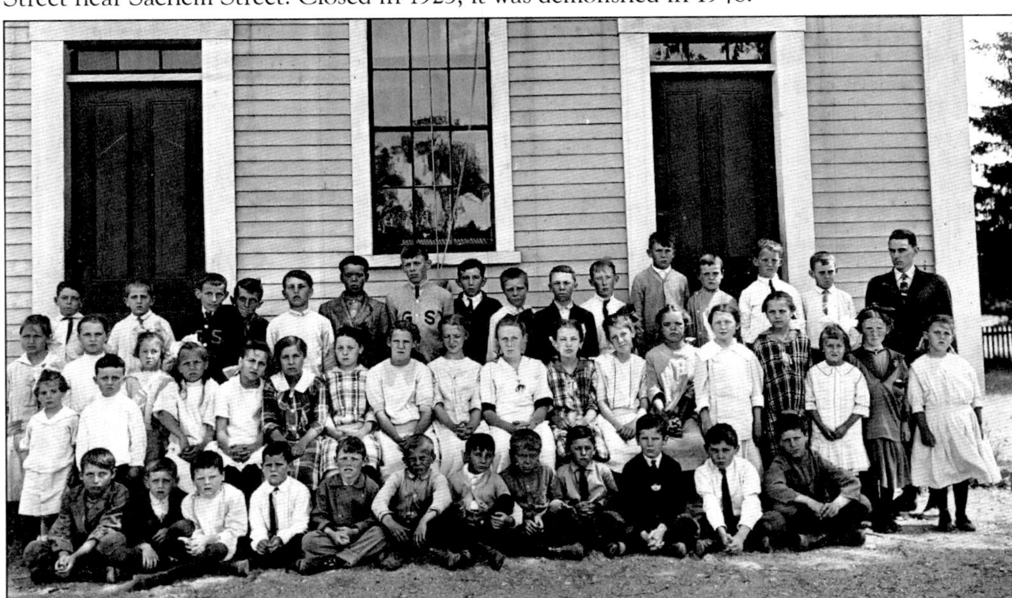

Multiple grades were taught in the one-room school with older children frequently assisting teachers with their younger charges. Over time, these one-room schools were consolidated into larger, more central schools at Middleborough center. Teacher Harold Striley poses about 1915 with his class at the Green School, another Sparrow-built school dating from 1872. Note the two boys who wear sweaters bearing the initials "GS."

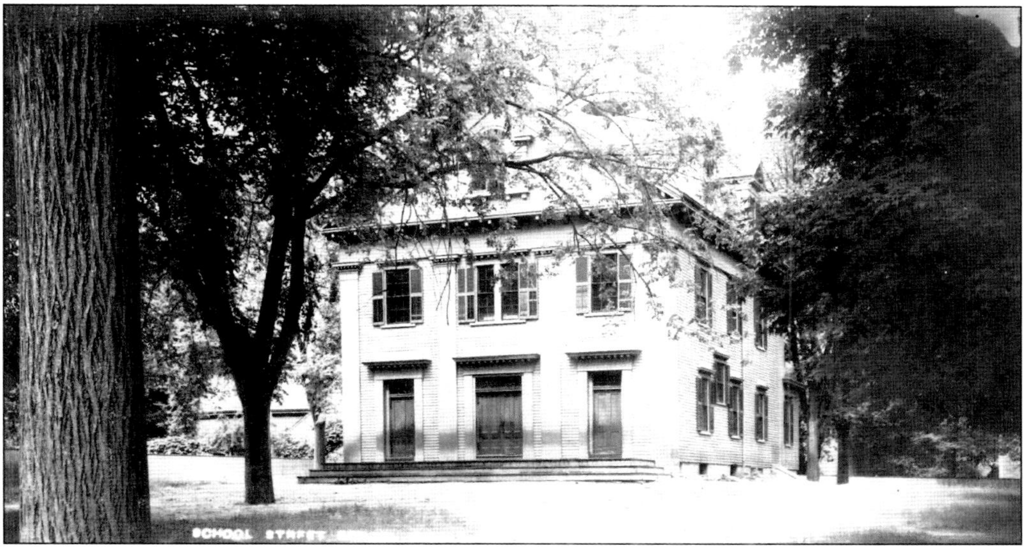

During the 1850–1851 school year, the School Street School was constructed to accommodate the children of Middleborough school district No. 18. At the time, it was the finest schoolhouse in Middleborough, and its presence provided the name for the street on which it stood. In 1907, when it was replaced by the current brick structure, the schoolhouse was moved to Center Street where it was converted to commercial use.

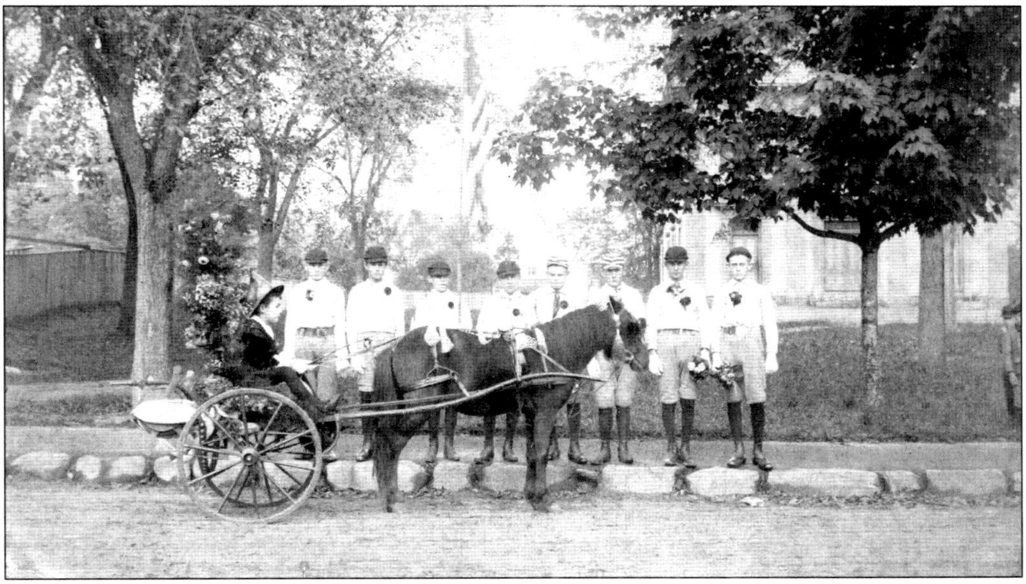

Undoubtedly inspired by the presence of Middleborough's central firehouse directly across the street, School Street School boys formed their own company. Pageants, celebrations, observances, and activities such as this were frequent in Middleborough's public schools throughout the era. School Street School children even mounted an impromptu Armistice Day parade in 1919 when word of the cessation of World War I reached the town. The school remains in operation.

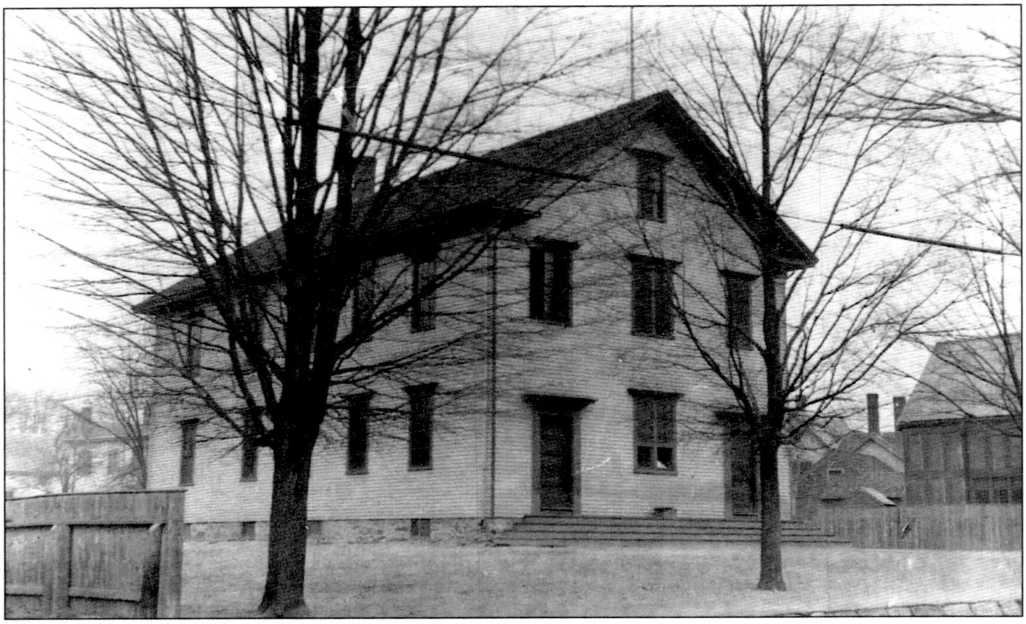

In the vicinity of Middleborough Four Corners, the growing population necessitated other multiroom graded schools such as the original Union Street School. Designed by Warren Homer Southworth and built in 1876, the wood-frame school building was greatly criticized for its plain style at the time, a marked contrast to the earlier School Street School. It was replaced in 1932 with an arte moderne–style building, now the Lincoln D. Lynch School.

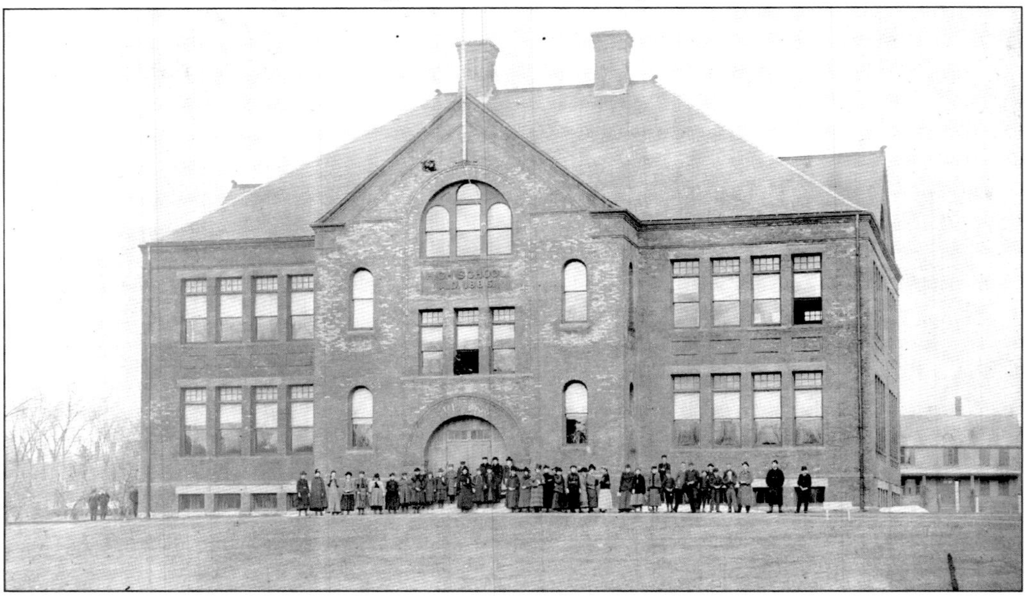

Middleborough's first public high school building was erected in 1887 on a lot adjoining the town hall and was used jointly until 1907 as a combined high school and grammar school. With the opening of the Memorial High School on North Main Street in 1927, this building was given over to exclusive use of the middle school and renamed the Bates School for former superintendent of schools Charles H. Bates.

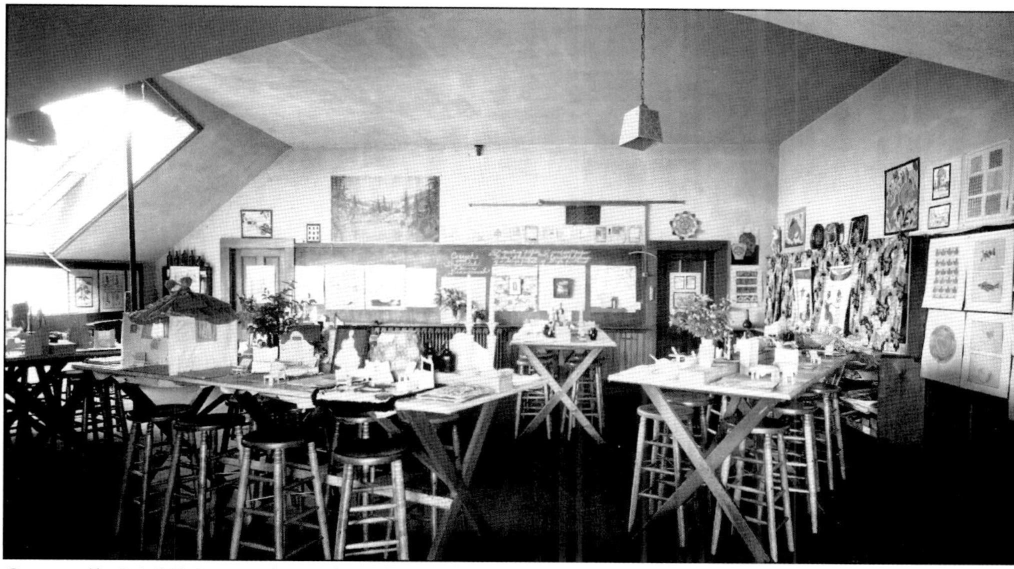

Originally Middleborough High School's chemistry laboratories were located in the basement, a situation that was described as "a menace to the health of those who have to work there." In 1899, they were relocated to the attic, where ventilation proved better. Later, when the building operated as the Bates School, the third-floor rooms were used for art classes, as seen above about 1930.

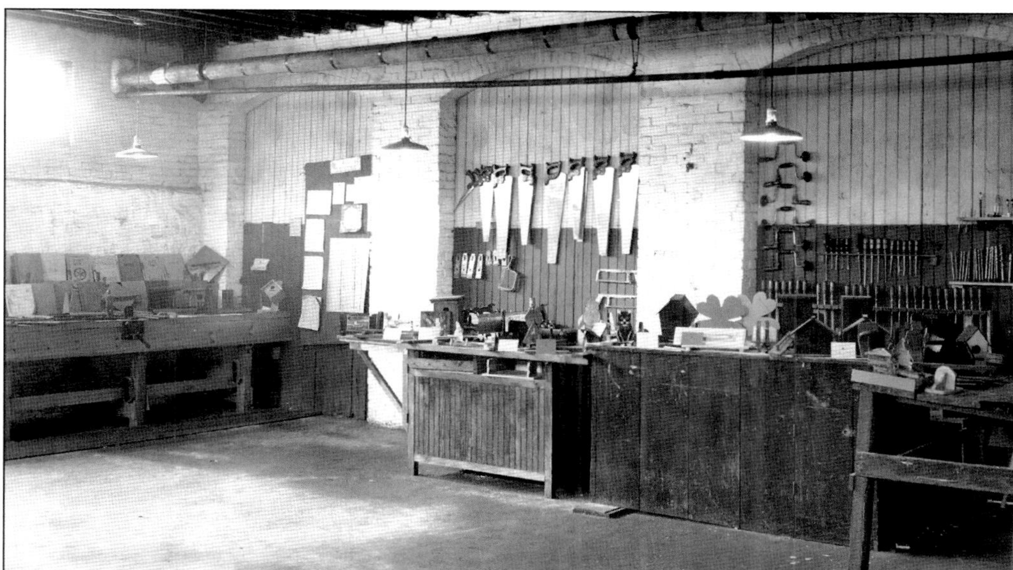

In 1897, calls were first heard for the introduction of a commercial course into the high school and were followed shortly thereafter by suggestions for the introduction of vocational classes into Middleborough schools. Ultimately, manual classes such as woodworking were introduced into the junior high school level, as represented by the wood shop in the Bates School basement, seen here about 1930.

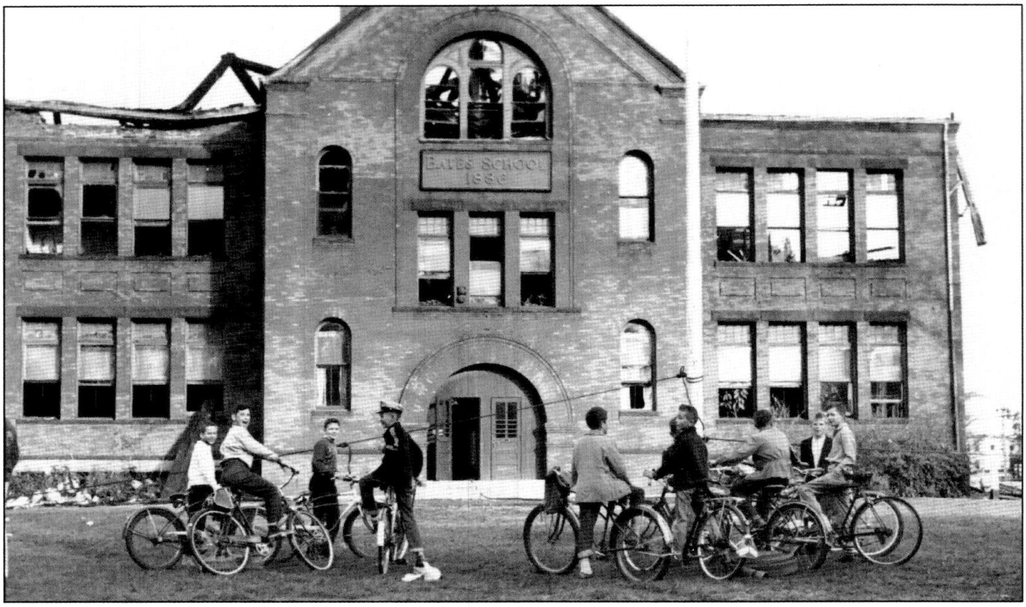

On September 20, 1954, during a firebug scare, an arsonist set fire to the Bates School, which was entirely gutted. Only the exterior walls remained, and they were demolished shortly thereafter for safety considerations. Despite its outdated infrastructure, the school was much beloved, and the shocking means of its destruction and its ultimate loss were deeply felt within the community. The Veterans' Memorial Park now occupies the site.

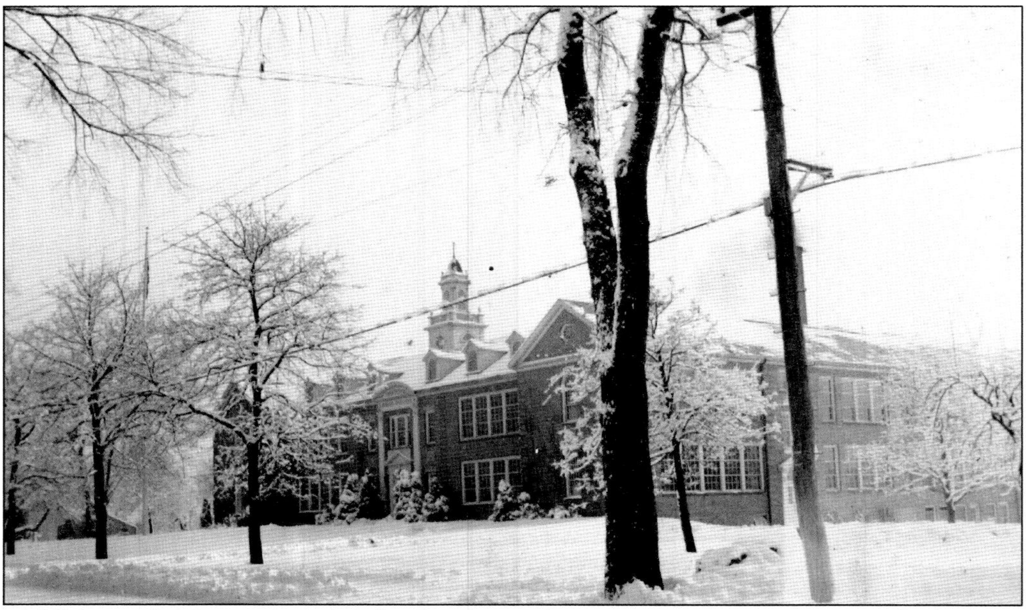

Middleborough Memorial High School is depicted on a snowy January 14, 1938. The building was erected in 1927 and served as the town's high school until 1971 when the present high school was opened on East Grove Street. Following that, this building served as the junior high school until being succeeded by the Nichols Middle School. Presently it fulfills its educational role as an early childhood education center.

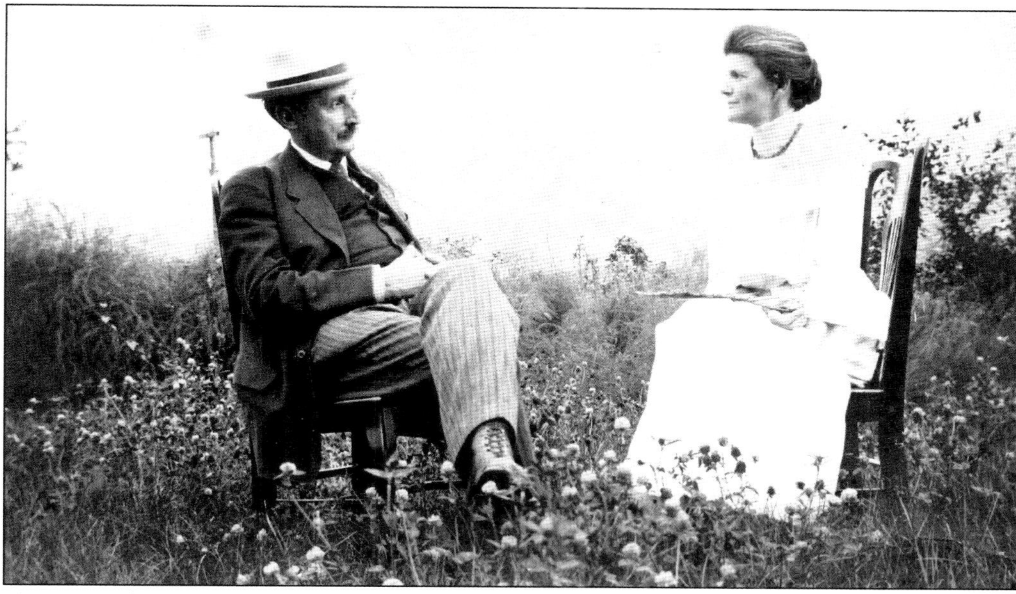

"Amateur photography in a Barnet clover field," wrote Walter Sampson (1862–1931), one of Middleborough's best remembered and best-loved educators, on the reverse of this early 1900s portrait of himself and his wife, Emma, in Vermont. Sampson served as principal of Middleborough High School for 33 years. An advocate of educator development as well, Sampson was a founder of the Middleboro Teachers' Association in 1920.

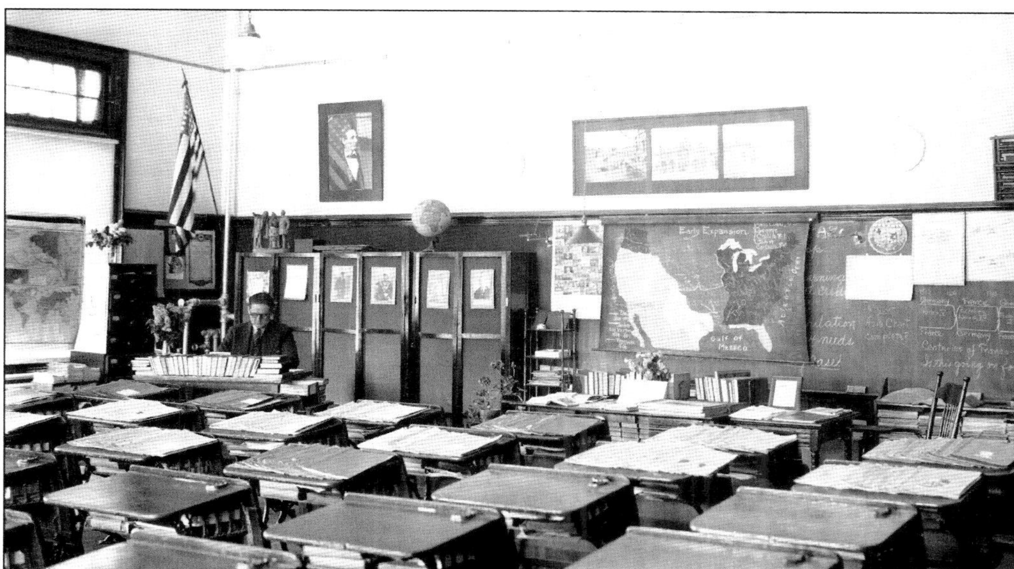

Like Sampson, Henry B. Burkland dedicated his life to the education of Middleborough's children, serving as a teacher and later as a middle school principal from 1928 until 1962. Here Burkland is depicted in the surroundings of his Bates School classroom. The school on Mayflower Avenue that replaced the Bates School was named the Henry B. Burkland School in his honor. Ironically, it too was leveled by fire in 1988.

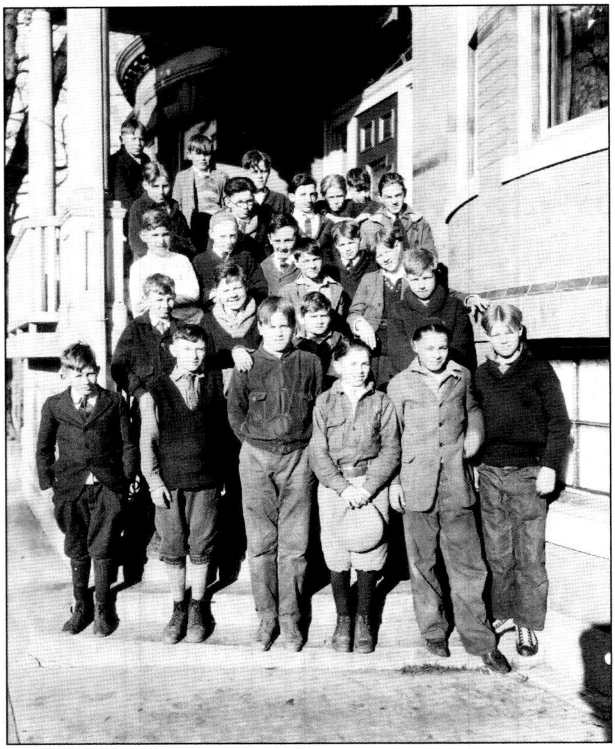

The local YMCA served an important role in the education of the community's children. Organized in 1883, it promoted athletics as well as educational courses for community members. So successful was this work that a substantial headquarters was constructed on North Main Street and opened in 1913. Here, young Depression-era Middleborough boys stand for a picture on the front steps of the building.

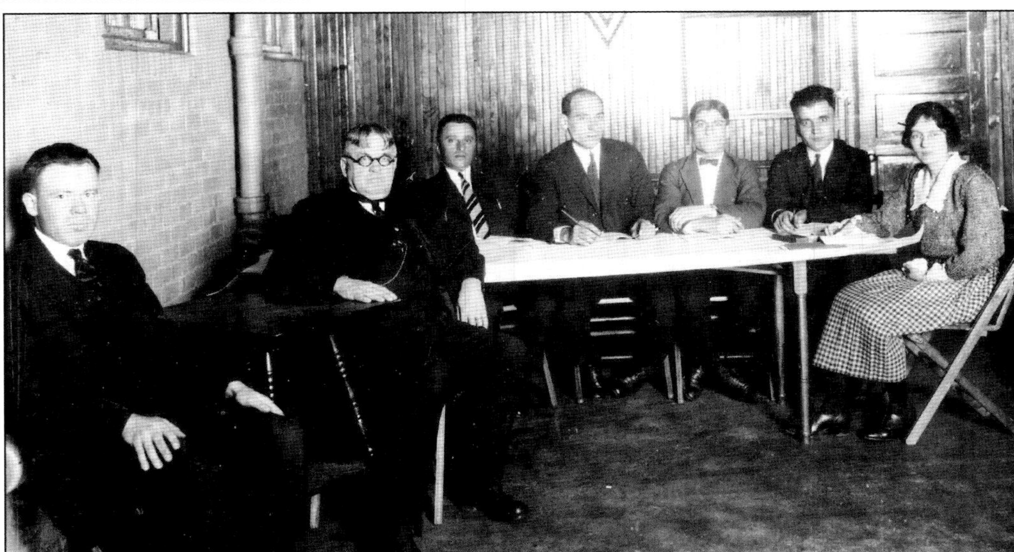

The local YMCA remained an important sponsor of adult educational classes as well, including this Americanization class from 1923, which assisted in acclimating more recent immigrants from southern and eastern Europe. Between 1894 and 1924, the community also sponsored a series of Citizens' Courses, comprised of lectures and concerts, and following 1917, chautauquas with their similar mix of education and entertainments were held in vast tents on the town hall grounds.

Nine

Religion

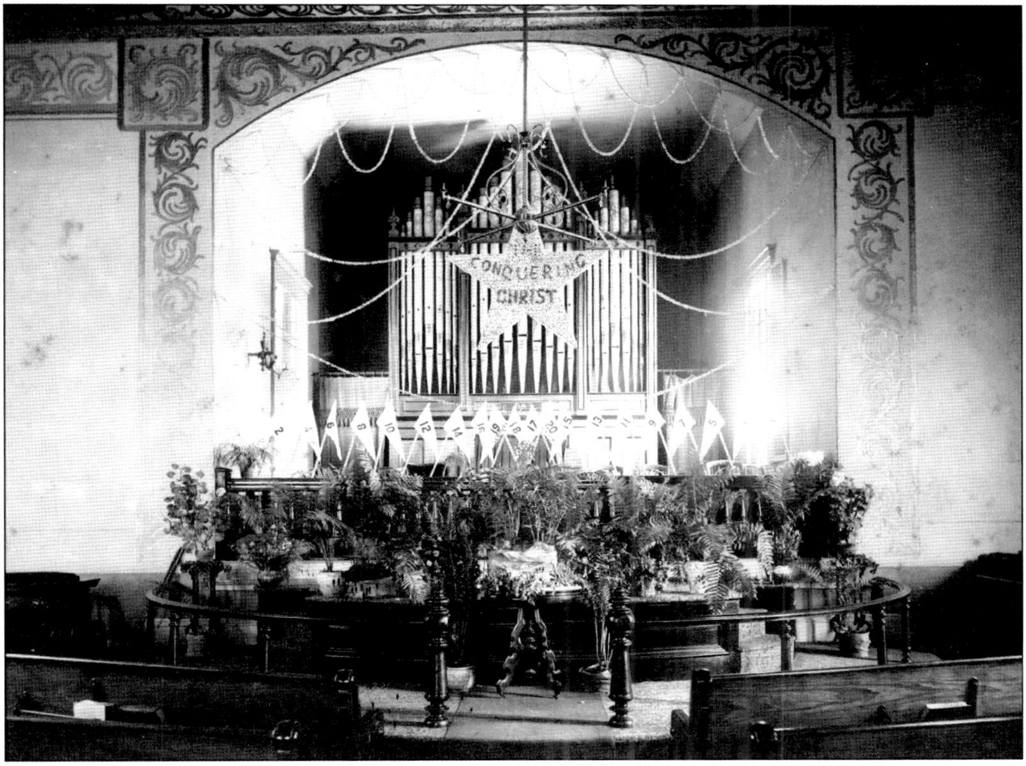

Middleborough was unique in Plymouth Colony for its early religious development. Although founded as a Congregational community, the town was soon home to three Baptist parishes. In the 19th century, these denominations were joined by Methodists, Unitarians, Catholics, and Episcopalians and later by Christian Scientists, Seventh Day Adventists, and Jehovah Witnesses. The sanctuary of the Central Methodist Church is decorated about 1900 to celebrate 19 centuries of Christianity.

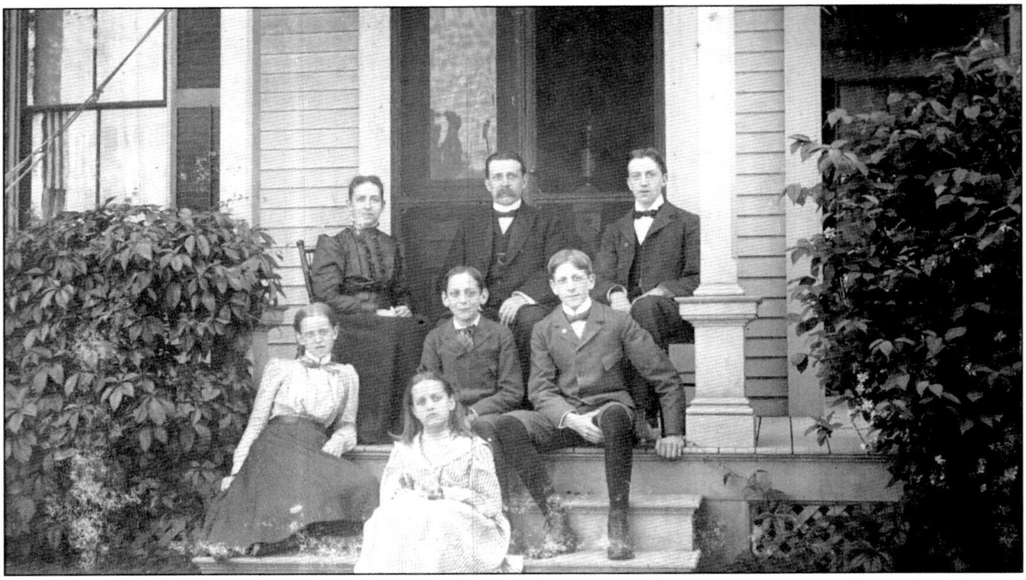

Middleborough's influential religious leaders have included Baptists Isaac Backus, George G. Fairbanks, and Robert Bisbee; Congregationalists Peter Thacher, Sylvanus Conant, Israel Putnam, and Isaiah C. Thatcher; and Episcopalian William Bayard Hale. Some of these men achieved national recognition. Rev. Richard G. Woodbridge, pictured above with his family about 1898, was one of the notable pastors of the Central Congregational Church and author of a New York Herald Prize sermon.

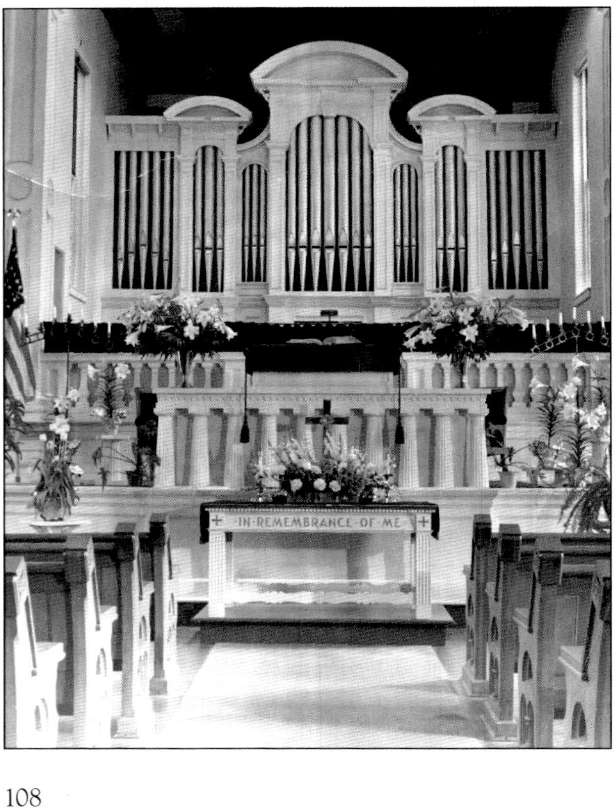

Easter remained the high point of the religious year for most Middleborough residents, who took the opportunity to attend services dressed in their Easter best. The churches were also dressed in their best finery, including the sanctuary of the Central Congregational Church, which is pictured adorned with lilies at Easter sometime during the 1940s.

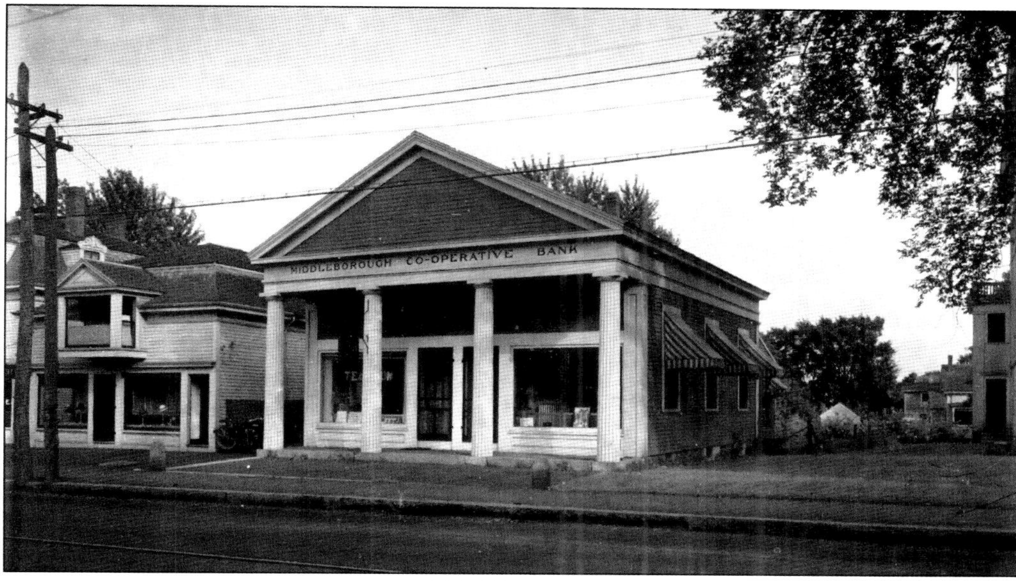

In 1842, the Congregationalists around Middleboro Four Corners constructed this small but elegant chapel building on South Main Street in which to conduct worship services. When the congregation outgrew the chapel, the present church was constructed in 1848. The chapel afterwards housed a number of tenants, including the Middleborough (now Mayflower) Cooperative Bank. When a new bank building was constructed, the chapel was moved to Webster Street where it still stands.

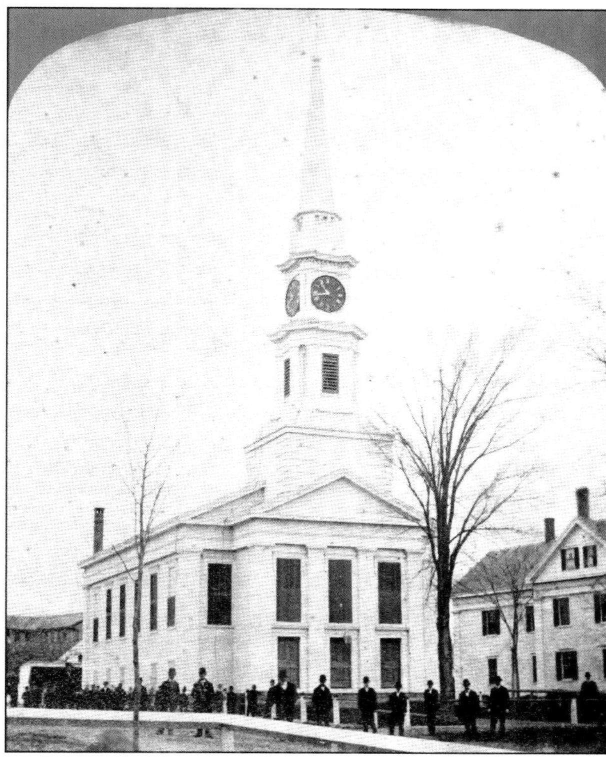

Nearby was the original Central Baptist Church, which was built in 1828 with funding from Levi Peirce. This was the earliest church established at Middleborough Four Corners, and it stood on the site of the present church. The approach to the church from South Main Street was known appropriately enough as Temple Place. The church became best known for the town clock that was installed in its tower in 1847.

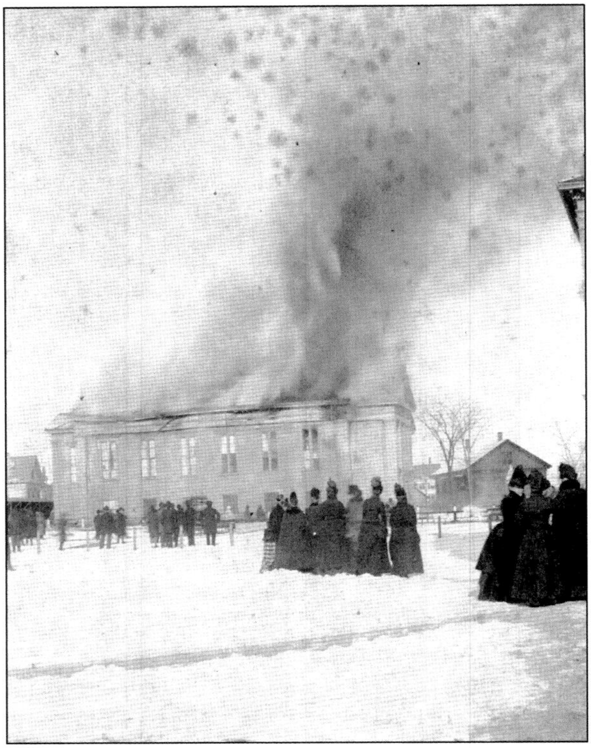

Perhaps the earliest photograph of a building fire at Middleborough, this view depicts the crowd that has assembled in the rear of Middleborough Town Hall to witness the destruction of the Central Baptist Church on Sunday, January 22, 1888, just after noon. The town clock in the steeple was said to have stopped precisely at 12:25 before crashing with the steeple into the interior of the church.

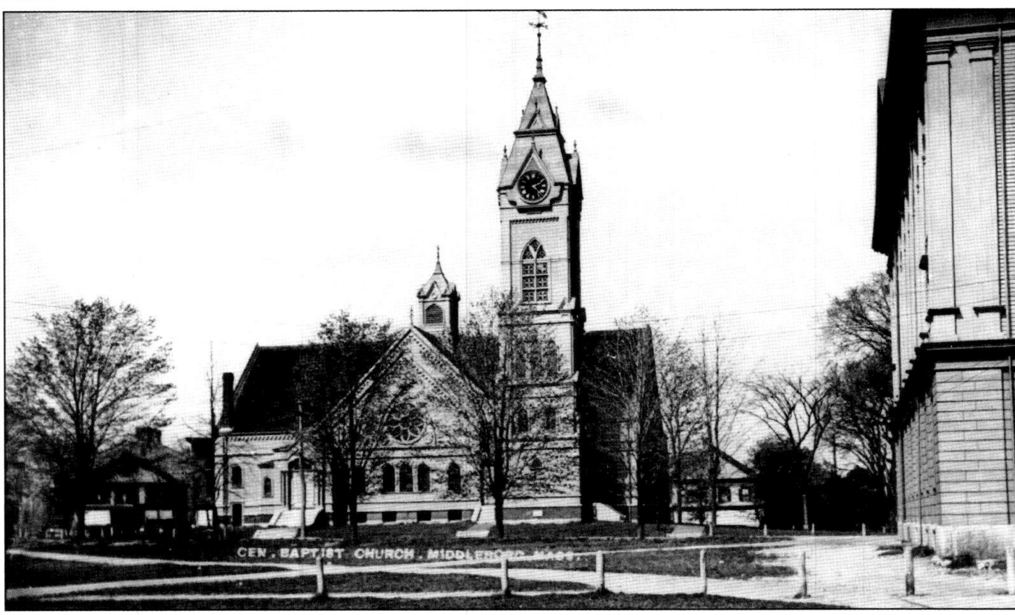

The church was replaced by a large Gothic Revival structure the following year, the Baptists joining the Central Congregational and Methodist churches in worship in the meantime. At the time of its completion, the new Central Baptist Church was pronounced "the admiration of the townspeople" and was noted as being among "the most remarked by strangers of any of the town's several fine public buildings."

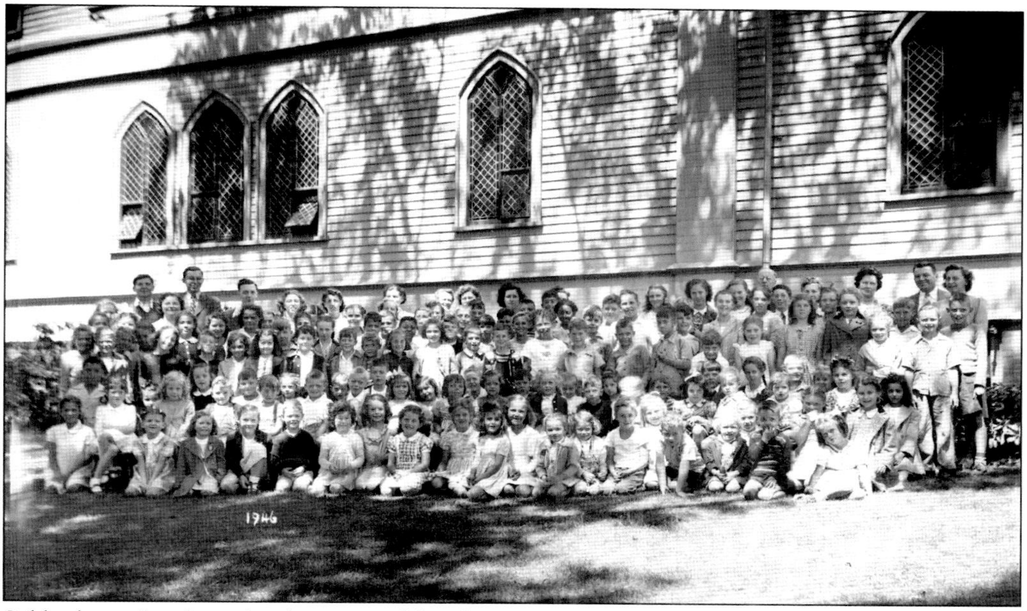

Sabbath or Sunday schools operated by the numerous churches remained popular from the 19th century onward, providing religious education for children and adults alike. Among the most well attended were those conducted by the Central Baptist Church. Here, the church's Summer Vacation Bible School class from 1946 gathers on the lawn outside the church. (Author's collection.)

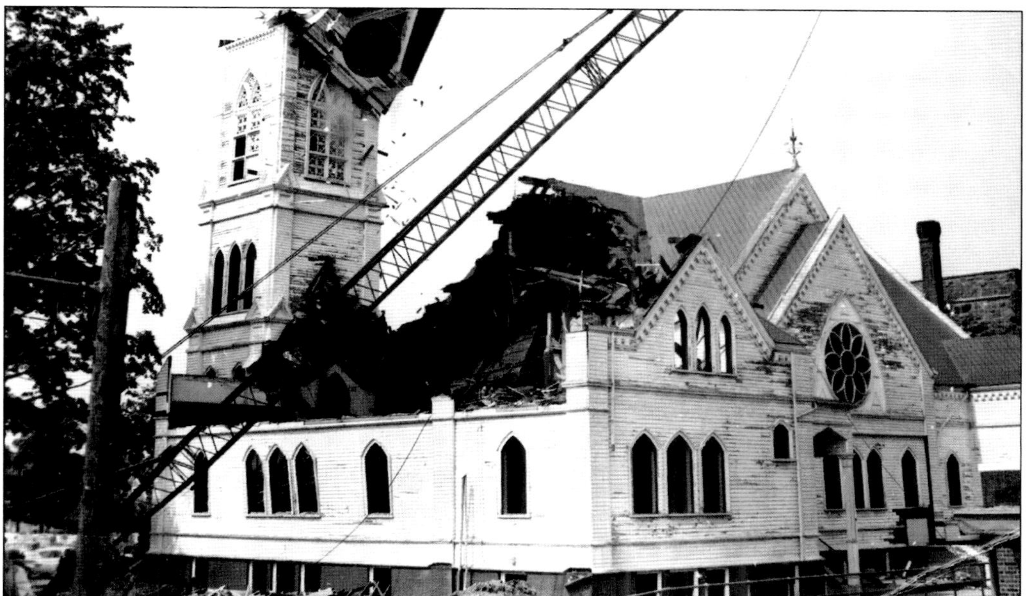

Despite the admiration that the community once held for the 1888–1889 Central Baptist Church, by the mid-20th century, it was considered outmoded, and plans were made for a modern Colonial-style brick church. To make way for the new structure, the old church was demolished in 1963. The crashing of its steeple into the body of the church was captured from this vantage point on Thatcher's Row.

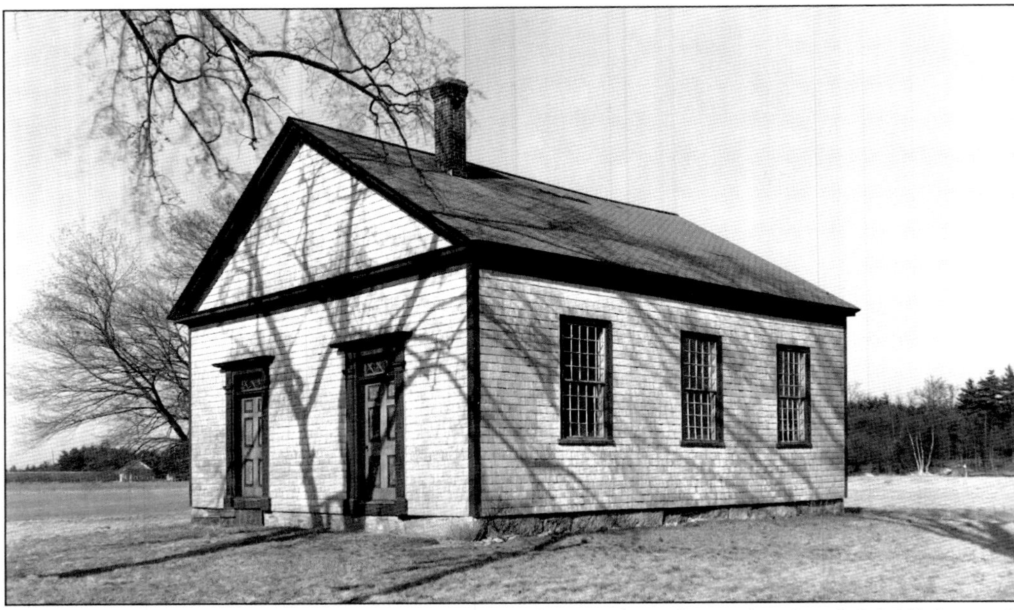

The earliest Methodist churches in Middleborough were those located at South Middleborough and Fall Brook. The Fall Brook chapel (above) stood on Cherry Street between Grove and Wareham Streets and served as the church for residents at Middleborough Four Corners. In the left distance are the greenhouses of the Leland Carnation Company. The chapel was taken down in the early 20th century.

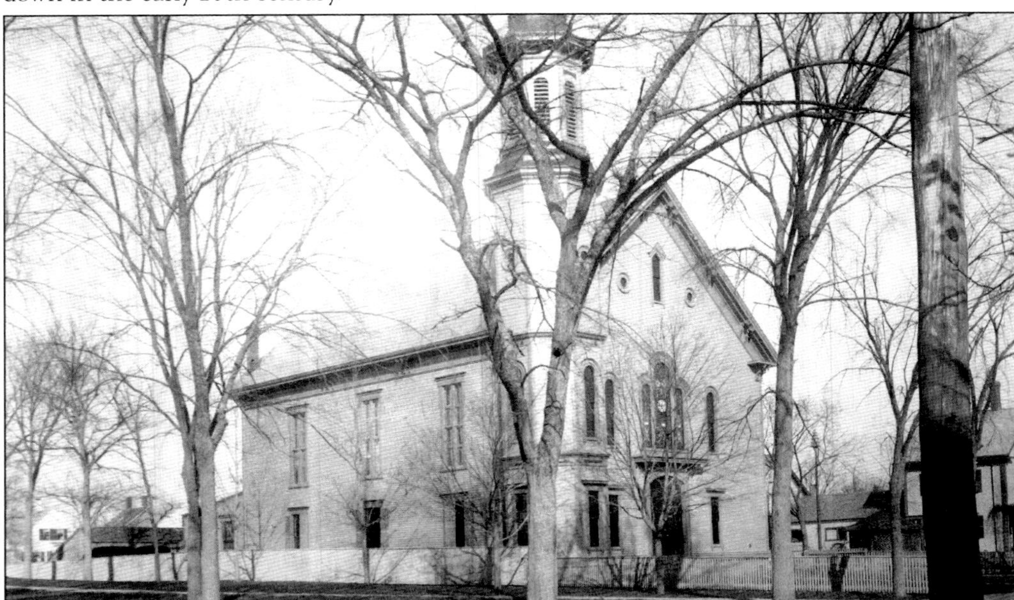

Because of the inconvenient location of the Fall Brook chapel to Middleborough center, the Central Methodist Church on School Street was built at a cost of $12,000 and dedicated in February 1869. Before remodeling following hurricane damage in 1956, the building featured a unique hexagonal corner tower. While the Methodists were relative latecomers to the local religious scene, energetic revivals in the mid-19th century built a large and active congregation.

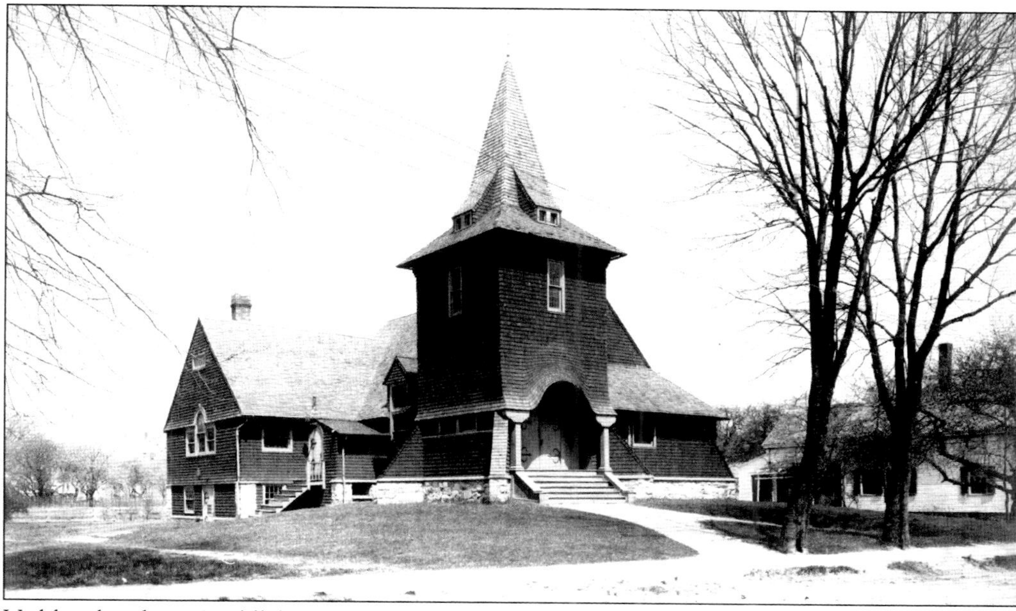

Unlike elsewhere, Middleborough was relatively untroubled by the theological dispute between Congregationalists and Unitarians, perhaps because Unitarianism, like Methodism, received a relatively late start in Middleborough. Established in 1889, the First Unitarian Society constructed a church on Pearl Street two years later in 1891. The church was designed by noted Boston architect William Ralph Emerson in a distinctive shingle style.

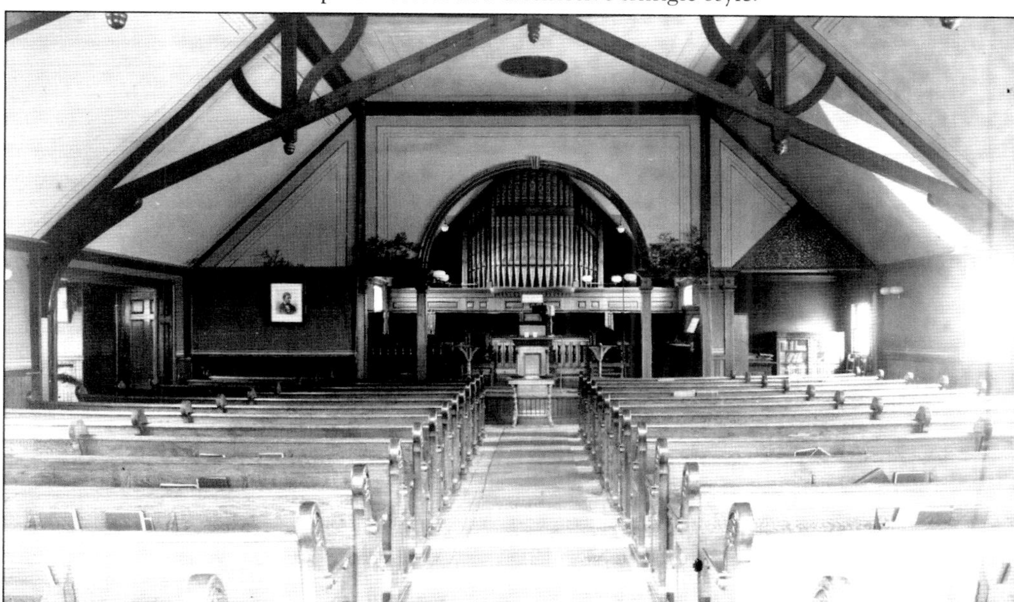

In 1907, the Unitarian church building, with its unusual auditorium that anticipated the craftsman style of design, was moved to its present South Main Street location between the Congregational and Baptist churches. In 1897 and 1898, a fourth church was added to this grouping when the architecturally notable Episcopal Church of Our Saviour, designed by Ralph Adams Cram, was built at Center and Union Streets.

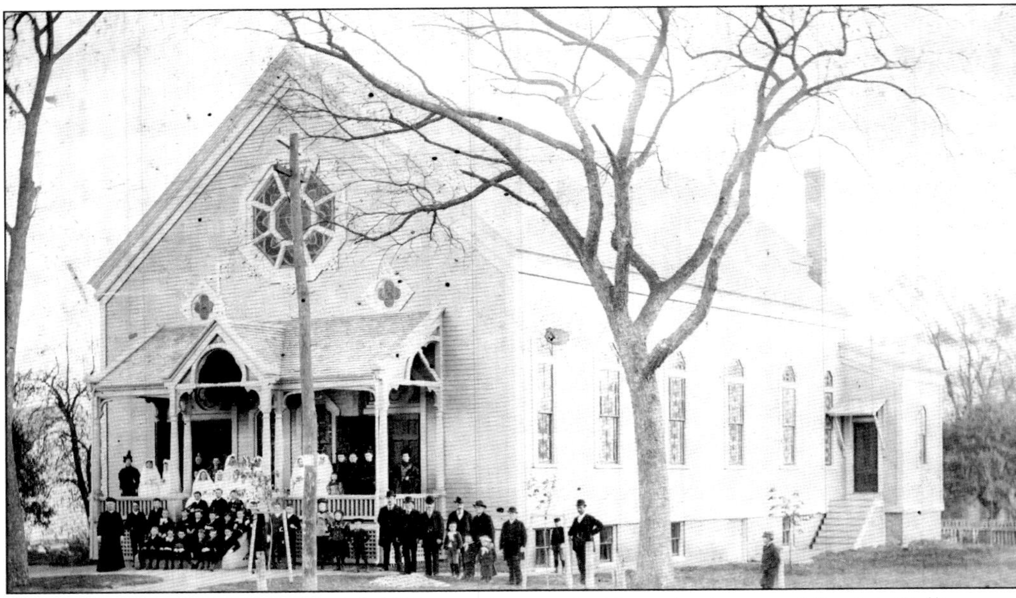

The first Catholic services in Middleborough were held in the home of Patrick Sullivan on Wareham Street in 1852. The influx of Catholic immigrants first from Ireland and then later Quebec, Italy, and Poland, however, brought with it a growing need for a place of worship. To meet this need, Sacred Heart Church was erected in 1880 and 1881. Pictured outside the church in the late 1800s is a first communion class.

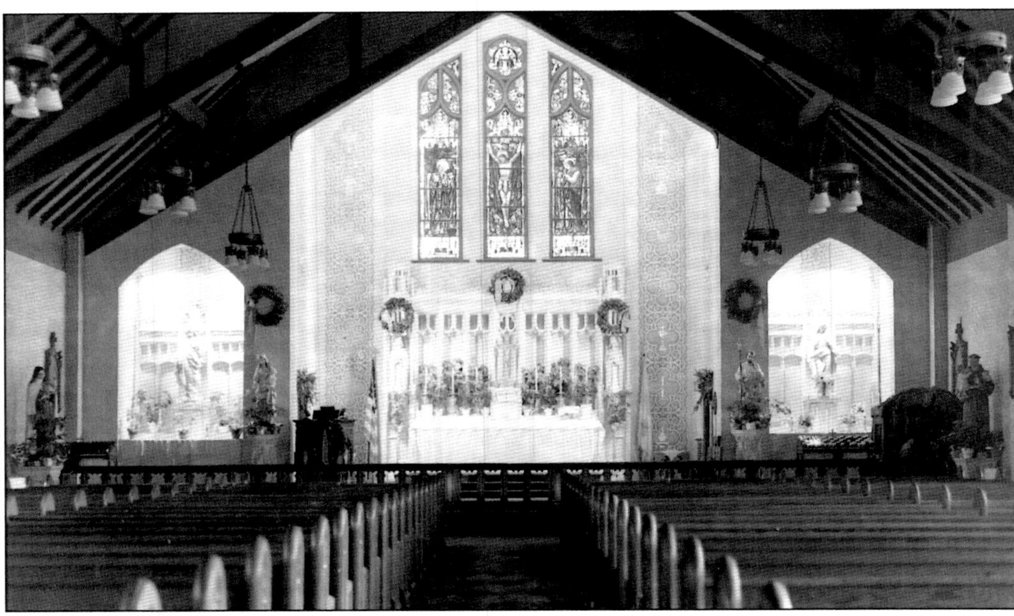

The original Sacred Heart Church, which stood upon the site of the present rectory parking lot, was replaced in 1917 and 1918 by a substantial English Gothic–style church in redbrick designed by Charles R. Greco of Boston. The new church featured a 70-foot tower, as well as beautiful stained-glass windows and interior frescoes seen here before interior remodelling in the 1950s altered the church's appearance.

Ten

LEISURE

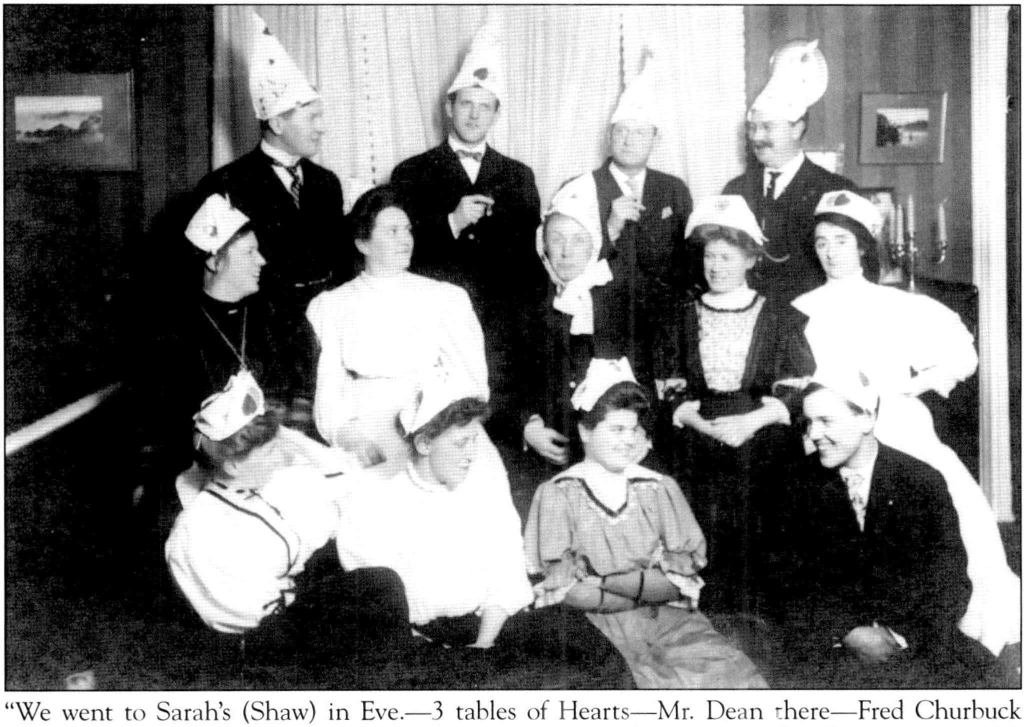

"We went to Sarah's (Shaw) in Eve.—3 tables of Hearts—Mr. Dean there—Fred Churbuck took our picture in paper nap caps," reads the caption on the reverse of this February 13, 1908, photograph. Informal neighborly gatherings such as this remained popular throughout the 19th and early-20th centuries, helping foster a strong sense of community.

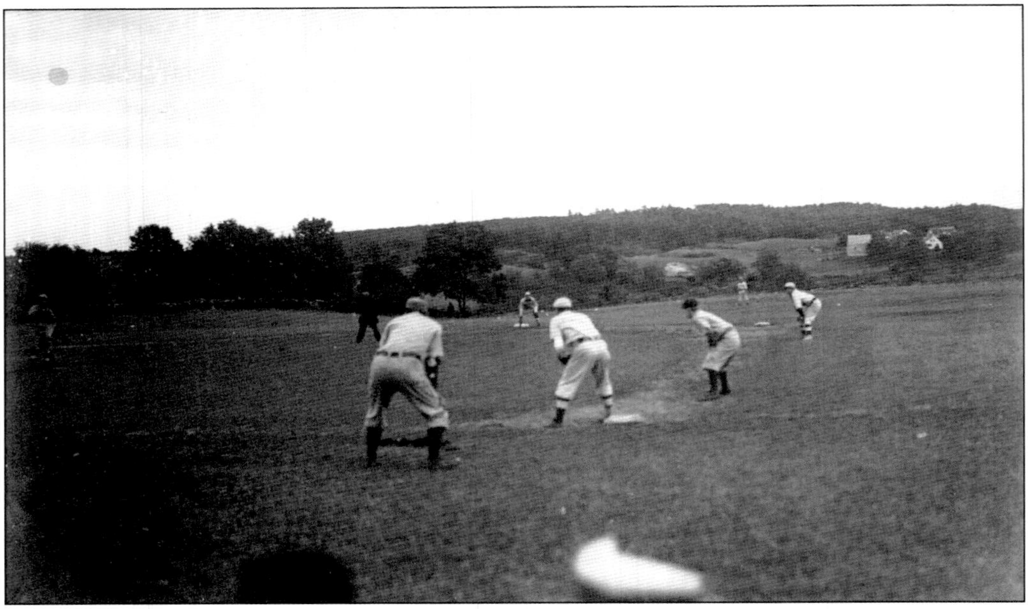

Baseball appears to have been first played in Middleborough as early as the late 1850s. Like elsewhere, the game grew in popularity with numerous teams—high school, amateur, and semiprofessional—entertaining local residents over the years. A succession of ball grounds hosted these early teams, which included the Sky Rockets, Adriatics, and Chemungs. Fred Churbuck captured a game in progress about 1900 at what are probably the North Street grounds.

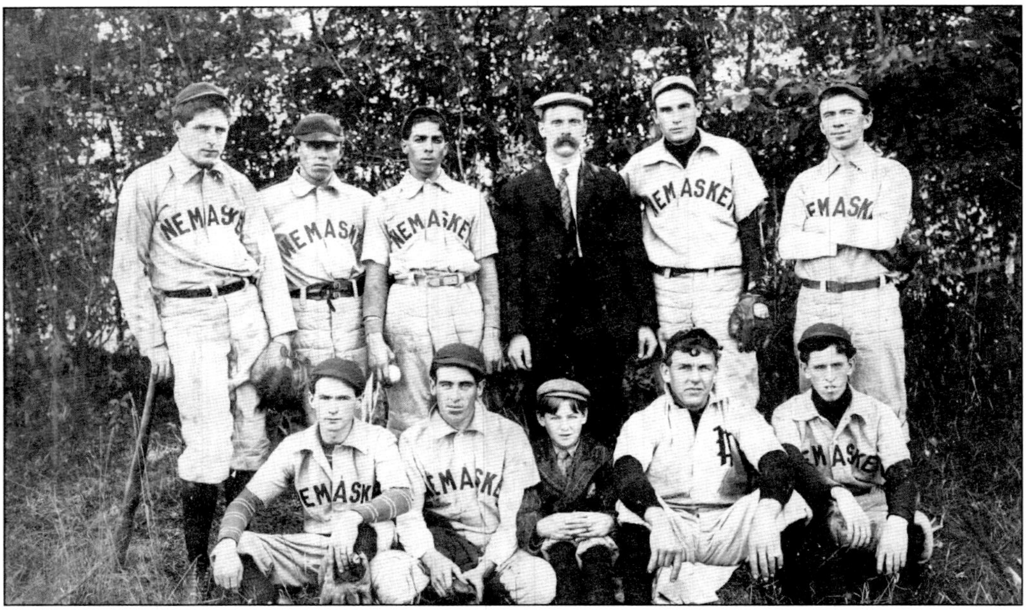

By the dawn of the 20th century, Middleborough's namesake team, the Nemaskets, were the preeminent force in local ball. Like today, the dream for many of these young men engaged in the sport was the majors. Some made it. In 1909, former Middleborough outfielder Gus Corcoran signed with the Philadelphia Athletics, and in 1921 Cyril (Cy) Morgan spent a year as a pitcher with the Boston Braves.

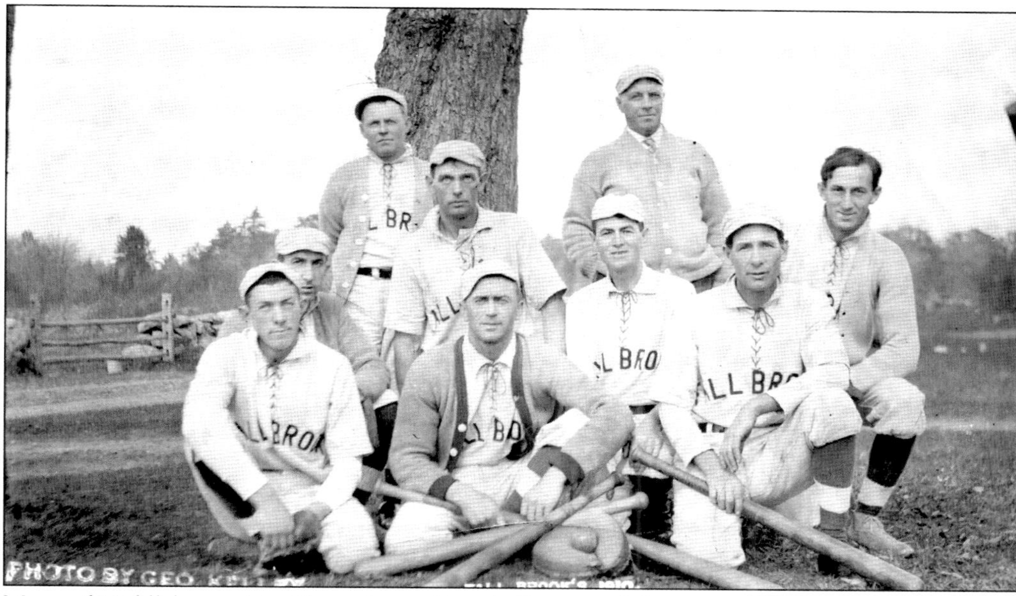

Many of Middleborough's villages formed baseball teams of their own. While most were amateur affairs, rivalries such as that between South Middleborough and Rock made for exciting matchups. Of them all, Fall Brook's team was undoubtedly the best. Formed in 1904 by Wilfred Cromwell, here the team from 1910 is pictured.

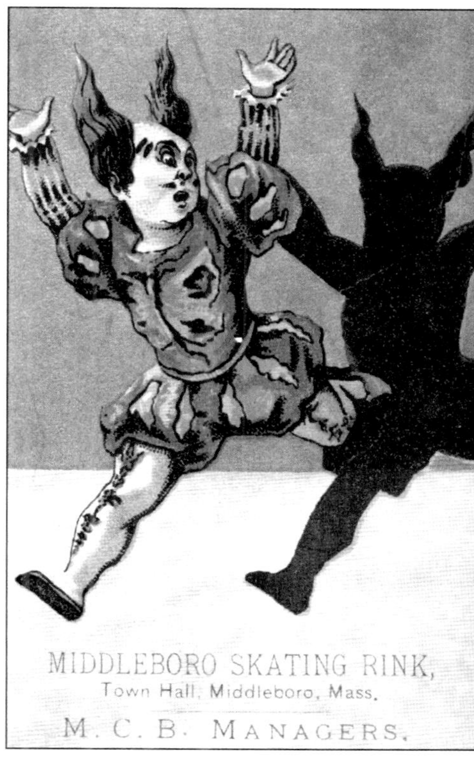

After baseball, one of the earliest forms of organized sports at Middleborough was roller polo, described as field hockey on roller-skates, which was popular in the last quarter of the 19th century. In the early 1880s, the Nemasket Skating Rink on Union Street was constructed to provide a venue for both roller-skating and polo, which had been conducted since Thanksgiving 1879 in the auditorium of Middleborough Town Hall, much to the detriment of the wooden floor there. The local rink was taken down in 1886.

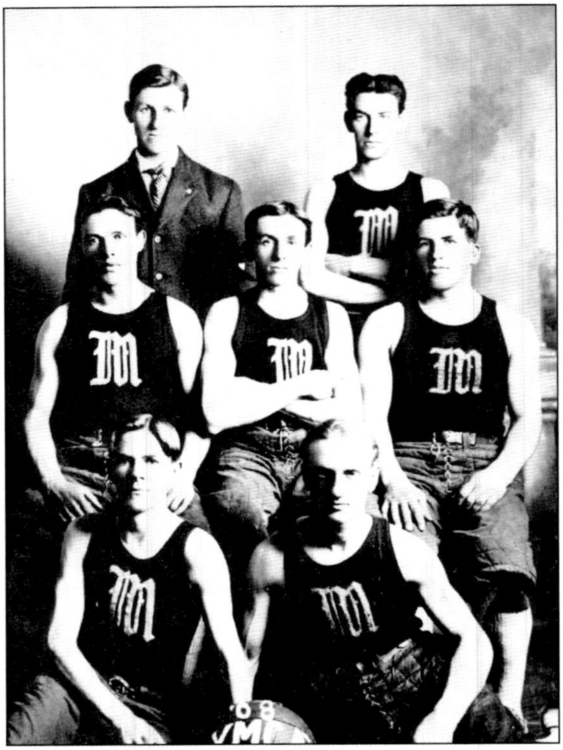

During the 1890s basketball developed, largely through the interest of Middleborough High School and the local YMCA, which became an important early local sponsor of amateur athletics. Here is a local YMCA team from the early 1900s. From left to right are (first row) Norton "Packy" Marshall and Elmer Gay; (second row) Ralph Kelley, Chester Churchill, and Harry Eaton; (third row) manager Charles "Bert" Sherman and Rodney MacDonald.

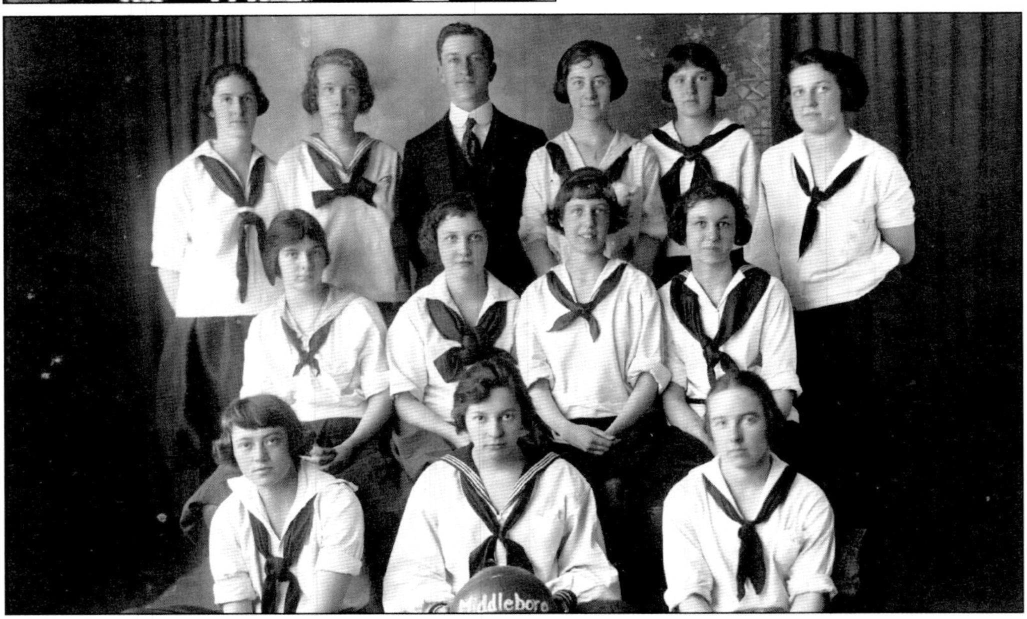

The YMCA also sponsored women's basketball teams, including "Cy's Dolls" during the 1920–1921 season. Ironically, as late as 1909, a local journalist had argued that women should confine their basketball playing to girls' schools so as not to "cheapen themselves by appearing as an entr'acte to a game between teams of young men, with the attendant coarseness and familiarity which is almost certain to be inflicted upon them."

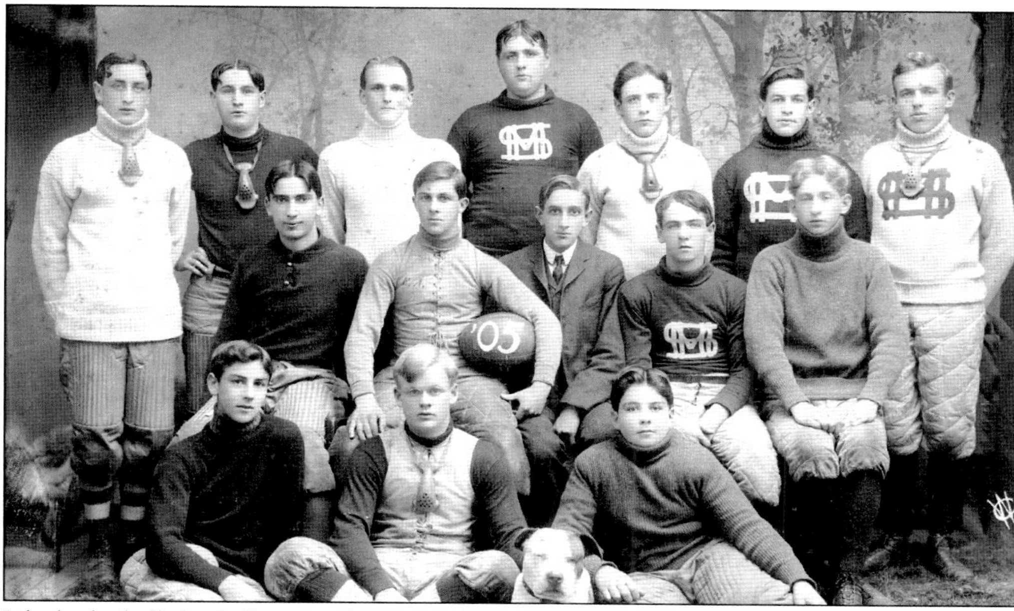

Like basketball, football emerged as a popular sport in the late 1800s largely through the efforts of Middleborough High School students who formed the first organized teams in town. The school's team from 1905 appears above. These early roots led to the growth of semiprofessional football in Middleborough following 1939, when the forerunner of the successful Michell Memorial Club Cobras team was formed.

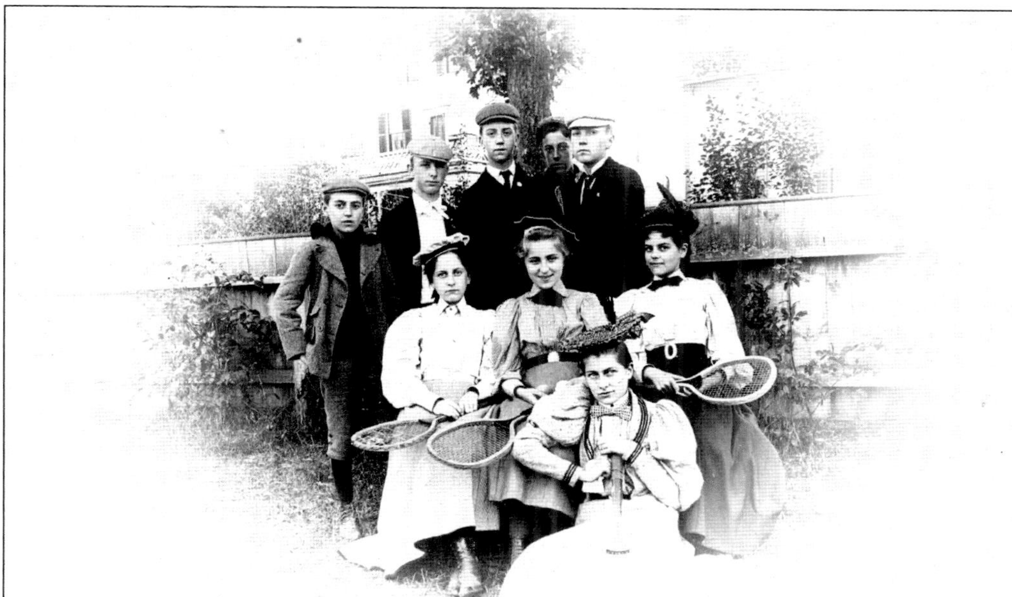

A more genteel diversion was lawn tennis, which was considered appropriate for ladies as well. Local clubs like the Nashawena Tennis Club (pictured) developed to cater to the community's desire to pursue the sport. Pictured are Theodore N. Wood, Charles Kingsley Woodbridge, George Arthur Shurtleff, Arthur Pierce Simmons, Leslie David Baldwin, Marion K. Tillson, Olive Willoughby Sullivan, Annie S. Cushman, and Lena Mae Baldwin.

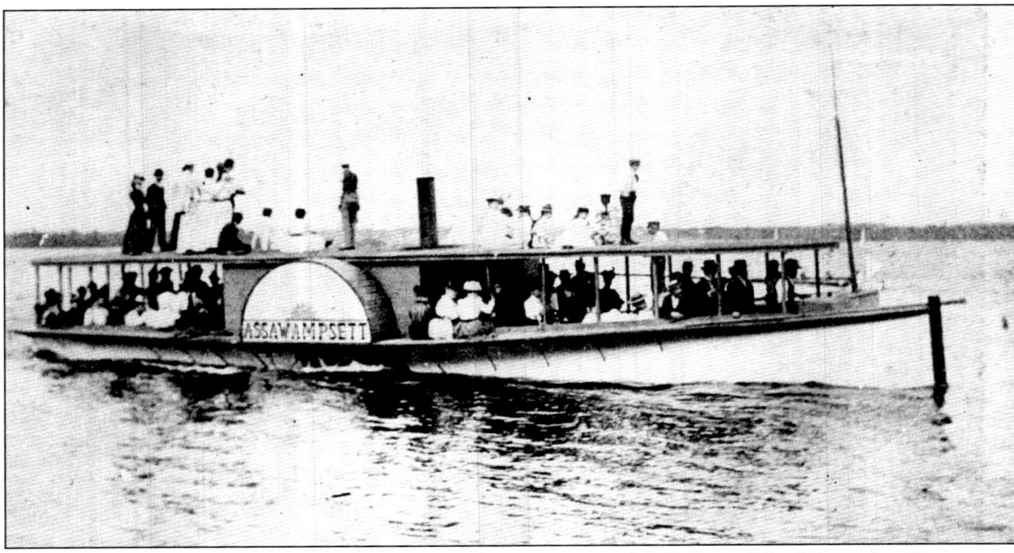

During the last quarter of the 19th century, the recreational delights of the Nemasket River were discovered. Between 1877 and 1895, John B. LeBaron operated steamboats including *Pioneer* and the larger *Assawampsett* on the river and offered various excursions on the adjacent lakes. So popular was steamboating that it was stated that if Middleborough "keeps on this way the town will get included in some future river and harbor bill."

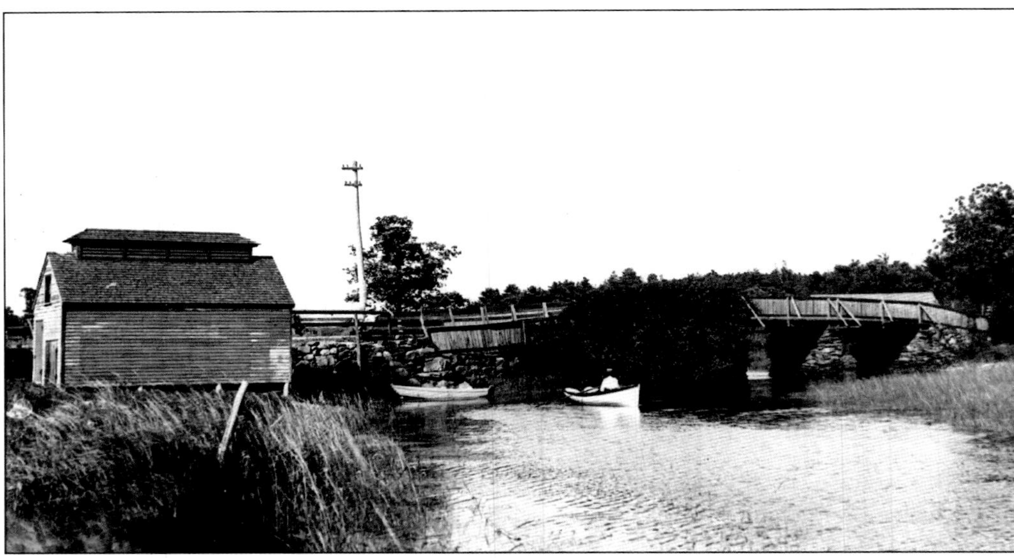

In the years surrounding 1900, rowing and canoeing on the Nemasket River came into vogue. The popularity of the river resulted in the construction of a number of boathouses where space could be rented by local residents, including the large house here seen on the south side of the graceful East Grove Street bridge. Like most of these structures, this one was abandoned and collapsed in the 1900s.

Summer was the high point of Middleborough's leisure season. Circuses were held in the large field at Everett Square later occupied by the A&P, field activities and sporting events were enjoyed at the Peirce Playground on North Main Street, and Independence Day celebrations featured parades, fireworks, concerts, and other activities. North Middleborough still holds an annual Fourth of July parade each year. (Courtesy of James G. MacDonald III.)

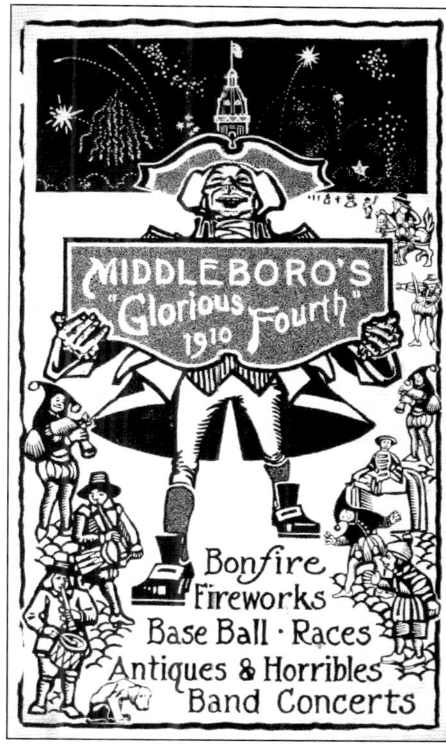

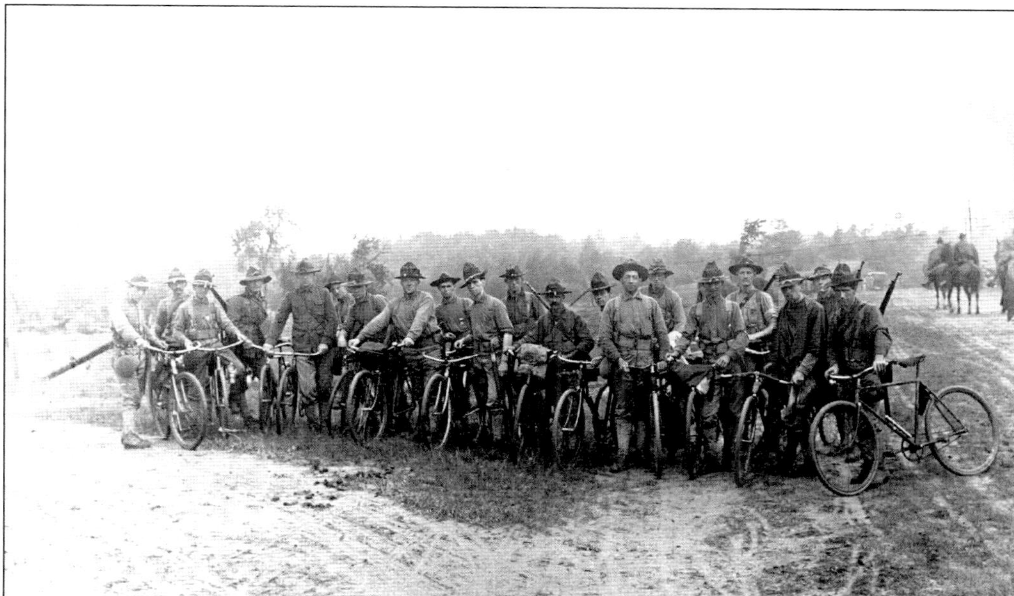

In 1909, 1913, and 1914, the U.S. Army conducted practice war games in the vicinity of Middleborough. While the activity was an important training exercise, it provided great diversion for most Middleborough residents at the time. Army adjustors followed the forces, compensating property owners for incurred damages. Local photographer Fred Churbuck captured soldiers during one of these maneuvers, putting a new spin on the cavalry.

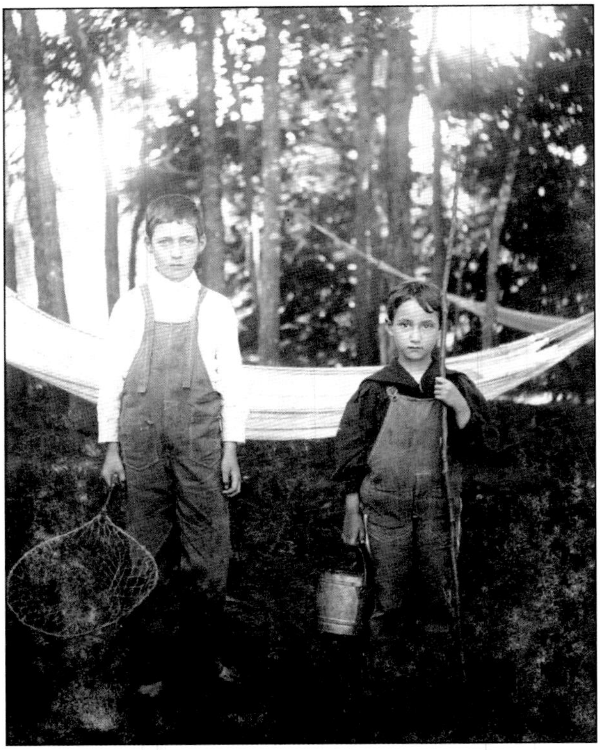

Informal summer pastimes included trips to the local swimming hole, either in the Nemasket River or one of the town's several ponds. The pleasure of river bathing waned following the opening of the Works Progress Administration–built town pool in the 1930s. Fishing, however, remained popular, as demonstrated by the two unidentified boys photographed in the late 1890s by John Belden with their net, pail, and homemade rod.

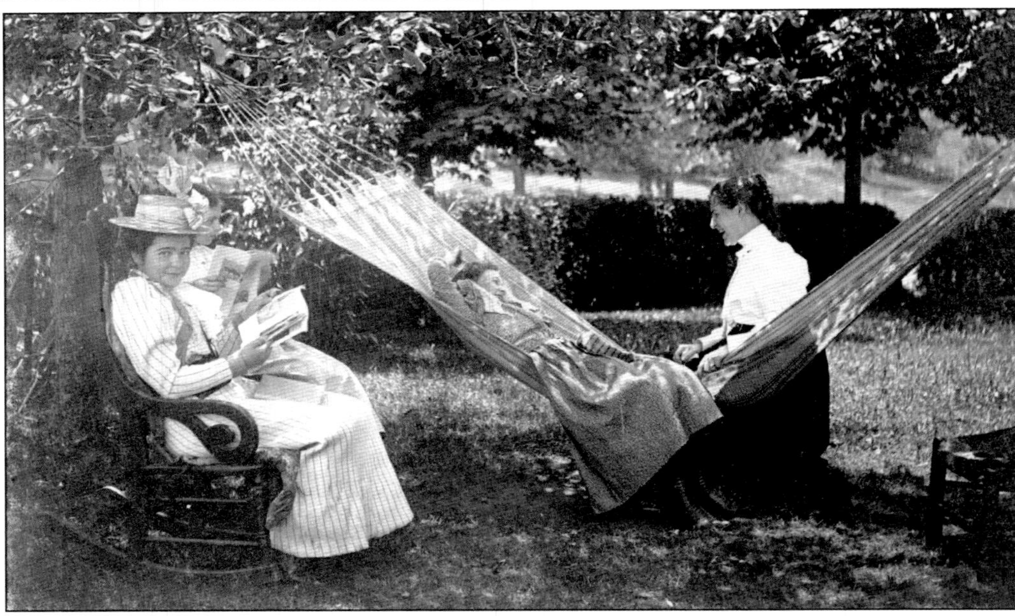

Formerly, summertime leisure frequently meant nothing more than a comfortable hammock, an interesting read, or good company, as depicted in this idyllic scene from the late 1890s captured by Belden. Lawn parties and home entertainments were popular at a time when transportation was limited. Eventually party wagons, trolleys, and the automobile made a much wider range of recreational opportunities available locally.

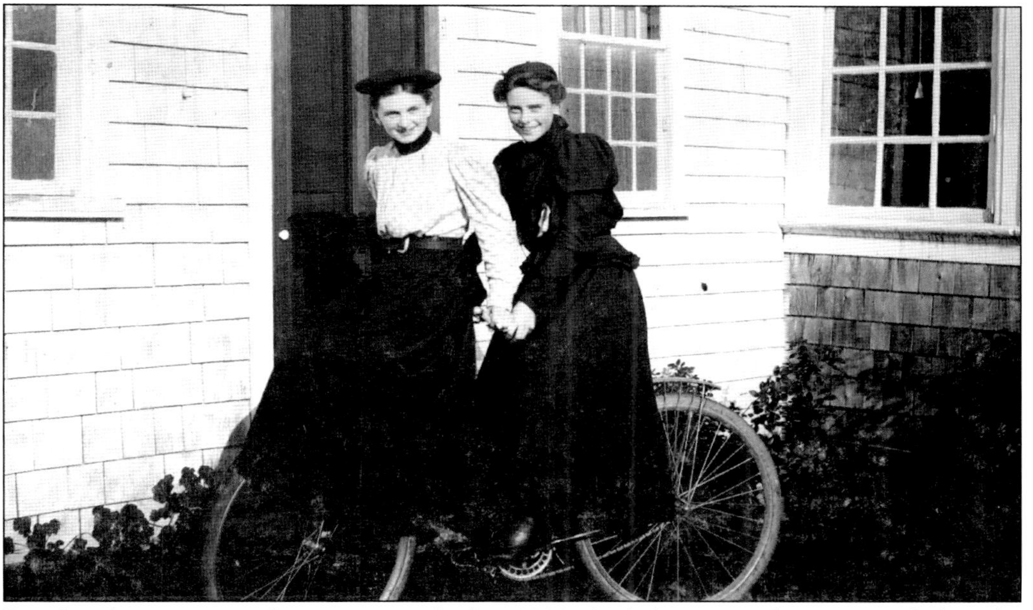

Bicycling became a popular pastime in the late 1800s, both for men and women, including the two young ladies photographed by Belden a few years prior to 1900. Bicycle racing also was pursued locally by such residents as Ben Chapman, James Sparrow, and William Simonds. To accommodate racing, a bicycle track was built at the Fall Brook Trotting Park, where harness horses were also raced until about 1906.

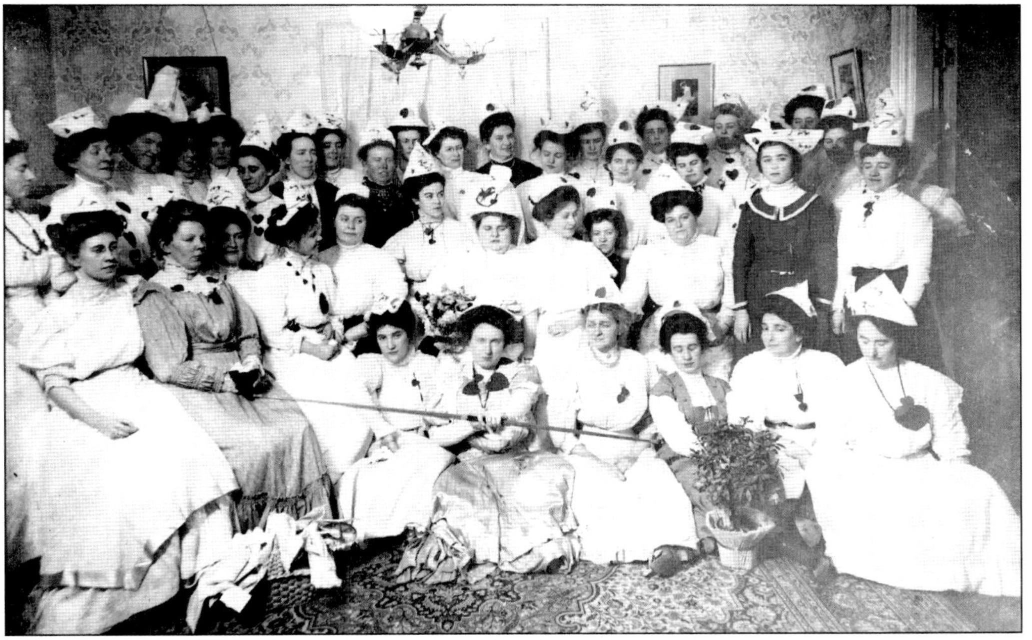

Funny paper hats apparently were de rigueur for social gatherings at the dawn of the 20th century. Here the ladies in attendance at a bridal shower have donned their decorated paper caps. Note the many paper hearts that emblazon the hats and bodices of the ladies, as well as the bow and arrow aimed at the photographer, undoubtedly meant to represent that of Cupid.

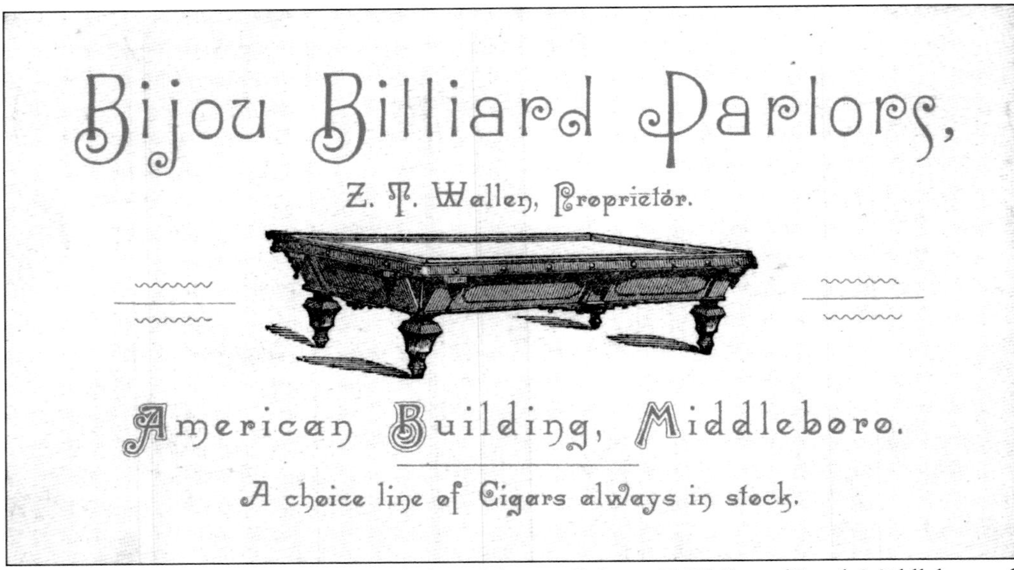

Playing billiards was definitely not for ladies of the era. Zalmon T. Wallen of South Middleborough operated a billiard parlor for gentlemen in the upstairs of the American Hall on South Main Street. Later, bowling alleys appeared at Middleborough center to provide indoor recreation and informal social gathering places. Most were a thing of the past by the mid-1900s.

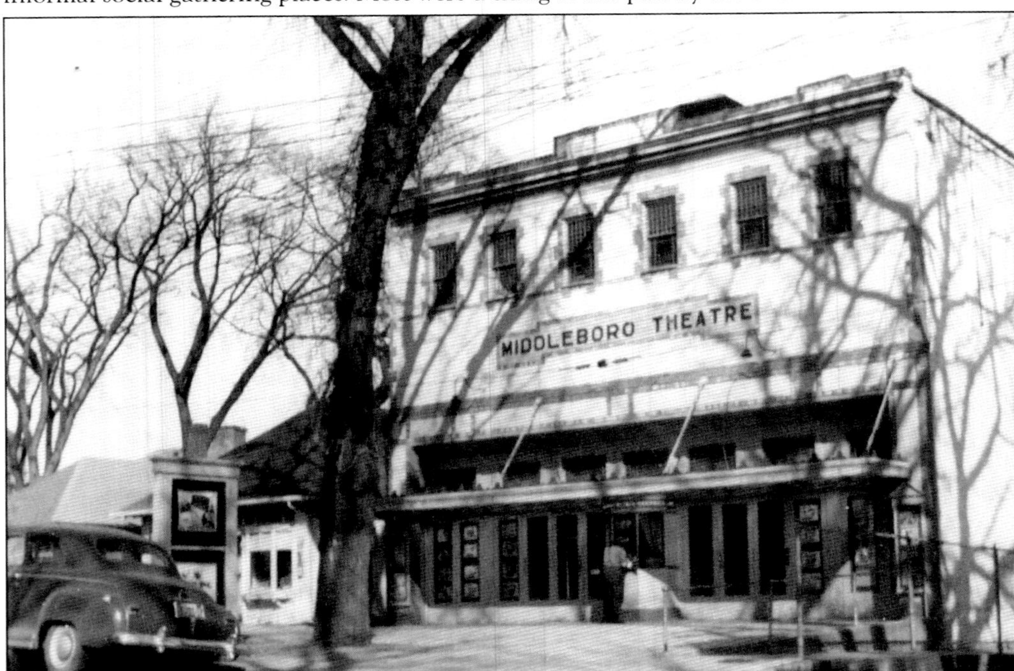

Films were first shown in Middleborough in 1907, and early theaters included the Star, the Lyric, and the town hall auditorium. In 1914 and 1915, the Park Theater on Nickerson Avenue was built as a motion picture house. Later operated as the Middleboro Theatre, it remained a popular entertainment venue for local residents through the 1950s when the Meadowbrook Drive-In on Route 44 helped bring an end to film-going downtown.

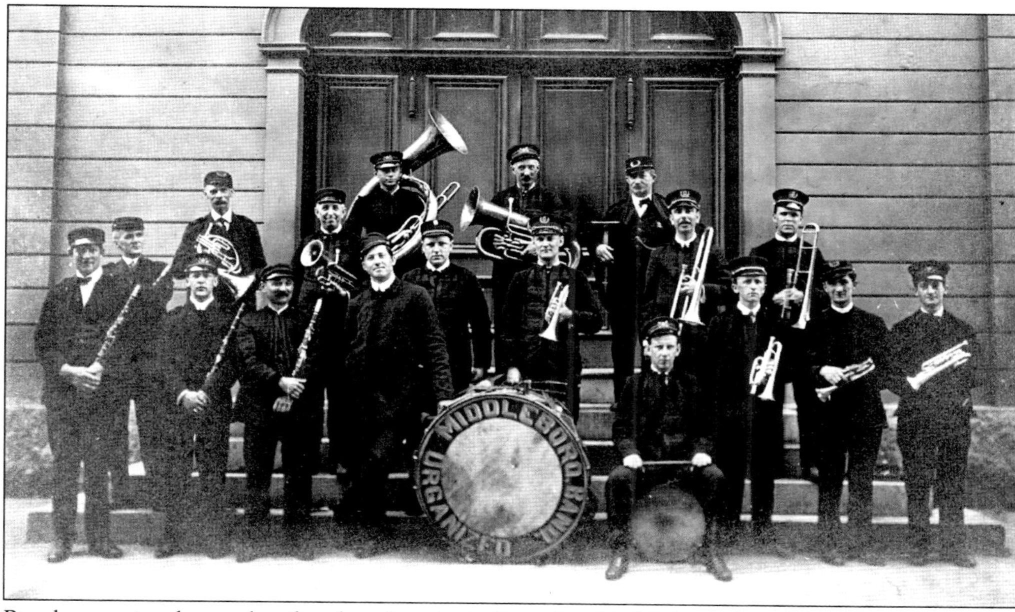

Bands remained popular for decades, including the Middleboro Band (organized in 1865) depicted above on the steps of Middleborough Town Hall. Other bands included the Bay State Band and the Middleboro Commercial Band. Middleborough's first bandstand on the site of the Savings Bank Building was succeeded by a second located in the rear of the town hall. This, in turn, was relocated to the Peirce Playground where it remains.

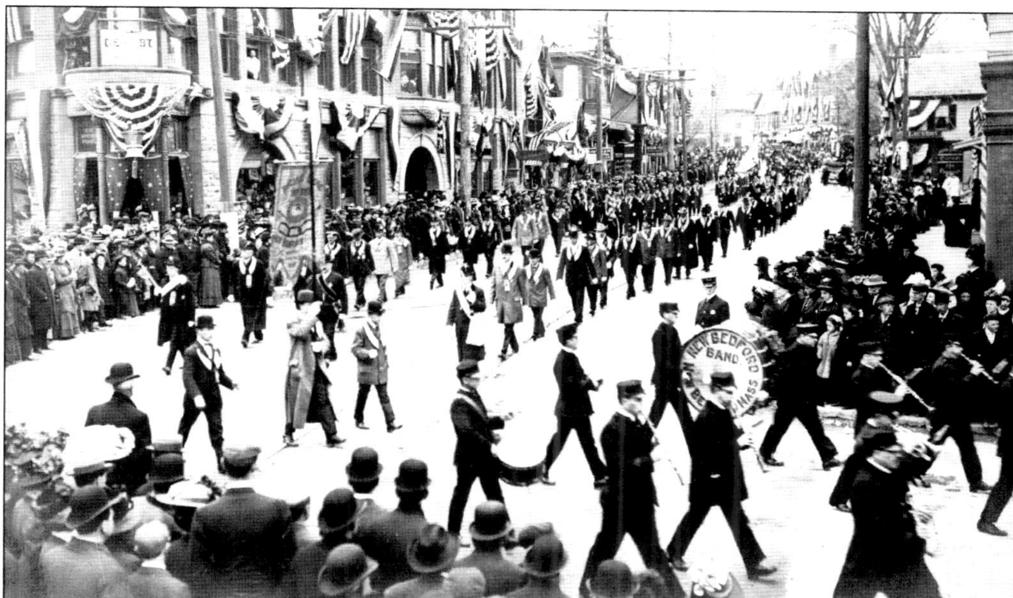

Middleborough was particularly noted for the scale of its celebrations, with particularly large ceremonies and parades being held in 1869, 1909, 1919, and 1969. Here, crowds line Center Street and the four corners to observe a parade in honor of the 25th anniversary of the local Independent Order of Odd Fellows lodge in April 1909. Middleborough continues to hold Memorial Day, Veterans' Day, and Christmas parades annually.

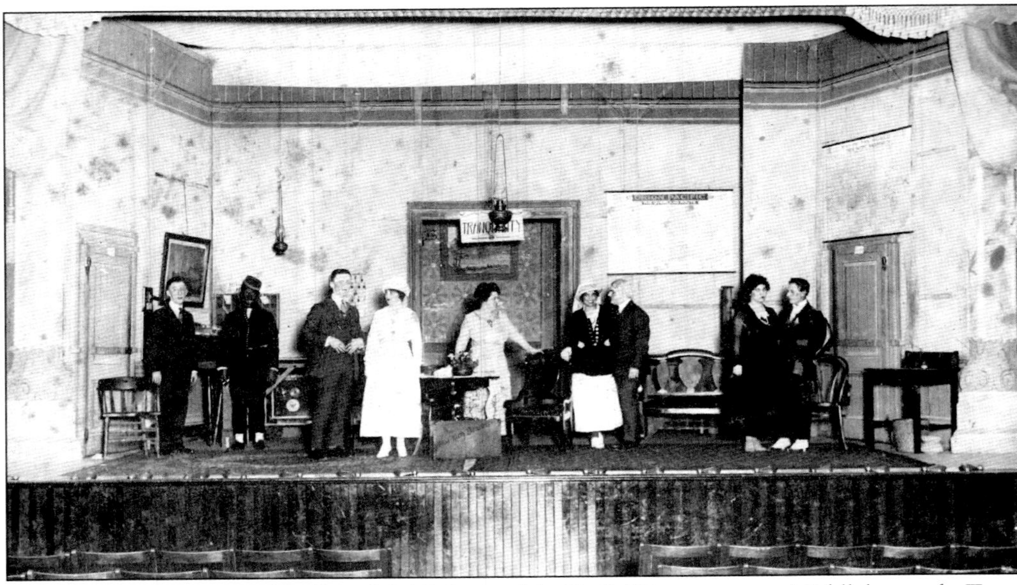

Designed as a memorial hall to Middleborough's Civil War veterans, Middleborough Town Hall's auditorium hosted numerous social functions over the years, including graduations, proms, lectures, dances, plays, concerts, roller-skating, and basketball. Theatrical productions, both professional and amateur, remained popular town hall attractions for years. Local residents Lillian (Phillips) Ball and Dalton Penniman are featured in this unidentified play from during the Depression, when such productions provided an inexpensive yet entertaining evening.

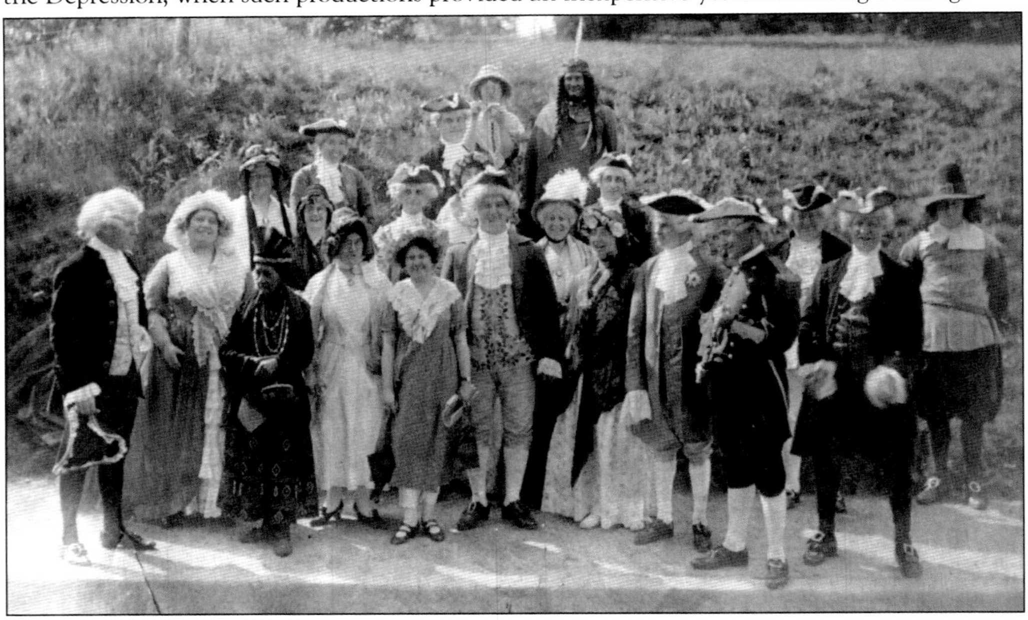

In 1921, the Ye Old Nemasket Choir float sponsored by the Nemasket Daughters of the American Revolution chapter won the $100 first prize during the Pilgrim tercentenary at Plymouth. The following year, the money was used to establish the Old Middleborough Historical Society, now the Middleborough Historical Association. The mission of the association is the preservation of the history of Middleborough and the education of the community in its past.

BIBLIOGRAPHY

Book of the First Church of Christ, in Middleborough, Plymouth County, Mass. With Notices of Other Churches in that Town. Boston, MA: C. C. P. Moody, 1852.

Breck, Sylvia. *Eddyville, Middleboro, Massachusetts 1661–1987*. Middleborough, MA: The Eddy Homestead Association, 1988.

Decas, George C. *Col. Peter H. Peirce (1788–1861): A Plymouth County Life*. Middleborough, MA: Middleborough Historical Association, Inc., 2001.

Eddy, Zachariah. "Sketches of the Early History of the Town of Middleborough, in the County of Plymouth." *New England Historic and Genealogical Register*. July and October, 1849.

Emery, S. Hopkins. *The History of the Church of North Middleborough, Massachusetts*. Middleborough, MA: Harlow and Thatcher, 1876.

Maddigan, Michael J. *An Illustrated History of the Rock Cemetery*. Middleborough, MA: Rock Cemetery Association, 2007.

North Middleborough Looks Back. Middleborough, MA: 1976.

Peirce, E. W. "History of Middleboro." In *The History of Plymouth County*. By D. Hamilton Hurd. Philadelphia: J. W. Lewis and Company, 1884.

Romaine, Mertie E. *General Tom Thumb and His Lady*. Taunton, MA: William S. Sullwold Publishing, Inc., 1976.

———. *History of the Town of Middleboro, Massachusetts*, Volume II. New Bedford, MA: Reynolds-DeWalt Printing, Inc., 1969.

Weston, Thomas. *History of the Town of Middleboro, Massachusetts*. Boston: Houghton, Mifflin and Company, 1906.

Witbeck, Mertie E. *History of the Central Congregational Church, Middleborough, Massachusetts 1847–1947*. Middleborough, MA: Central Congregational Society, 1947.